WINSTON
CHURCHILL

WINSTON CHURCHILL

THE FLAWED GENIUS
OF WORLD WAR II

Christopher Catherwood

BERKLEY CALIBER, NEW YORK

THE BERKLEY PUBLISHING GROUP
Published by the Penguin Group
Penguin Group (USA) Inc.
375 Hudson Street, New York, New York 10014, USA
Penguin Group (Canada), 90 Eglinton Avenue East, Suite 700, Toronto, Ontario M4P 2Y3, Canada
(a division of Pearson Penguin Canada Inc.)
Penguin Books Ltd., 80 Strand, London WC2R 0RL, England
Penguin Group Ireland, 25 St. Stephen's Green, Dublin 2, Ireland (a division of Penguin Books Ltd.)
Penguin Group (Australia), 250 Camberwell Road, Camberwell, Victoria 3124, Australia
(a division of Pearson Australia Group Pty. Ltd.)
Penguin Books India Pvt. Ltd., 11 Community Centre, Panchsheel Park, New Delhi—110 017, India
Penguin Group (NZ), 67 Apollo Drive, Rosedale, North Shore 0632, New Zealand
(a division of Pearson New Zealand Ltd.)
Penguin Books (South Africa) (Pty.) Ltd., 24 Sturdee Avenue, Rosebank, Johannesburg 2196,
South Africa

Penguin Books Ltd., Registered Offices: 80 Strand, London WC2R 0RL, England

This book is an original publication of The Berkley Publishing Group.

First edition: March 2009

Library of Congress Cataloging-in-Publication Data

Catherwood, Christopher.
    Winston Churchill : the flawed genius of WWII / Christopher Catherwood.
      p.   cm.
    Includes bibliographical references and index.
    ISBN 978-0-425-22572-1
    1. Churchill, Winston, Sir, 1874–1965—Military leadership.   2. World War, 1939–1945—Great
Britain.   3. Great Britain—Politics and government—1936–1945.   4. Great Britain—Foreign
relations—1936–1945.   I. Title.

    DA566.9.C5C33 2009
    940.53'41092—dc22
    [B]
                                                                              2008047654

PRINTED IN THE UNITED STATES OF AMERICA

10   9   8   7   6   5   4   3   2   1

CONTENTS

Preface

O F THE MAKING of many books there is no end, and the sheer volume of books on a struggle as titanic and world-changing as the Second World War is on a scale epic enough in size to match the importance of the years that they describe.

Consequently in writing on Winston Churchill—about whom whole libraries full of books have been composed—I have had to be more than selective, otherwise this work too would have run into many volumes. Frequently, therefore, I have taken just a paragraph, or sometimes a few pages, or even a whole chapter, to narrate what other authors have written whole volumes on, often in minute detail.

As a result, this book has left out more than it has left in, and so what you have is not a simple chronological account but a story with a purpose, an argument, a tale that has a moral to it.

I would have loved to include far more about the war in the Pacific, as that is a topic naturally of huge interest to Americans, and was, for the United States, a very considerable part of the war indeed. In many of the wartime discussions, the issues of Europe and the Pacific were closely interwoven, including in terms of supplies and logistics. Not only that but, for example, Roosevelt disagreed strongly with Churchill over the prime minister's quixotic defense of the Indian Empire, the Raj, which Roosevelt rightly saw as an institution whose time should long since have gone—and, indeed, it did go in 1947, since the postwar Labour government fully agreed with the president on such issues.

I should also add that southern and eastern Asia, major additions to the narrative of this book, are beyond your author's sphere of knowledge, which is not the case with either Europe or the Middle East. I can write with understanding about, for instance, the Ljubljana Gap in the Adriatic, an area of much strategic dispute between Churchill and the Americans, not only because I have studied the region academically but because I have also been there personally, not to mention to the beaches of Normandy where D-day was fought, or to various Middle Eastern deserts where battles have been fought not just in the 1940s but for millennia. Of the Burma Road or the Andaman Islands, or of such places famous in US history as Corregidor or the Coral Sea, I am sadly unfamiliar.

So this book, while not short, is by nature selective. But I think it tells a fascinating tale, one that shaped the world we live in today; even well into the twenty-first century we remain as much as ever in the world created by the way in which the Second World War was fought and won, and by the decisions that giants such as Winston Churchill in particular made.

Churchill would himself start each of his wartime volumes with a theme of the work. Perhaps we can do the same here, and in the same style:

How Winston Churchill Was Right over Munich
Understood the Real Issues About Hitler
Realized War Was About Actually Fighting Your Enemy
Saved Britain from Defeat from the Nazis in 1940
Knew That Victory Would Only Come with American Help
Gave the British the Morale to Hang On Until Then
And Proved Forever His Sheer Genius
Nevertheless Made Some Big Strategic Blunders in 1941
Rejoiced When America Finally Entered the War
Yet Tragically Failed to Understand
How Truly Powerful on an Unprecedented Scale
And How Transformative America Would Be
So Kept to the Old War-Winning Ways of
His Great Ancestors and Britons Before Him
And in so Doing
Delayed the US Military Plans That Would
In All Likelihood Have Won the War Years Earlier
And Saved Millions of Lives in the Process
Including Those of Countless Jews
and also
As Churchill Finally Saw
Would Have Prevented Stalin from Being
The Real Winner of the War in Europe
Because Victory There Had Been Delayed
And by so Doing
Showed His Tragic Flaws

That, to use the Churchillian way of stating it, is the moral of this book!

INTRODUCTION

Setting the Scene

IT WAS DECEMBER 1941. News from North Africa was bad. "Strategic withdrawals," otherwise known as military defeats, were the order of the day. It was more than likely that Moscow would also fall, and the USSR, Britain's only ally of any significance, would disintegrate, leaving Hitler an empire stretching from the Atlantic coast to the Pacific Ocean. The British were hanging on, but by a thread.

So when a Welsh physician turned in excitement to his teenage daughter and said, "Now we will win the war!" people would have had good cause to believe him sadly deluded.

But the Welshman, Dr. Martyn Lloyd-Jones, who had written a book during the London Blitz, *Why Does God Allow War?*, was right when he told his daughter, my mother, the good news. For the war was now won—the United States had finally decided to enter in on Britain's side, and the United Kingdom was no longer in danger of defeat. Hitler's decision to declare war on the United States was an answer to all Britain's hopes and dreams since Churchill had become prime minister in May 1940, and a vindication for those who saw the war as a struggle between freedom and tyranny. The most powerful democracy in the world was engaged at last. Victory was still a long way off—not until May 1945 in Europe and later still in the Pacific—but *eventual* victory was now certain.

There are many myths about the Second World War. One of these is that Churchill was the victor, the man who won it for freedom, democracy, and liberty from tyranny. But as we shall see, this is nowhere near the case, courageous and daring as Churchill most certainly was.

For the truth is otherwise—the *real* winners of World War II were the United States and the Soviet Union, the two postwar superpowers, and, as is obvious, only the first of these two nations was a democracy. The two major fronts of the war were the Americans against the Japanese in the Pacific, and the Russians against the Germans in Europe, on the *Eastern* Front. While Ike, Montgomery, and the sixty or so divisions under their command in Western Europe were fighting the Germans, *four hundred* divisions were engaged in a vicious, Darwinian struggle between Hitler's Reich on the one hand and Stalin's Soviet Union on the other. Compared to that struggle, and the large-scale barbarity and carelessness for human life with which it was fought, even D-day and the Battle of the Bulge were, in comparison, small potatoes.

So while this book is going to concentrate on Churchill heavily, and the decisions that he made, we do need first to set Churchill in the wider context of the Second World War itself, since we in the West are still, decades later, prone to believe convenient myths, as opposed to what *really* happened during the war; fans of Churchill, like myself, sadly being among the worst offenders.

A few statistics (courtesy of Norman Davies's definitive book *Europe at War*) show this beyond question.

Between 1939 and 1945 around 144,000 British servicemen lost their lives in the European part of the conflict. Between 1941 and 1945, a shorter period, 143,000 Americans similarly died. However, Soviet deaths numbered *eleven million*, which is just under forty times as many fatalities as the British and American losses combined.

Churchill was rightly proud of the wonderful British victory at El Alamein in 1942, the final turning of the tide against Rommel's Afrika Korps, and a victory that caused Churchill to order the ringing of bells across Britain. It was a much-needed boost to sagging British morale, and has been rightly remembered by people in the United Kingdom ever since, especially as it was probably the last major battle won by Britain without US aid during the rest of the war.

But the total death toll for El Alamein was 4,650. Take another Allied campaign we all know in the West: Market Garden, the failure to capture Arnhem, the famous "Bridge Too Far" in the book and film of the same name. There total deaths were 16,000, a toll almost four times as high.

Take by contrast some of the battles between Germany and Russia on the Eastern Front.

The battle of Kursk, in 1943—which we will see later on as possibly the most important in the whole war in Europe—saw 325,000 deaths, or, to put it another way, just over twenty times as many fatalities as Market Garden, and *seventy times* as many as the battle of El Alamein, an encounter far more famous in the West than the infinitely more important and considerably more bloodthirsty battle of Kursk, just a few months later.

We have now heard of the siege of Stalingrad, perhaps because of the recent well-received movie *Enemy at the Gates,* which does actually manage to give a good account, for a Hollywood production, of the chaos and terror that the siege of Stalingrad must have engendered among its participants. It is reckoned that in the siege alone some 973,000 people died (and possibly more than that).

Contrast that to the 132,000 deaths in Operation Overlord in 1944, or the 38,000 deaths during the Battle of the Bulge. Now, 132,000 Allied losses on the beaches of Normandy is a lot of people, and we do not need to have watched *Saving Private Ryan* to know the bravery and heroism of those who stormed the beaches and who gave their lives to create a bridgehead in France that would take the liberation of Western Europe one stage further. But the total mortalities come to just under an eighth of the figure at Stalingrad. This gives us a very different perspective altogether. To put it another way, of the 3,500,000 German soldiers who were killed in battle, only 15 percent were killed at the hands of American troops. I was engrossed by the superb TV series *Band of Brothers*, but Soviet troops killed well over five times as many Germans as their brave American equivalents did (taking into account those Germans killed by British and other Allied forces).

At their peak, the Americans were producing a new tank every five *minutes*. Only one other country came anything close to this staggering level of logistical production, and that was the Soviet Union, mobilized to the very fullest possible capacity because of the totalitarian nature of the regime. Norman Davies's *Europe at War*, Richard Overy's exhaustive *Why the Allies Won*, and more detailed studies, such as Rodric Braithwaite's exciting *Moscow 1941*, show this very clearly. We tend to think of wars being won on the field of battle, and it is certainly true that logistical history, describing tank production, aircraft statistics, and the like, is nowhere near as good a read as tales of bravery on the battlefield.

But without the equipment, no soldier, sailor, or pilot can ever win anything. As Richard Overy demonstrates, the fact that by the end of the war, the Allies could replicate all their tank losses, whereas the Germans were not merely unable to do the same but were also running out of fuel and still having to use horses (which needed increasingly nonexistent fodder to stay alive), shows that however boring statistical history might be in comparison, factories are every bit as vital for winning modern technological warfare as generals and soldiers on the ground.

(Much of this also applies to the war in the Pacific, with which most American readers of this book are doubtless very familiar. I will deal with the conflict against Japan in parts of this book, as it is vital to gaining a proper perspective of the whole struggle. I do have to admit, however, that my knowledge of Europe is far greater than that of Asia, and correspondingly of the war in those places as well. My coverage will therefore be more political than technical/strategic, which I hope that Asia specialists among my readers will forgive.)

We are all rightly and regularly reminded of the six million entirely innocent Jews butchered in the Shoah, or Holocaust. We should certainly never forget them, and twenty-first-century Europe is massively the poorer culturally, artistically, and in countless other ways for its drastically reduced Jewish population, the fundamental immorality of the killing quite apart.

But how many of us know that twenty-seven million Russians were also killed (civilians as well as military) during the same time period? That is four and a half times as many Russian deaths as Jewish if taken literally, although there must be some double counting in those statistics somewhere. Either way, though, the number of Russians killed exceeds that of Jewish deaths by a considerable margin. To the Nazis, Slavs were as much *Untermenschen*, or inferior human beings, as Jews; and as Laurence Rees's book and TV series, *War of the Century*, reminds us, German troops, or the Wehrmacht, as well as the SS, did not hesitate to massacre Russians wholesale with the same deliberate zeal and callousness with which they put Jews into concentration camps and killed them there.

Here though we come to one of the key myths of the Second World War.

Here too we come to an area where I disagree strongly with those "revisionists" who seek to criticize Churchill, especially for his conduct during the war. As will be apparent, I am no apologist for Churchill, or for many of his wartime mistakes. But the reason why this book is called *Winston Churchill: The Flawed Genius of World War II* is that, perhaps for the first time, you can read an account of not just why he was wrong—as the revisionists have done, the distinguished British historian John Charmley included—but also *where he was right*.

This is therefore an unashamedly *postrevisionist* book, and in that light I am so grateful to my publishers for giving the book a title that is both accurate and helpful. Early lives tend, alas, to be hagiographies of a hero with no faults, and, in the case of Churchill, a genuine hero who set the tone for what followed by his own monumental *History of the Second World War*, which for millions of people around the world became the definitive account, all the more so because Roosevelt died before the war ended and thus left no memoirs, and Stalin, almost by definition, was a Soviet dictator who kept truth ruthlessly suppressed, as did his successors right through until the Gorbachev era of openness in the 1980s. For many today, therefore, as well as for the immediate postwar generation of grateful survivors, Churchill's version is *the* story of what happened and why.

It was not until the 1960s that Britain became more liberal in what it allowed historians to see, with a rule introduced that would make public all but the most secret intelligence archives thirty years after the original documents were written. In the case of World War II, however, the British government of the day in fact permitted all declassified documents out early, to the great joy of historians everywhere.

Churchill of course had no idea that this would happen when he penned his six-volume history back in the 1940s and 1950s, so he equally had no inkling that his very selective quotations, all of which put him in the most favorable light possible, would ever be available in their original form to future generations, who could then read them to check the veracity of what he was writing. Now we can do this, and thanks to Cambridge historian David Reynolds's book *In Command of History*, based upon the Churchill archives in that city, we can now tell very precisely indeed how Churchill doctored the wartime story for publication, and which documents he quoted only selectively or studiously ignored.

Needless to say, when historians did see the real originals, from the early 1970s onwards, they realized how selective Churchill had been. So we then had a new generation of writers who put Churchill in a very different light, not always to his advantage. Unfortunately, while some, most notably John Charmley, were scholarly, others, such as Alan Clark, one of Margaret Thatcher's more notorious and louche ministers, were sensationalist, arguing, for example, that Britain should have done a deal with Hitler in 1940 rather than continue the conflict. There was also a strong anti-American tone in these books, regretting the fact that the war made the United States the overwhelmingly predominant global power, as if Britain could have continued some kind of parity or even superiority, as was the case pre-1914.

Unfortunately for getting an objective overview of Churchill, the sheer immorality of Clark's suggestion of a deal with Hitler, and the utter fantasy that Britain could somehow have kept its empire and maintained parity with the United States (the latter case being made even by serious historians) blinded people to Churchill's very real flaws. Since those who criticized him were often people with unacceptable views, the Churchillian version of events remained unchallenged.

What has surely made a real difference is twofold, and this is important in terms of the background to this book.

First, since Gorbachev liberalized the USSR in the 1980s, we have been able to find out what really happened on the Eastern Front from 1941 to 1945 (and somewhat before, such as in 1938). This has challenged the Churchill version as well as the complete Western myopia on the overwhelming contribution that the Soviets made to Allied victory, and against Germany in particular. The casualties I quoted at the beginning of this introduction tell it all, and do so, for the first time, in proper perspective. As I said some pages back, the reality is that the Americans won against the Japanese and the Soviets against the Germans, and all else were really sideshows in comparison to those two titanic struggles. To the ultimate victory, Churchill's brave stand against Hitler was pivotal in 1940 and 1941, when Britain was at its direst hour of peril, but after that the big victories and the final ending were all down not to Britain but to the United States and the USSR, not coincidentally the two postwar superpowers.

Second, the works of pioneer historians such as the late Robert Rhodes James, whose 1970 *Churchill: A Study in Failure, 1900–1939* showed that you do not have to denigrate Churchill in 1940 to show that up until that date, he had, to say the very least of it, an erratic and deeply checkered career. Those who regarded him up until 1940 as a dangerous and unreliable buccaneer had a good point. They had plenty of evidence to back their hypothesis.

But just because he was an egotistical adventurer until 1940 does not take away from his transformative ability to rescue Britain from Nazi conquest in 1940–41.

In other words, as this book will tell, he was both *flawed* and a *genius* in equal measure at the same time. A university contemporary has gained enormous academic coverage of his "new perspective" on the theologically involved subject of Second Temple Judaism and its ramifications for how we perceive the New Testament. What you are about to read is, I trust, a sympathetic but not uncritical *new perspective on Churchill in the Second World War,* and in his relations with the United States in particular.

So, with the critical background now laid, let us get on with the story.

CHAPTER ONE

Stopping Hitler in 1938:
When Churchill Got It Right

T HE PAPERBACK VERSION of the official biography of Winston
Churchill, by Martin Gilbert, has the right title for its fifth volume: *The Wilderness Years*. From 1931 to 1939, Churchill's party was
in office but he was not.

The notion of the prophet in the wilderness, the lone voice of
truth, crying out the dangers of Hitler and the Third Reich is a very
romantic one, and it is the view of Churchill that prevails in the popular imagination, and with excellent cause. Churchill *was* right about
Hitler and the Nazi menace, and had he been listened to, instead of
being ignored as some kind of extinct volcano, as was the case, life
would have been mightily different indeed, and all for the better.

However, as we will see throughout this book, things were not
that simple, as they never are.

Historiography—the study of the writing of history—is like all
such disciplines often something tediously boring and read only by

specialists. Since, despite being a professional historian myself, I tend to empathize with such a view, I will avoid as much as possible what is often a fairly arcane and obscure debate, in order to concentrate on the real story. But in the case of Winston Churchill, so great and towering a figure of the twentieth century, our subject has attracted so much controversy over the years that we cannot avoid the debate about how he has been seen by historians in the forty-plus years since his death in 1965.

Churchill was himself an historian—his epic multivolume life of his illustrious ancestor, John Churchill, first Duke of Marlborough, one of the most successful and outstanding military commanders Britain has ever produced, forms one of the best historical biographies ever written, even despite the natural bias of the author, since there was no prouder a descendant of Marlborough than Winston Churchill himself.

So when it came to describing the story of World War II, Churchill immediately realized the importance of history itself. He more than most statesmen was aware how vital it was to be seen by historians to be right, and for your own version of events to be seen as the only one possible. All politicians, not to mention those in all spheres of life, writing their autobiography do this. But as Churchill added, history would be on *his* side because he was the person who would write the history.

For this, lesser lights, your own author included, have profound cause to be thankful. Churchill kept as many documents as possible, every one with an eye to the history books he would write once the war was over. In fact, even as early as the First World War he was already doing this—as a former prime minister, Arthur Balfour, once quipped, Churchill was writing a book about himself and calling it *The World Crisis*. Few people have written as many volumes of autobiography as Churchill, and he did so unhesitatingly from his early twenties, with his exploits on colonial battlefields, onwards.

Therefore for many of us, our view of the buildup to World War II, and of the events during it, including the wartime origins of the subsequent Cold War, are all formed by Winston Churchill's own magnum opus, his majestic six-volume work, *The Second World War.* The fact that he gave it such a title is in itself significant. What appears to be an objective history of the war—rather like the countless official histories that military historians produced in both Britain and the United States in the 1950s and 1960s—is in essence nothing of the kind. It is, in reality, Churchill's war memoirs, not so much an overall picture of the war but about his own, completely vital and pivotal role within it, as the man who was right about Hitler in the 1930s, to his amazing years in command of the United Kingdom as prime minister and minister of defense from 1940 to 1945.

When Churchill wrote it, with the very considerable help of many able assistants, he never presumed that the archives upon which he based the work would ever be seen by anyone else. (The fact that he was able to keep thousands of wartime archives was in itself highly unusual—all of them were the property of the state, and, as we will see later, that is quite a story in itself.) Churchill quoted reams of his own wartime missives, memoranda, and position papers, and, not surprisingly, all of them put him in the most excellent light.

Now of course, many of you will be thinking, *he was right.*

Needless to say, on *the* two absolutely pivotal issues of World War Two—resisting Hitler in 1940–41, whatever the cost, and the fact that without the United States, Britain had not the faintest chance of survival—I would agree that Churchill was, beyond question, right in every possible way. For Britain to have surrendered to a monster such as Adolf Hitler (which would in effect have given the Nazis complete and perpetual power over continental Europe, from Calais in the west to Vladivostok in the east) would have been an act of such monumental folly and sheer immorality that history would probably never have seen its equal.

Likewise, it is amazing—some would say miraculous—that Britain managed to hang in there alone and unconquered between the fall of France in 1940 and the American entry into the war at the end of 1941. (As we shall see, Britain was profoundly lucky here too since, if Hitler had not declared war on the United States shortly after Pearl Harbor, those Americans wanting Japan, not Germany, to be the main enemy would have prevailed, and Britain would have continued to be in dire straits for many more years to come.) To use a phrase employed about another war, the fact that Britain did not succumb to a Nazi invasion in the summer of 1940 was a close run thing, and was far from inevitable.

So what is the fuss?

The extraordinary thing about the Churchillian decisions to oppose Hitler from 1933 onwards, to resist him steadfastly in 1940, and to live in hope of American aid is that, while most of us take them for granted, they are all in fact now highly controversial.

In this, Churchill is far from being a special case. So often some famous figure is lauded to the skies, reverential biographies are written, and then, all of a sudden, that person goes out of vogue. Highly critical studies replace hagiographies, the subject's every decision is scrutinized and then torn apart, and their reputation sinks, as often as not beyond repair.

So too with Churchill, especially after the British government decided in the 1960s to open all the Second World War archives to researchers. What Churchill had thought was secret in perpetuity was now open for all to read.

Here we will look at two aspects of Churchill—his life before 1939, and the way in which he wrote his history of the war, not just to tell the story from his own vantage point but to make his own current *political* position secure.

First, when the archives were opened, as David Reynolds's book *In Command of History* usefully reminds us, Churchill's own view of the war now came up for microscopic examination and critical scrutiny.

The truth, however uncomfortable, is that Churchill was far from straight in his autobiography.

Next, while most politicians pen their memoirs after they have fully retired, Churchill was an active and practicing politician throughout the time he wrote his history volumes. From 1945 to 1951 he was leader of the opposition, hoping once again to be prime minister, and then from 1951 to 1955 he presided over his Conservative government as a peacetime politically partisan prime minister.

Beginning in 1953 his wartime colleague Dwight Eisenhower was president of the United States, just as Churchill was beginning to write about the delicate Allied partnership of D-day and after, in which Eisenhower played the pivotal military role. Churchill the politician in 1953–55 urgently needed Eisenhower the president's goodwill, so anything in the history that criticized Eisenhower the Supreme Allied Commander 1943–45 had to be written with kid gloves, to say the very least of it.

In other words, because Churchill remained a politician throughout the entire period of writing the history, with many of the key players, such as Eisenhower, equally active and powerful, a fully truthful account, one that took no prisoners and gave full vent to what Churchill felt *at the time*, back in the war, was thus impossible.

Just to take another example, between becoming prime minister again in late 1951 and Stalin's death in early 1953, Churchill was keen to bring about some kind of rapprochement between the West and the USSR. Churchill was the man who popularized the term "Iron Curtain" and applied it to the Cold War. But he still believed in peace and global harmony, and in talking to Stalin without weakening the West. So inevitably this colored what he wrote about his dealings with Stalin during the war.

We cannot therefore rely on what Churchill wrote about himself to get the full picture of what was actually happening in that time, however much we would like to believe the legend.

On the other hand, nor should we commit the sin that the revisionists have done, and say that because Churchill did make numerous mistakes, he was wrong about the greatest achievement of all, his defense of Britain against Nazi tyranny and invasion in 1940–41, or about his resolute opposition to appeasement before the war.

For this is what the revisionist writers—from professional historians such as John Charmley to the Holocaust denier David Irving—are now beginning to do. Neville Chamberlain, the architect of the Munich settlement of 1938 and prime minister from 1937 to 1940, is, they say, a much maligned and misunderstood man, a politician of rare principle whose sole desire was to prevent war and to defend Britain's historic interests, both at home and in the preservation of the British Empire. Not only that, they argue, but the net effect of Churchill hanging on in 1940 was that Hitler was prevented from wiping out the USSR, and that Britain was so bankrupt in 1945 that the United States inevitably took her place as the number one global economic and political power.

I am inevitably simplifying a complex argument—brilliantly outlined in, for example, John Charmley's well-researched and provocatively written works, not to mention those of Correlli Barnett, who, in a wonderful example of irony, spent the last working years of his life as keeper of the Churchill Archives at Churchill College, Cambridge, where this chapter is itself being written.

Furthermore there are some areas in which they are right. What was the *main* reason that Churchill was initially excluded from office between 1931 and 1939? The answer has nothing to do with appeasement, since Hitler did not take power until 1933. The actual answer is that Churchill's "Wilderness Years" began as a result of his fanatical, obsessive opposition even to the very mildest form of independence for India, this being a subject on which he railed repeatedly against the government during the passing of the India legislation between 1931 and 1935. Churchill was perceived as the worst kind of reactionary, a fossil from a bygone age, an adventurer whose time in office, back in World War I, had led to the massive defeat and fiasco of the Dardanelles project, sure proof, if any were needed, that Churchill was all hot air and most certainly unreliable.

Churchill was, in other words, that tragic figure, the little boy who cried wolf. In 1936, for instance, when he had arranged a major gathering in favor of rearmament, he also declared his support for the deeply controversial monarch King Edward VIII, which caused an enormous stir and utterly deflected from all the right things he was saying about the urgent need for Britain to rearm in the face of the growing Nazi menace.

Furthermore, back in the 1920s, both as secretary of state for war and then as chancellor of the exchequer, in charge of the nation's finances, no one had done more than Churchill to destroy Britain's military and naval strength. Although he was not the person who introduced the infamous "Ten-Year Rule," which automatically presumed that Britain would not need a large army because war was unlikely to break out for at least another ten years into the future, he was, as chancellor, the man who made it permanent. So why was

Britain so pathetically unready in its army, navy, and air force in the 1930s? It was because Churchill had cut all the services to the bare minimum in the decade before. Yes, he was totally right on the need to rearm to fight fascism after 1933, but the real thing he was asking of his colleagues in Parliament was, in effect, to undo the hideous damage he had done himself to British defenses between 1919 and 1929.

On all this the revisionists are therefore correct—the facts stand out for themselves. Churchill was simply not trusted, since on issue after issue he was completely wrong or contradicted his earlier self. The idea that so old a civilization as India was unfit for ruling itself is outrageous—as, indeed, Franklin Roosevelt and most decent-thinking people on both sides of the Atlantic held it to be. Churchill's views were imperialistic and archaic of the worst kind.

This, therefore, is the true tragedy of Churchill's Wilderness Years—that when he *was* right, over Nazism and the need for Britain to confront the horrors of Hitler, his colleagues rejected him because they distrusted him so deeply over issues over which they were right and he was wrong. When we look at Churchill during the 1930s we tend to see everything, understandably so, in the light of 1940 rather than in the context of *how people perceived Churchill at the time*, which was as a spent volcano, a relic from a bygone imperial age, no longer in tune with the times and whose ranting on all subjects, from India to Germany, could best be safely ignored.

However, we can now depart from revisionist territory.

(I am here setting aside mavericks such as the Holocaust denier David Irving, who has written copiously on Churchill but whose denial of the very evident deaths of over six million Jews, not to mention countless socialists, gypsies, and homosexuals, surely puts him outside the consideration of most people. It is writers such as Alan

Clark, Thomas Fleming, and John Charmley who I am taking seriously here, not to mention historians on the British political left, not known in the United States, whose opposition to Churchill is more ideologically based.)

One of the most insightful books ever written about Churchill deals solely with his career up to the opening of World War II. This is Robert Rhodes James's work *Winston Churchill: A Study in Failure, 1900–1939.*

Note the dates of above: *1900–1939.* They are vitally important. We judge Churchill entirely in the light of *after 1939,* and in particular, of his triumphant achievement of 1940–41, without which I would probably not be writing this book, since Hitler would have won the war.

What the late Robert Rhodes James was saying (in his book and to those who knew him) was that if Churchill had died on September 2, 1939, he would have been seen as a failure—a brilliant one, a gifted orator, a superb historian—but a basically failed politician nonetheless.

What made Churchill, and the reputation he has had since, is that after 1939 he was able, as First Lord of the Admiralty from 1939 to 1940 and then as prime minister (and, significantly, minister of defense) in 1940 to 1945, to do something about the one issue upon which he had been right since 1933. Not only that, but the very archaic sense of British might and imperial grandeur that he possessed, which made him look so utterly irrelevant and archaic in opposing the right of Indian people to rule themselves, became his most wonderful oratory in defense of decency, civilization, and freedom itself in 1940 and 1941, a point made by biographers such as Geoffrey Best, John Keegan, Roy Jenkins, William Roger Louis, Warren Kimball, and many others in their lives of the great man. As the legendary American broadcaster

Ed Murrow put it, Churchill mobilized the English language and sent it into war.

We will see in looking at Churchill in 1940–41 that the revisionists are surely wrong morally, apart from anything else, to say we should have done a deal with Hitler in 1940, to allow him to go east while we preserved the British Empire.

But on the issue of the West's betrayal of the one solid democracy in Central and Eastern Europe in 1938, Czechoslovakia, Churchill has now been proved more right than even he knew at the time, which makes his defense of that brave and unfortunate country all the more perspicacious and our wicked desertion of it to Hitler far worse.

This is because we now know (to use the title of John Lewis Gaddis's book on the Cold War) what the Soviets were thinking at the time. This makes an enormous difference. Up until Gorbachev in the 1980s we could read our own archives but not those of our Soviet wartime ally or those of countries that became Soviet satellite states after 1945. Some historians, such as Britain's John Erickson, were able to consult some, but, by and large, extensive and free research in such archives—essential to gaining a true perspective—was impossible. This is no longer true and many historians, such as Michael Jabara Carley, Jonathan Haslam, and Gabriel Gorodetsky have been able to examine what was hitherto forbidden.[1] While the main changes to our new knowledge have been in studies of the Cold War, it has also had a major impact on our understanding of what was happening in the USSR in the period 1938–1941.

In particular we can now see what the Russians (as Churchill always called them) were thinking during the Czechoslovakian crisis of 1938 and, equally important, in the discussions that led to the Molotov-Ribbentrop Pact of 1939, the key event that enabled Hitler to launch what soon became World War II.

On both issues, Churchill is triumphantly vindicated, both in his outrage at our shoddy betrayal of the Czechs in 1938 and also in the need to bring the USSR in on our side against Hitler in 1939, especially after the Nazi conquest of the rump of Czechoslovakia in March 1939 convinced even Chamberlain that Hitler could no longer be trusted and that war of some kind was probably inevitable.

For not only should we have gone to the aid of the Czechs, morally speaking, but their defenses would have been such as to make a German blitzkrieg against them very difficult, and immensely costly to the Nazi invaders. The Czechs could certainly have held out far longer than the Poles in 1939, Poland being a country with virtually no natural frontiers, and, unlike Czechoslovakia, a nation without massive fortifications, which the Czechs would have used against a German invasion in 1938, but which Chamberlain in effect handed over to the Third Reich at Munich.

In addition, in 1938 the internal debate in the USSR was not over. Maksim Litvinov, who was Jewish, had not yet been dismissed as foreign commissar, and was thus still in place to argue for an effective antifascist front, of which the Soviet Union was in a position to play a pivotal part. While the Poles were, for understandable historical reasons, as wary of the USSR as they were of the Third Reich, it now seems to be the case that other Central and Eastern European countries would, albeit nervously, have given the USSR overflight rights, which would have enabled at least some direct assistance to the Czechs, even if falling short of sending an actual army to their aid.

But Chamberlain, who wrote to his sister about his "most profound distrust of the Soviet," ruthlessly excluded not only the poor Czechs themselves from the deliberations and decisions of 1938, but also the USSR. This, the new documentary evidence seems to show, was critical in the internal Soviet debate. It persuaded Stalin, who held the ultimate power, to side with those who wished to do a protective deal with Hitler. He felt this would allow the USSR to rearm (rather important after his catastrophic and bloodthirsty purges of the Red Army) and potentially allow the capitalist powers to destroy each other, thereby making the Soviet Union all the more powerful in the aftermath.

In 1939 Litvinov made way for Vyacheslav Molotov, who, while negotiating with the West, also negotiated with Hitler, in the Molotov-Ribbentrop Pact (also known as the Nazi-Soviet or Hitler-Stalin Pact) of August 1939. Hitler was thus able to invade Poland, *in collaboration with the Soviet Union in 1939;* this also allowed Hitler not to have to worry about his eastern front in 1940, enabling Germany to conquer France that year.

If, however, Hitler had had to fight a hard campaign against the Czechs in *1938*, with a hostile rather than neutral/friendly USSR, things would have been dramatically different. It might, in fact, have ended the war if not that year, 1938, but a very great deal earlier than proved to be the case.

Churchill had his secret sources within the Air Ministry, so knew many British defense secrets. But he did not know of the items at which we have just looked. No one in London knew of the internal Soviet discussions, which remained secret until the files opened in the 1980s and 1990s. *But on the two key issues—the need to defend Czechoslovakia and the importance of including the USSR in an antifascist alliance, Churchill was supremely right.*

One of the key themes of this book is that if Churchill had listened to General George C. Marshall, the Second World War would have ended in 1943, rather than in 1945, and with dramatically different results.

But it is also worth saying that I state this in the light of several facts: the war started in 1939, the Americans did not enter until late 1941, and Chamberlain's policies, even after fighting began, were so dreadful that Churchill inherited an almost impossible hand in 1940.

This is why those revisionists who praise Chamberlain and want to restore his shattered reputation are, to me, so completely wrong. For the reason why Britain had to cede global supremacy to the United States—as if such a thing would not have happened sooner or later anyway—is that by 1940, so terrible was Britain's position, and so hor-rifyingly close was the United Kingdom, let alone its empire, to utter defeat and ruin, that, as Churchill knew, the only possible hope of survival was the entry of the United States into the war on the Allied side. The only options were American rescue and subsequent hege-mony, or conquest by the Third Reich. Looking at all the evidence, there is no third solution, as simple as that.

Chamberlain told his sisters that one could only count on the Americans for words, and nothing else. It seems extraordinary today, after nearly seventy years of America as the greatest power in the West, that serious politicians, such as those who ran Britain in the period 1933–40, could honestly exclude the United States utterly from their decisions. Yet such is indeed the case with the Chamberlain gov-ernment, with its firm rejection of all Roosevelt's offers of mediation.

(To be fair, things were not helped by Joseph Kennedy, the US ambassador in London, who regularly wrote off Britain's chances of survival, to the horror of his pro-British son Jack. President Kennedy's making of Winston Churchill an honorary US citizen in 1963 is seen by many as filial atonement for Ambassador Kennedy's record back in 1940.)

So although Churchill, when finally in office, unwittingly pro-longed the war, had he been prime minister in 1938, Hitler would have lost it that year, the Holocaust would never have taken place, and

Central and Eastern Europe would never have suffered under Soviet rule for over forty years. We would thus never have had the Cold War either. Sooner or later Britan would have been obliged to give up its empire, but it would not have become as spectacularly financially bankrupt as proved to be the case in 1945 after six years of global conflict. The United States would surely have emerged as the world's premier superpower, but through inevitable economic growth and development, instead of as the result of the biggest war in history.

For as the historian Michael Jabara Carley shows in his book *1939*, the "orthodox opinion...that Britain had few policy options" is complete nonsense.[2] What Carley shows is that both Britain and France in effect shut the USSR out of the political system from around 1935 onwards, and this in turn ruined the standing within the Soviet Union of those like Litvinov who wanted a firm antifascist alliance with the West. Chamberlain showed his utter contempt for the Soviets by excluding them from Munich, so the Russians under Stalin simply took their revenge by signing the Molotov-Ribbentrop Pact with Hitler in August 1939. The West had been appeasing Hitler for years to save itself from war with the Nazis; now, Stalin was saying in effect, it is our turn.

(Historians, says Carley, who look solely at Western negotiations with the Soviets in the March–August 1939 period—that between the Nazi conquest of the rump of Czechoslovakia and the signing of the pact—are ignoring all that went before, including the West's deliberate spurning of the Soviet option.)

What is especially important to remember is how violently anti-Soviet Churchill had been until well into the 1930s. Between 1918 and 1920 there was no greater supporter of actual military intervention against the infant USSR by British troops than Churchill himself—an obsession, according to the then prime minister, David Lloyd

George, that many found annoying.[3] Churchill had wanted armed action against the Bolsheviks in the Russian civil war, and no one could outdo him in terms of anti-Communism, not just in rhetoric but in what he hoped would be a decisive war to strangle the Soviet Union at birth.

Ideologically speaking, therefore, the very fact that it is Churchill, *the* anti-Bolshevik, with a track record no other British Conservative politician could match, who came out for an alliance *with* Stalin, against Hitler, shows how far Churchill had come and how acutely he, as opposed to all the other French and British politicians of his time, saw the real facts and the overwhelming danger to the West that the Nazis posed.

The supreme irony of the 1938–39 period is that it was the anti-Communists such as Neville Chamberlain who, precisely because they excluded the Soviets during this time, ensured that it was Stalin who won World War II. There was indeed a European-based superpower in 1945, with a vast empire, but that was Stalin's USSR, the victor of the land struggle against the Third Reich, and not the fading, economically broken Britain and its empire.

Chamberlain's defenders blame Churchill for this; following Carley and those who have actually read the Soviet archives I would do exactly the opposite. In 1938–39 Britain *did* have options. But Chamberlain threw them away, first at Munich in 1938 by destroying the one democratic power in Central Europe with strong defenses and a real army—Czechoslovakia—and thereafter by pursuing will o' the wisp talks with countries in Central Europe, such as Poland or Romania, that militarily Britain could never defend against Nazi aggression, thereby antagonizing the one power that could, the USSR. As Soviet Commissar Maksim Litvinov told the French ambassador to Moscow, Robert Coulondre, in 1937, the Soviets, faced with the obvious Nazi threat to peace in Europe, felt like Cassandra, the Trojan priestess who warned against the impending invasion from the Greeks. But no one was listening and the Soviets were beginning to feel bitter.

Carley suggests with considerable merit that "the root of failure of Anglo-Franco-Soviet cooperation against Nazism was anti-communism."[4] The letters Neville Chamberlain wrote regularly to his sisters are strongly anti-Bolshevik, and, as Carley shows in more detail in *1939*, the French elite were as anti-Communist as their British counterparts. Indeed, the very existence of the quasi-fascist Vichy regime in France post-1940 shows that for many French patriots, conquest by Hitler was preferable to alliance with Stalin. It is Churchill's ability to conquer his own earlier anti-Bolshevism in the threat of Nazism that makes him so impressive in this period, precisely because so many of his own social class and background were the other way around, fearing Stalin more than Hitler.

Carley's book deals with the failed negotiations of 1939, between the British and French on the one hand, and the Soviets on the other, and does so for the first time in the knowledge of the internal debates in the Kremlin. So when he deals with how things could have been different, he does so in the context of how Poland's fate in 1939— attacked and conquered by both the Soviet Union from the east and the Nazis from the west—would have been drastically different. He writes:

> In the scenario that never happened, victorious French and Polish armies would have stood with British, US, and Soviet forces, and—especially the Poles—would have blocked unwanted communist expansion in Europe. Soviet prestige would have grown,

but Soviet communism would not have expanded into the void created by the Polish and French debacles.[5]

Carley rightly takes us back in his book to the West's rejection of Soviet collective security offers against Germany, going back to 1934–35. I would take my 1939 scenario to 1938, a year earlier. The Czechs did not fear the Soviets in the way that the Poles did (and with good historic reasons, in the Polish case), and their army was better—in 1939 incredibly brave Polish cavalry fought German tanks from on horseback, a noble but ultimately foolish and fatal gesture. A war in 1938 would have been even more successful than Carley's imagined British/French/Polish/Russian defeat of Hitler in 1939 and, since Czechoslovakia was a full-fledged democracy, one based on stronger moral grounds as well.

It is surely no coincidence that Churchill was writing his epic biography of Britain's greatest general, John Churchill, Duke of Marlborough, victor of the battle of Blenheim in 1702, just as he, the duke's twentieth-century descendant, was opposing appeasement in the House of Commons.

We will look at the strategic implications of what Churchill learned in more detail elsewhere. But the key thing is that *Churchill knew that without continental allies, Britain was far more vulnerable than if she had them.*

Churchill was above all a patriot, however old-fashioned. The virtue of this was that he understood the nature of the threat Nazism posed to British freedom itself far better than most of his contemporaries did. They were worried about Bolshevism, whereas he, no friend of Communism, knew that it was Hitler not Stalin that posed the vital strategic threat to Britain in the 1930s. There was no chance that Soviet planes and tanks would attempt to attack the United Kingdom, whereas Nazi domination of continental Europe would result either in conquest or, at the least, in total emasculation of Britain and its empire.

(This is why, when we come to 1940, he understood so correctly that to allow Hitler to rule as far as Calais would so seriously weaken Britain that even nominal independence was quite out of the question, something that many of his colleagues, such as Foreign Secretary Lord Halifax, entirely failed to grasp.)

Sometimes, as happened to Britain in 1756 (when the United Kingdom switched its major continental ally from Austria to the upstart Kingdom of Prussia), one has to jettison old prejudices in favor of new geopolitical realities. As in the eighteenth century so in the 1930s: Hitler's Germany was the menace, and Britain, as was historically always the case, needed allies.[6]

Thus when Churchill became prime minister in 1940, he was a man left with no options, since Chamberlain (and his French equivalents) had destroyed them all in 1938, and for sure in their failure to prosecute the war effectively against Germany when they could have in 1939–40. By 1940 it was survival with American help or disaster. That is the full horror of Chamberlain's mistake and blindness to both history and global realities.

The tragedy I deal with in this book is that in 1941 Churchill did not understand the full extent of what American involvement could now offer. Poor, battered Britain in 1940 had just one real choice—hang in there until America came to the rescue or suffer the French fate and be ruled by Hitler. But after 1941 the full military might of the greatest economic power in the world, that of the United States, was now fighting side by side with Britain.

Having now dealt with the background, let us look at precisely what happened at Munich, to see two things:

a. Why it was that Churchill was proved correct

b. The devastating long-term effect this was to have on Britain's ability to fight the war, not just after 1939 but especially after 1940, by which time Churchill was prime minister

Accounts of the Munich tragedy are many, with strong arguments on both sides, both for Neville Chamberlain and against. But perhaps one of the best is by a former US Army brigadier-general and subsequent academic, Telford Taylor: *Munich: The Price of Peace.*[7]

Taylor, while recognizing that Chamberlain and others did have a case—namely, that Munich bought time—is nevertheless devastating in his critique of this view, and on that he is surely right.[8]

In 1939 the Soviet Union was neutral, having been appalled at the West's behavior toward the Czechs. So Stalin did his deal with Hitler, and as a result the Germans only had to fight a one-front war, which they won. Had we defended the Czechs, that would not have been the case—the USSR would either have gone directly to Czechoslovakia's aid or at least been active somehow on the side of the West. Germany would have had to fight a two-front war, and that in itself would have made the fighting very different. As Taylor correctly points out, in "terms of the balance of forces, and the Second Front [i.e., two-front war] which the Chiefs of Staff ardently desired in 1939, Britain and France would have been better off in 1938."

In terms of the *naval* balance of power, all too often ignored in the equation—though not by Churchill—the Royal Navy's preponderance in terms of ships and submarines would also have been far greater, since by 1939 Germany had been able to augment its navy considerably. Britain's power to mount an economic blockade of Germany was thus far more considerable in 1938 than a year later.

While the British and French armies were not in particularly great shape in 1938, Taylor shows that in 1938–39, the Wehrmacht made enormous strides, partly in divisional strength—just four extra—but above all in armor: German armed strength *doubled* in panzer forces alone, enabling the winning blitzkriegs of 1939–40 to take place successfully. Not only that, but when it invaded France the German army had 335 *former Czech* tanks, all of which were now used against the West instead of on the West's side, as would have been the case had we aided the Czechs as we could and should have done in 1938.

(In fact the Czech army was even better equipped than that—as we shall see.)

While it is entirely true to say that the RAF had a dramatic increase in 1938–39, and one that made perhaps a crucial difference in the airborne Battle of Britain in 1940, it is also the case that the increase in size of the Luftwaffe in the same period was equally significant. So the *net* balance is equal on both sides, and thus one cannot argue that postponing the war a year altered the outcome of the air campaigns.

However, as Taylor points out, in "every other important military aspect, they [the Allies] would have been better off had they fought in support of Czechoslovakia in 1938 instead of throwing her to the wolves." Taylor, a former general as well as an academic, knows of what he speaks.

We also know from Field Marshal Keitel's memoirs that the Czech defenses were very powerful indeed in 1938, and thus drastically different from the far less impressive Polish military in 1939, not to forget the fact that Czechoslovakia had strong natural defenses in its mountains—the part we forced the Czechs to give to Hitler in 1938—whereas Poland's plains and marshes had no such obstacles against an invading army.

As Keitel wrote in his memoirs, the Wehrmacht was "truly surprised by the strength of the larger forts and military emplacements."[9] While it is possible that the Czechoslovakian army would have been overrun eventually, the consensus seems to be that they would have held out for a great deal longer than the Poles managed in 1939, and there it is vital to remember that the Poles were defending themselves on two fronts—against the Soviets from the east as well as the Germans from the west—whereas the Czechs would have been fighting only one enemy.

Not only that, but the Czechs would have been an asset to the West in any war in 1938, not just in how long they would have held out. We see this in how much Czech weaponry the Germans gained in 1939, when the rump Czechoslovakia fell to the Nazis in March that year. The Third Reich gained 1,600 aircraft, 550 antitank guns, some 2,175 artillery pieces, and no less than 43,000 machine guns (and the Czech Skoda Works were, I would add, reckoned to be the best arms manufacturers in the world), along with 469 tanks and armored cars.[10] In March 1939 all this went onto the debit side from the credit side so far as the Western Allies were concerned.

Furthermore, we also now know that because the weather over Czechoslovakia was terrible in the relevant days in the fall of 1938,[11] the Luftwaffe would have had serious losses if they had been obliged to invade Czechoslovakia in September/October 1938 instead of being given the key defensive areas on a plate by Neville Chamberlain.

Finally, Taylor is surely right to argue that Hitler would have had to keep many army divisions on his eastern borders in a war in 1938, out of fear of possible Soviet action, as was *not* the case in the real war that broke out in 1939, for the reasons we have seen.[12] Although Taylor and others (such as Paul Kennedy) are surely right to say that the fall of France in 1940 was due to sheer French military incompetence,[13] one could argue that at least the French would have faced fewer German troops and have had more time to get their act together.

As Correlli (Bill) Barnett, former keeper of the Churchill Archives, concludes:

> The war itself was begun under the worst strategic circumstances. In 1936, when the French army was strong and the German army was weak, the British had not even tried to persuade the French to mobilise and put an end to the illegal German re-militarization of the Rhineland; on the contrary. In 1938, in the Munich crisis, under the spell of bomber-funk [the fear of former Prime Minister Stanley Baldwin that "the bomber would always get through"[14]] and military weakness, the British government had bartered a fine Czech army in exchange for Hitler's promises of goodwill. Now in 1939 the British had elected to fight when the military balance had tipped further in the German favour, for the years 1936–1939 [for which Telford Taylor blames Chamberlain more than Baldwin] had marked the progressive weakening and obsolescence of the French army *vis-à-vis* the German, and the progressive erosion of the French will to fight.[15]

One could not put it better.

All this means, I would argue, that when war *did* come, Neville Chamberlain had thrown away any prospect of Britain winning. Thus when Churchill finally achieved his lifelong ambition, in May

1940, and became prime minister, he could not have done so in worse circumstances. By then, Churchill was very much in the right—he had demonstrated beyond peradventure that Britain should have increased its armed forces and stood up to Hitler.

The tragic irony, as Barnett and others have reminded us, is that it was *Churchill* who as chancellor of the exchequer had denuded us of the necessary armed forces back in the 1920s.[16] But it was evident from 1933 onwards that the happier times of the 1920s had changed, and that if Churchill had been right to cut the size of the armed forces after 1918, they had now to be restored to the kind of level that would enable Britain to fight its enemies in full-scale war. Churchill was now on the side of the angels, but with nowhere near the number of tools, as he would put it, to finish the job.

Why was Churchill so ignored? Here I think we can agree with Professor John Charmley, Churchill's most eminent critic and Neville Chamberlain's foremost defender. Charmley's comments are correct in this instance, and worth quoting at length, because the issue is something that not only Churchill overlooks in his own history of this period but also most people for whom Churchill's exile from power is a mystery:

> The darker tone with which Churchill portrayed the contemporary world was to be evident from 1933 onwards, but the very bitterness with which he pursued Baldwin prevented his message from being effective. It was regarded by many as a "die-hard" view of the world, which it was; but many liberal-Conservatives [such as Duff Cooper, who resigned over Munich] felt themselves cut off from Churchill by the fact that those who supported him on India were the sort of antique right-wingers whose influence on Conservative counsels was deplored by liberal opinion. Churchill was in a

vicious circle: he could not fight India without the "Blimps" [a 1930s term for rabid reactionaries, after a mythical "Colonel Blimp"], but many of these did not share his views on the dangers to be apprehended from the Continent; whilst those who shared his views on the latter deplored his associates and actions over India. As long as Churchill could be portrayed as being more interested in wrecking the Government than he was in India, then his position would be a difficult one and his word would be set at discount.[17]

This is precisely what happened, so that as the menace from Nazi Germany grew ever more terrible, no one who should have listened was taking any notice of Churchill because of his wholly reactionary—one could even say racist and primeval—attitude toward India and its desire to be free of foreign colonial rule. This is all airbrushed out of the great Churchill myth of the voice crying in the wilderness, but if we look at Churchill honestly, we have to take this very strongly into account. He was ignored where he was right because he shouted so loudly over things upon which he was manifestly wrong.

But on the rest of what follows, one cannot in all conscience agree with Churchill's critics—for instance, the next chapter in Charmley's account of this period is called "The Myths of Munich."[18] But as we have just seen, the *real* myth is in fact the one that Chamberlain's supporters issued at the time and which the revisionists have expounded since, that Munich gained Britain time. In fact it is now clear that the opposite is true and that the democracies were in a far *worse* position in relation to Germany in September 1939 than they would have been in October 1938.

Churchill instinctively knew this, so let us see how he reacted to the events as they tragically unfolded during 1938.

Churchill had no doubts that Czechoslovakia was a true beacon of democracy. As he told an audience in Bristol, in the west of England, toward the beginning of the crisis on May 16, 1938:

> I see no reason why the Sudeten Deutsche [*sic*] should not become trusted and honoured partners in what is, after all, the most progressive and democratic of the new States in Europe...It is a dark hour in which to proclaim...[a pro–League of Nations Covenant] policy, but I believe that with wisdom and resolution all that has been lost might be recovered.[19]

Churchill believed that Germany was not ready for war in 1938—something that subsequent research has proved to be entirely correct. But in this, alas, he was often a lone voice. Furthermore, as we have seen, in predicting the opposite of what most people said at the time—that *Britain* would grow proportionately stronger in 1938–39 (the "time for rearmament" argument made by the appeasers then and their apologists since)—and insisting that our enemies were the ones who would become militarily readier and more powerful, Churchill was being truly prophetic. As he told his constituency in Chingford later that month:

> High authorities consider that Germany is not ready for a land war. There is a shortage of food and of raw materials. The German Army is not fully officered. In these circumstances, unless the rulers of Germany go mad, we should have a further breathing space. But what is going to happen next year and in 1940? The German Army will be much relatively stronger than that of France and the British Air Force is not catching up. Indeed, at the present time we are falling further behind. Unless, therefore, we can gain other Powers to the side of peace, disaster may occur.

As history now knows, this is exactly what happened. Germany caught up and overtook the democracies, Chamberlain signed away the one true and fully armed democracy in Central Europe, and in 1939 war broke out at a moment seriously disadvantageous to the democratic West.

Churchill had foreseen all of it, and was utterly ignored. What a tragedy, we say today, and on this issue rightly so. But we forget that people were not listening to the man who was right about Hitler, but to the bungler of the Dardanelles and Gallipoli in the First World War, a man who had changed his political party twice, who had spent most of the 1930s opposing even home rule for India and who had been the loyal supporter of the degenerate King Edward VIII. This is the true tragedy of the child who cried wolf, since as the tale concludes, finally the wolf *did* come but no one believed the child.

Thankfully for posterity, Churchill was thick-skinned enough to continue regardless. As he warned a meeting of League of Nations enthusiasts in Birmingham (Neville Chamberlain's home city and a major manufacturing town) on June 2, 1938:

> The idea that dictators can be appeased by kind words and concessions is doomed to disappointment. Volcanic forces are moving in Europe and sombre figures are at the head of the most powerful races. The dictator countries are prepared night and day to advance their ambition, if possible by peace, if necessary by war. I am under the impression that we and other countries stand in great danger...our air forces, on which so much depends, are actually falling farther and farther behind.

By September, Neville Chamberlain was doing all possible to prevent war by betraying the Czechs, thereby, unknown to anyone in Britain, greatly strengthening the position of those in the Soviet Union who wanted to keep out of conflict and let the capitalist powers destroy each other, rather than those, such as Foreign Minister Litvinov, for whom an antifascist alliance was the key to peace.

Churchill issued a statement to the Press Association in London on September 21, which showed that, unlike the prime minister, he truly understood the issues at stake:

> It is necessary that the nation should realise the magnitude of the disaster into which we are being led. The partition of Czechoslovakia under Anglo-French pressure amounts to a complete surrender by the Western Democracies to the Nazi threat of force. Such a collapse will not bring peace or safety to Great Britain and France. On the contrary, it will bring both countries into a position of ever increasing weakness and danger. The neutralisation of Czechoslovakia alone means the liberation of 25 German divisions to threaten the Western front. The path to the Black Sea will be laid wide open to triumphant Nazism.... The idea that safety can be purchased by throwing a small State to the wolves is a fatal delusion. The German war power will grow faster than the French and British can complete their preparations for defence.

Tragically for the Czechs, the few British cabinet ministers who wavered at the sheer scale of the betrayal proved no match for Neville Chamberlain, with only Duff Cooper, the First Lord of the Admiralty, finally having the courage to resign.

By the time Parliament eventually assembled on October 5, 1938, it was too late—the Germans had moved into the areas they wanted and Hitler's bloodless triumph was complete.

In the debate that took place, Churchill was under no illusions that the idea that Britain had won "peace with honor"—Chamberlain's infamous phrase on returning from Germany—was utter nonsense. In saying what he did, Churchill was not only right but also brave, since the overwhelming popular mood in the country was relief at there being no war, with absolutely no concept whatsoever of the cost of what the West's betrayal of their fellow democracy would now entail. Chamberlain was cheered in the streets, and seldom can a nation have been so delusional as was the United Kingdom that October.

So Churchill knew that he was in a small minority on the Conservative benches when he got up to speak, saying:

> I will, therefore, begin by saying the most unpopular and unwelcome thing. I will begin by saying what everybody would like to ignore or forget but which must nevertheless be stated, namely, that we have sustained a total and unmitigated defeat, and that France has suffered even more than we have.

At this point, Viscountess Astor, the American-born first woman member of Parliament, shouted out, "Nonsense!"

(It was Lady Astor who told him once that he was drunk. He replied that *she* was ugly, but that *he* would be sober in the morning.)

Churchill continued unaffected. Had Britain and France come together with Russia, he argued, things could have been very different—but this had not even been tried. Instead:

> All is over. Silent, mournful, abandoned, broken, Czechoslovakia recedes into the darkness. She has suffered in every respect by her association with the Western Powers and with the League of Nations... [and] in particular from her association with France.

This, to Churchill and others, was what was so monstrous—that democracies that had promised to protect their friends (and by guarantee in the case of France and the now rump remains of Czechoslovakia)—had now forced their vulnerable ally into the hands of the Nazi dictatorship.

Churchill knew exactly what this would now mean:

> We are in the presence of a disaster of the first magnitude which has befallen Great Britain and France. Do not let us blind ourselves to that. It must now be accepted that all the countries of Central and Eastern Europe will make the best terms they can with the triumphant Nazi Power. The system of alliances in Central Europe upon which France has relied for her safety has been swept away, and I can see no means by which it can be reconstituted.

Not only that, Churchill pointed out, but Hitler would now step up his demands, and Britain, whose rearmament process was nowhere near along what it should have been, might find it impossible to refuse.

As he concluded (some of these words he would use for his history of Britain before the war):

> This is only the beginning of the reckoning. This is only the first sip, the first foretaste of a bitter cup which will be proffered to us year by year unless by a supreme recovery of moral health and martial vigour, we arise and take our stand for freedom as in the olden time.

In this famous speech Churchill also made a point that those who feel we should have done a deal with Hitler in 1940 should ponder closely. One point is a moral one; the other asks the legitimate question: so, if we allow Hitler to accomplish what he wants and on his terms, what kind of Britain will remain? A powerful nation with a mighty empire? Supporters of appeasement always point out that Hitler would have allowed the United Kingdom to keep its colonies in places such as Africa and the Raj. Or would it be something else, a state in theory strong, but in reality weak and dependent? Churchill saw the truth on both issues, first on the moral question:

> You have to consider the character of the Nazi movement and the rule which it implies. The Prime Minister desires to see cordial relations between this country and Germany. There is no difficulty at all in having cordial relations with the German people. Our hearts go out to them. But they have no power. You must have diplomatic and correct relations, but there can never be friendship between the British democracy and the Nazi Power, that Power which vaunts the spirit of aggression and conquest, which derives strength and perverted pleasure from persecution, and uses, as we have seen, with pitiless brutality the threat of murderous force. That Power cannot ever be the trusted friend of British democracy.

Churchill continued on the theme of Britain's fate if appeasement continued:

> What I find unendurable is the sense of our country falling into the power, into the orbit and influence of Nazi Germany, and of our existence becoming dependent on their good will or pleasure.

His pleas for effective rearmament had "all been in vain." A nightmare now stood before Britain:

We do not want to be led upon the high road to becoming a satellite of the German Nazi system of European domination.

As Churchill would have known, the London *Times* already censored reports from its correspondents that might upset Hitler, and Churchill foresaw this becoming the norm if things developed on their present course. One only has to see the way in which states in Central Europe were taken over piecemeal, first by the Nazis in the 1930s and then by Stalin in the 1940s, to see how easily this could happen, to know that Churchill was being no scaremonger.

But for the time being he was a lone voice. As he told his constituents in Chingford on December 11, in an end-of-year speech to supporters of the League of Nations:

This has been a year of disaster and humiliation the like of which Great Britain has not known for many generations. An even more unpromising phase lies before us. We are told our policy was appeasement. If that is true it is obviously failing.

Had Neville Chamberlain succumbed to Conservative Party pressure and called a special general election after Munich there is no doubt that Churchill would have been finished, since he would, in all likelihood, have lost his seat. His own constituency party only agreed that he could continue as its candidate (and thus member of Parliament) by three votes to two.

This is something we should remember, for it had strong repercussions even while Churchill was prime minister and, notionally at least, leader of the Conservative Party after Chamberlain's death in late 1940. Since Churchill was on the right of the party over issues such as India, many of the more moderate anti-appeasers looked to the glamorous figure of Anthony Eden for leadership, and kept as far away from Churchill as possible. But Eden, if one can be so bold, was surely a wimp, someone whose opposition to Munich was so nuanced as to be unrecognizable, and certainly no threat to the prime minister. In fact Eden was wanting to get back into the government, and therefore always pulled his punches, something of which Chamberlain was aware, and which enabled the prime minister therefore to ignore criticism coming from that quarter.

The bulk of the party was, however, firmly behind Chamberlain, and regarded Churchill with grave suspicion and scorn.[20]

When he did finally achieve the premiership in 1940, since there had been no general election, the parliamentary Conservative Party remained those mainly pro-Baldwin and pro-Chamberlain members who had been elected in 1935. Fantastic as it may now seem to us, and to present-day Conservatives in Britain (not to mention countless small c conservatives in the United States) for whom Churchill is the ultimate icon, the fact is that most Conservatives *at that time* despised him and all his works, and indeed continued to do so even after May 1940.[21]

In fact, as biographers on Eden have shown, it was Anthony Eden rather than Winston Churchill to whom many of the dynamic young Conservatives looked,[22] however extraordinary this might seem to us in the hindsight of how disastrous a prime minister Eden proved to be (as Churchill had guessed) when he finally achieved that office in 1955, only to resign in ignominy in 1957. Had Eden, who had been foreign secretary as recently as February 1938, when he resigned, pushed himself with any degree of vigor, the prize would quite possibly have been his in 1940, and not Churchill's. But, as time was to show, Eden was not the stuff of which leaders were made, something that was reflected as soon as September 1939, when Chamberlain felt obliged to have Churchill in the war cabinet, as First Lord of the Admiralty, but Eden outside it, in charge of links with the Dominions, away from the management of war.

What changed everything was the callous Nazi invasion of the rump of the Czechoslovakian state on March 14, 1939. Suddenly the Emperor, Chamberlain, was seen as he really was, without any clothes. Appeasement was over.

However, although the policy was now seen to have failed, its practitioners retained their full grip on power, with even more disastrous results.

Meanwhile, Churchill did not hesitate to remind his constituents of the horrors that now awaited them after the destruction of Czechoslovakia and that country's total removal from the map. As he told them, the "entire balance of Europe" had been changed, and for Britain in particular:

Although we can do nothing to stop it [i.e., help the Czechs], we shall be sufferers on a very great scale. We shall have to make all kinds of sacrifices for our own defence that would have been unnecessary if a firm resolve had been made at an earlier stage. We shall have to make sacrifices not only of money, but of personal service in order to make up for what we have lost. This is even more true of the French than of ourselves.

Attacking those in his own constituency who had tried to deselect him, he pointed out that "everything I said has already proved true": his stand back in October 1938 was entirely vindicated.

When war began, a devastated Neville Chamberlain confessed to the House of Commons:

[E]verything that I have worked for, everything that I have hoped for, everything that I have believed in during my public life, has crashed into ruins. There is only one thing left for me to do: that is, to devote what strength and powers I have to forwarding the victory of the cause for which we have to sacrifice so much. I cannot tell what part I may be allowed to play: I trust that I may live to see the day when Hitlerism has been destroyed, and a liberated Europe has been re-established.[23]

Since Chamberlain died little over a year later, his wish did not come to pass.

His protagonists have seen him as a tragic figure, as can be seen in the name of one later biography: *Chamberlain and the Lost Peace*, at the end of which the above quote is given as a tragic epigraph to a man who loved peace above war.[24]

The real problem with such a view is that Adolf Hitler and the nature of the Nazi regime gave no choice—*there never was going to be a peace so long as Hitler was around and Nazism was conquering Europe.* As we also saw, Churchill knew that no deal with Hitler was *politically* possible let alone morally defensible. Since there was going to be no peace, Chamberlain's policy was doomed from the start. In fact, Lord Swinton, the man who did more than anything to try to make sure that we had a Royal Air Force capable of defending Britain, discovered that Chamberlain did all possible to sabotage his efforts at national defense.

One Churchill critic has written that to "fight a war was, in a sense, already to have lost it," since economically Britain simply did not have the resources to fight the war upon which it now embarked.[25]

In terms of the *sustained* spending which war required, we should of course remember that this view is sound economics—Britain was nearly bankrupted by the end of the First World War (as Churchill knew well) and was going to have its economy completely devastated by the end of the Second.

But what good would being the helpless satellite of a victorious and mighty Third Reich have been? Surely Churchill was right to see that "victory whatever the cost" (as he was to put it) was better than that. Furthermore, as Hitler had proved notoriously unreliable, who could trust his promises that the British Empire would be left alone while he ruled the Continent, massacring its Jews and Slavs with equal hatred? How long might Britain's timorous satellite status have lasted until Hitler imposed direct rule, and all that that implied? Not only that, but how would the United States, the country Chamberlain wrongly so despised,[26] have been able to liberate Europe from Nazism without the launchpad of the United Kingdom? It might have happened, but it would have been infinitely more difficult.

In any case, the Americans realized what Churchill, with his notoriously antediluvian views, failed to see—the British *Empire* was surely not worth saving *as an imperial domain*. The days of such empires were over, as Roosevelt understood, but both Chamberlain and Churchill, with their Victorian mindsets, utterly failed to see it.

Britain could not have avoided war with Germany, the long-term future of the British Empire upon which the sun famously never set was over, *and* the United States was already, though it did not know it until 1943 or 1944, the mightiest nation on earth. All these things were inevitable and no amount of wishful thinking or nostalgic fantasy for better times would put it right for Britain.

(One could say that the British supremacy was doomed as soon as war broke out in *1914*, since economically speaking the United Kingdom and its empire were never as prosperous or as powerful thereafter.)

Chamberlain, for all the sincerity of his efforts—and one should not begrudge him that—was therefore destroying all he believed in *himself* by the policies that he adopted. Had rearmament truly been increased after he became prime minister; had he stood by democratic Czechoslovakia; had he spoken to and tried to involve the Soviet Union, however distasteful; had he heeded the world's greatest democracy, the United States: how very different indeed, and for the better, things would have been then. But the former Lord Mayor of Birmingham knew better, and in September 1939 Britain finally entered into conflict with Germany with the worst of all possible hands.

Chamberlain now formed a ministry—but not an all-party coalition of the kind that had won the First World War, the kind that under Churchill would be on the winning side in the Second. It was an emphatically Conservative government, made different really only by the appointment of Winston Churchill as First Lord of the Admiralty, a post that Churchill had last held, alas so disastrously, back in 1911–15.

(Since the main theme of this book focuses on Churchill as prime minister I am not going to give enormous detail about his time at the Admiralty, toward the end of which he also became chairman of the committee of defense ministers—Admiralty, War Office, and Air Office. The official history of the campaign in Norway is very helpful for those who want to read more, along with Stephen Roskill's definitive first volume of *The War at Sea*.)[27]

Even a resolute defender of Churchill's war record cannot truly claim that Churchill's brief time at the Admiralty was a stunning success. For example, it is clear that he did not understand the devastating effect of air power on vulnerable battleships—something that was not an issue when he was first appointed in 1911. As we shall see later on, this was to have catastrophic results in December 1941.[28] Nor it seems did he really grasp the significance of convoys, which were to be so vital after 1942 in conveying American troops to come to the rescue in Europe.

In the spring of 1940, Churchill, desperate for British troops actually to attack the German enemy—something they were certainly not doing during this period, often called the Phony War—dreamed up a scheme that would do just this. This would involve both the Royal Navy and ultimately British Army forces, as well as breaching Norwegian neutrality (the Scandinavian countries were doing their best to keep out of the conflict, and Sweden was to remain neutral throughout the war).

The plan was typically Churchillian—bold and innovative. But it was also a disaster, just as so many of his bright schemes had been during World War I, such as that at Gallipoli.

One interesting point, though, does need to be made: although the Germans were able to win and capture Norway, their fleet was devastated. They thus lost control of the Atlantic and, come the evacuation of British forces from Dunkirk later that year, the German fleet was in no position to stop the escaping French and British troops. So there was a silver lining to the very dark Norwegian cloud.[29]

But fate now played an extraordinary turn, one that in fact went on to save Britain from certain defeat at the hands of the Nazis.

In the debate in the House of Commons in May 1940, it was Churchill who had to be the government's main defender against a motion of censure put out by the opposition. Back in 1915–16, such a mess had cost him his career. Now it was to make him prime minister. For it was obvious that while the actual debacle in Norway was Churchill's fault, nonetheless, the *real* problem was the continuation of Neville Chamberlain as prime minister, and of an administration that was entirely partisan in nature and not the cross-party coalition needed in wartime.

So while Churchill did his best to defend the government, numerous Conservative MPs voted against their own party and with the opposition. As a result, the government's normal three-figure majority plummeted, and Chamberlain realized at long last that he needed to resign.

It was in fact touch and go whether Churchill would be prime minister, since the establishment favorite was Lord Halifax, the foreign secretary. But not only was Halifax a peer, in the House of Lords, but, as he understood about himself, he simply did not have the stomach to be a wartime leader. This was just as well—as Richard Holmes has rightly said, it does not bear thinking about what would have happened to Britain after the fall of France later that year if Halifax rather than Churchill had become prime minister.

Fortunately Churchill was the one King George VI chose to form a government. He now proceeded to do so, calling on all the talents and parties as well, with senior Labour Party leaders now included.

So Churchill was prime minister at last. As he famously recorded in *The Gathering Storm*:

During these last crowded days of the political crisis my pulse had not quickened at any moment. I took it all as it came. But I cannot conceal from the reader of this truthful account that as I went to bed at about 3 am, I was conscious of a profound sense of relief. At last I had the authority to give directions over the whole scene. I felt as if I were walking with destiny, and that all my past life had been but a preparation for this hour and this trial. Eleven years in the political wilderness had freed me from ordinary Party antagonisms. My warnings over the last six years had been so numerous, so detailed, that no one could gainsay me. I could not be reproached for making the war or with want of preparation for it. I thought I knew a good deal about it all, and I was sure I should not fail. Therefore, although impatient for the morning, I slept soundly and had no need for cheering dreams. Facts are better than dreams.[30]

This is of course the Churchill legend at its best, and is oft-quoted by those who, rightly, admire the great man as the savior of his country. He was, though, being disingenuous. Plenty other than opposition to appeasement had kept him out of power from 1931 to 1939, and this he ignores. His truculence on India was to have serious ramifications during the war, as we shall see. But one could also say that in being excluded so ruthlessly from office by MacDonald, Baldwin, and Chamberlain he had been supremely lucky.

Appeasement had not merely failed but done so spectacularly, and in Churchill there was now a leader of his people, a father of the nation, who had both opposed it and, *among many other issues*, been refused power because of it. His slate was clean, he was uncontaminated by the past, and he could lead a new government with a clear conscience in a way that would have been impossible for, say, someone such as Eden had he become prime minister instead. Whatever Churchill's faults, and we should not forget them, what did, for example, India matter now that Britain was alone against the most deadly enemy in its national history? In May 1940 no other issues mattered any more than the one on which Churchill had been supremely, utterly, and completely right.

CHAPTER TWO

Britain Alone and Churchill's Fatal Error

O N MAY 10, 1940, Winston Churchill achieved his lifetime ambition: he was prime minister and First Lord of the Treasury. Destiny had smiled upon him at last, though as John Charmley has put it: "If Destiny was walking with Churchill, it had brought him into something which resembled a trap."[1]

Professor Charmley, whose views on Britain in May 1940 have, over the years, become controversial, is in fact correct on this issue. But another biographer, David Reynolds, is also right to say that it is for this glorious period, 1940 and the decision to fight on, that Churchill is best and most rightly remembered: "the apex of his career and one of the most epic moments in British history."[2] Or as Richard Holmes puts it, the "event of May 1940 and the two years that followed are the most studied in the entire history of Britain."[3]

They are also some of the most controversial, since both serious historians such as John Charmley and renegade politicians such as Pat

Buchanan have accused Churchill of making the wrong choice. (Even novelists are now doing this.) Britain, they believe, still had an empire, one worth defending and keeping. Churchill was to proclaim "victory whatever the cost" and for some this was a cost too high.

(While reviewers, such as one in the *New York Review of Books* in 2008, lump John Charmley together with the right-wing revisionists, your author disagrees. Charmley, for example, believes that Churchill should have enabled Britain to play its full role in Europe after 1945, and that his belief in the Special Relationship blinded him to the need for the United Kingdom to take its proper place in the new European unity that arose as a result of the war. This I think automatically puts John Charmley into a different category of critic, since one of the main features of most of the ultra-right-wing revisionists is their Europhobia. Nevertheless, while Charmley's case is based on decades of solid research, his position on 1940 is not the one followed here, as will become obvious.)

Here we come into a minefield: do morals play a role in history, and in its writing? Surely the answer when dealing with 1940 would have to be "yes they do," and that in turn changes our perspective on Churchill and the actions he took in the key weeks in 1940 that saved Britain from Nazi conquest and enabled the British people to retain their independence from one of the most odious tyrannies the world has ever seen.

In fact Churchill's decision was even braver than he allowed us to believe from his memoirs of those valiant days.

In the second volume of his memoirs, *Their Finest Hour,* he writes of the time just before the French surrender:

Future generations may deem it noteworthy that the supreme question of whether we should fight on alone never found a place upon the War Cabinet agenda. It was taken for granted and as a matter of course by these men of all parties in the State, and we were much too busy to waste time upon such unreal, academic issues. We were united also in viewing the new phase with good confidence...I was invited to send a message in the same sense to President Roosevelt.[4]

This sounds very heroic! Unquestionably it was the right decision, since the idea that Britain could keep its empire and have a genuine degree of independence from a Third Reich that controlled the entire continent is surely a fantasy of the largest magnitude, as I have said elsewhere. But it is alas completely untrue.

To begin with, Churchill took power, as we saw, initially only with Conservative support, and it was only when he had actually become prime minister that he brought the Labour and Liberal parties in with him to form the coalition government that was to last until the fall of Germany in 1945.[5] Not only that but Chamberlain was still leader of the Conservative Party, and thus the wielder of enormous political power.

We can see this in the diaries of John Colville, later an ardent Churchillian (and effective cofounder of Churchill College at Cambridge) but back in May 1940 someone as enthusiastically pro-Chamberlain as most of the British establishment at the time (King George VI, for example, and Queen Elizabeth very much included). Colville is important as not only was he at the heart of the Whitehall/ Court nexus (grandson of a former cabinet minister, a page when a child to King George V), but also, in 1940, a promising diplomat and one of the young assistant private secretaries at 10 Downing Street.

On Friday, May 10, he was to record in his diary that if Chamberlain "does go I am afraid it *must* be Winston" [his italics].[6] When it was final that Churchill was indeed to be prime minister, Colville wrote of his Downing Street colleagues that "[e]verybody is in despair about the prospect." In fact, Colville's view of Churchill, which was typical of the upper reaches of society at the time, was:

> He may, of course, be the man of drive and energy the country believes him to be and he may be able to speed up our creaking military and industrial machinery; but it is a terrible risk, it involves the danger of rash and spectacular exploits, and I cannot help fearing that this country may be manoeuvred into the most dangerous position it has ever been in.[7]

Colville was indeed right about Britain's perilous plight, which, with the fall of France, was to get even worse. But the irony was that it was Colville's hero, Neville Chamberlain, and not Churchill, who had put the country there. But at the time, R.A. Butler, then parliamentary undersecretary of state to Halifax at the Foreign Office, represented the majority view when he told a depressed Colville the "sudden coup of Winston and his rabble was a serious disaster and an unnecessary one," that Churchill was a "half-breed American" and "the greatest adventurer in modern political history."[8]

In fact, as the eminent military historian (and biographer of both Winston Churchill and his ancestor John Churchill, Duke of Marlborough) Richard Holmes has shown, it was Churchill's sheer energy from day one that made the crucial difference from the lackluster regime of Chamberlain and the fainthearted, which was now thankfully gone.[9] We can be thankful that at the hour of greatest peril, someone who knew what he was doing and who believed that victory, however unlikely, was possible, now had the charge of the nation's destiny.

Much has been made of the fact that when on May 13 both Chamberlain and Churchill entered the House of Commons, it was Chamberlain not Churchill whom the Conservative backbenches cheered to the rafters.[10] This was not unnoticed by Churchill himself, and this in turn affected how he took his decisions.[11]

While we now therefore see this time as Churchill's greatest hour, this was emphatically not how it was perceived at the time.

Two of the main appeasers, Chamberlain and Halifax, remained in the cabinet: Chamberlain in the ancient post of Lord President of the Council, and Halifax even continuing in his prewar job as foreign secretary. The other two cabinet members were Clement Attlee, the leader of the Labour Party, and his deputy, Anthony Greenwood. Churchill was therefore the only anti-appeasement Conservative to hold cabinet rank.

His political room for maneuvering and what he was able to achieve were thus considerably circumscribed. By the end of the year Chamberlain was dead and Churchill his successor as the leader of the Conservative Party. Lord Halifax was safely thousands of miles away as British ambassador to the United States. But in May 1940 it was very different.

So, in fact, discussions did take place on what on earth to do now that our one major military continental ally, France, was about to crumble, with British troops being evacuated from Dunkirk, and Hitler's triumph in Western Europe seemingly complete. These were the war cabinet discussions on May 26, 27, and 28, 1940, with the rest of the new government brought in at the end.[12] Halifax for one was not keen to see the needless destruction of the British Empire, and was open to peace feelers, perhaps through Italy, which was then technically neutral. Halifax thought Churchill was speaking "the most frightful rot" and was listening only to his emotions, and not to reason.

This might sound the worst kind of appeasement, giving in to

Hitler. Yet if one thinks about it logically, as Halifax would have liked Churchill to do, how on earth Britain could have contemplated beating Hitler in May–June 1940—the fall of France only confirmed what everyone was expecting during the war cabinet discussions—is in actuality a complete mystery. Britain had disarmed heavily after the First World War, and after losing so much equipment at Dunkirk now had even less with which to fight the widely expected Nazi invasion. Yet Churchill was *in public* making some of the greatest speeches of his long career and, according to one later Conservative politician-cum-historian, Sir Robert Rhodes James, "one of the most crucial in modern history" on May 13, 1940:

> I would say to the House, as I said to those who have joined this Government: "I have nothing to offer but blood, toil, tears and sweat." We have before us an ordeal of the most grievous kind. We have before us many, many long months of struggle and suffering. You ask, what is our policy? I can say: it is to wage war, by sea, land and air, with all our might and with all the strength that God can give us; to wage war against a monstrous tyranny, never surpassed in the dark lamentable catalogue of human crime. This is our policy. You ask, what is our aim? I can answer in one word: It is victory, victory at all costs, victory in spite of all the terror, victory, however long and hard the road may be; for without victory, there is no survival. Let that be realized; no survival for the British Empire, no survival for all that the British Empire has stood for, no survival for the urge and impulse of the ages, that mankind will move forward to its goal. But I take up my task with buoyancy and hope. I feel sure that our cause will not be suffered to fall among men. At this time I feel entitled to claim the aid of all, and I say, "Come, let us go forward together with our united strength."[13]

(When a member of my family who survived the London Blitz saw Churchill's original notes for this speech in the Churchill Archives, she had goose bumps! It is difficult not to react in the same way nearly seventy years later. But one should add one important point: people remember these parliamentary speeches with awe and admiration, as they should. But unless they were in the House of Commons *at the time* they did not actually *hear* them live—broadcasting was forbidden in Parliament for several further decades. Rather they were broadcast later, and it is their *subsequent* broadcasts that people old enough actually recall.)

On May 19 Churchill broadcast one of his first speeches to the nation (which therefore those listening to the radio *did* hear live). He did not disguise the dire position in which Britain found itself: "It would be foolish...to disguise the gravity of the hour." But this speech presumed a stabilization "on the Western Front," and within days British troops were embarking on little boats across the Channel, all their vital equipment left behind for their enemies to use.

Churchill's policy was thus in tatters—there was no Western Front! As Richard Holmes is so right to comment: "It does not bear thinking about what would have happened had Chamberlain still been in place during the collapse of France,"[14] nor, one might add, if Halifax had been appointed prime minister only a few days earlier.

The reason is that when France fell only a month later, centuries of British foreign and defense policy vanished with the loss of the United Kingdom's one great continental ally. No one knew history better than Churchill, since he had written so much of it himself. He knew how his ancestor, the great John Churchill, first Duke of Marlborough, had managed to beat the aggressor of his time, King Louis XIV of France, and had done so in large part because of Great Britain's continental allies, especially the Dutch republic and the imperial forces under the command of Prince Eugene of Savoy. Without these allies, Britain would have had no chance against Louis XIV, whose power was greater than any other single power on the European continent. Marlborough was not merely captain general of an army but in effect also a diplomat holding a war coalition together, rather in the way that Eisenhower would find himself having to do in very different circumstances in 1944–45.

For the first month of Churchill's new premiership, this was not evident, since France was still in the war. The historic British policy—a large interocean navy and a small land force for use on the Continent alongside key allies—was still in place. Then all changed, and considerably for the worse.

Was Churchill being two-faced: making great speeches of defiance in public but allowing discussion of peace terms in private? I think not. There is little doubt that he himself opposed such surrender resolutely, telling his personal Chief of Staff, General Ismay, that he expected both of them to be dead within three months if the Nazis did land: one can imagine Churchill, gun in hand, fighting the invaders to the last ditch![15]

In fact, although it is evident from the archives that Churchill fiercely opposed a policy of surrender—in particular to Hitler—he really did not have much other option but to hope for the best. In terms of realpolitik Halifax was right: Britain's chances of survival were effectively nil. As we saw in the last chapter, this was because Chamberlain had all but destroyed them by betraying Czechoslovakia in 1938, thereby creating the circumstances that led to Stalin opting for Hitler rather than for alliance with the West in 1939. Everything then depended on the broken reed of the French army, which decades of studies have shown was not made of the kind of material necessary to resist the kind of onslaught a now enlarged and battle-ready German Wehrmacht could mount.

Not only that, but as Mark Mazower has pointed out in *Hitler's*

Empire, his recent study of Nazi-occupied Europe, many in France preferred, as they saw it, Hitler to Stalin, and so the will to stand up to, let alone to defeat, the invasion of their country did not exist.[16] Against such defeatism from within there is little defense.

So how did Churchill think Britain could continue?

First, and rather ironically, in view of his deposition of the former prime minister, much of Churchill's hope lay in economics: the possibility that an economic blockade of Germany would work and that the Third Reich would eventually collapse from within.[17] This was also Chamberlain's view, and it explains the crazy decision not to invade Germany when war began in 1939. We saw that such a policy was catastrophic in that it allowed Hitler the free hand he wanted, to invade and crush Poland in collaboration with the Soviet Union, without for a minute having to worry about his Western Front with France. Indeed the Phony War, as it was soon nicknamed, was surely one of the greatest missed opportunities in the history of war, one for which millions would soon be paying with their lives.

Here one should make an extra comment. In *1940* and *after* France had fallen such a policy does make some kind of sense, since direct war between Britain and Germany on the soil of continental Europe was now impossible. The British, having been successfully beaten by the Germans off the Continent, were certainly in no position whatsoever to go back without any allies worth the name. (The Canadians and other Dominion forces were ready and willing to help, but their armies were much too small to make an effective difference.)

In September 1939, however, such a move would have made every sense, since it would have been hard, as we saw, for Hitler to fight what was every German ruler's nightmare, a two-front war. So once again, Chamberlain's criminal negligence had left Churchill with an impossible hand.

Linked to the economic argument is that of bombing—the idea beloved of the Royal Air Force that Germany could be defeated by aerial bombardment alone. As the war progressed, this would be believed in ever more deeply by Bomber Command, as the citizens of Dresden would find out to their cost toward its end.

All this ties in with traditional British policy—to have a comparatively small army. The United Kingdom had used economic blockade before, notably during the Napoleonic Wars in the late eighteenth and early nineteenth centuries, and the Royal Navy had played a pivotal role in ensuring that such a blockade could be rigorously enforced upon the high seas. In 1940 the sea was still the major form of international long-distance transport, as Britain was to discover when the German U-boat campaign did so much damage to the supplies the United States was sending to its besieged ally.

In retrospect both of these notions seem quaint, namely, that blockade and a tiny army would work against a behemoth such as Nazi Germany. For now we know that the only way to defeat Hitler was with the full, frontal assault we finally witnessed on D-day. One of the main themes of this book is that Churchill was if anything too much of an historian, overwedded to the past, and thus utterly unable to see the life-changing, war-winning difference that US entry into the war would make.

But from June 1940 to December 1941 Britain was utterly alone. So from a purely military and survival point of view, Churchill really had no other option but these two ways of fighting the now mighty Third Reich. Surrender or some kind of sordid deal was the only other option, and this, thankfully for Western civilization and the cause of democracy, was one that he emphatically rejected as morally unacceptable.

(In his very darkest hours he did contemplate a deal with, say, a post-Hitler military regime, if such ever arose,[18] but since the Munich settlement of 1938 had rescued the Nazis from the possibility of a coup, it was not until Germany was losing in 1944 that such an outcome became possible: and by that time the Allies were both winning and had declared for unconditional surrender.)

This was not to say that German and British forces could not, however, meet on the field of battle somewhere.

One of these options was Churchill's idea of setting Europe ablaze—with the Special Operations Executive, commandolike forces acting behind enemy lines in sabotage and subversion. This was a typically brave Churchillian move, an important innovation that some of those who were actually involved in such clandestine activities in wartime now think, despite all its glamour and heroics, was actually a well-meant but terrible mistake.

Churchill had been involved in the Boer war, against the Afrikaners (or Boers, as they were sometimes called) in 1899–1902. He was captured during the conflict, and famously escaped from a train and returned to freedom. He had been highly impressed with the guerrilla activity of the Boers against the British, and in his usual way of wanting to learn from the lessons of history, thought it a great idea if equally brave British (and allied—French, Polish, Czech, for example) special agents could be sent behind enemy lines to, as he famously put it, "set Europe ablaze."

Movies galore have been made of the intrepid exploits of the men—and women—agents of SOE, from *Ill Met by Moonlight,* starring Dirk Bogarde as the real-life and uniquely brave British agent Patrick Leigh Fermor, to fictional accounts, including the recent *Charlotte Gray,* set in France and with Cate Blanchett in the main role. (I think we can also include movies such as *Force 10 from Navarone* with Harrison Ford in this list, as the heroes were in well-known SOE territory in Yugoslavia, where their most famous actions took place.)

However, despite all the glamour and excitement, we can also say that SOE, while doubtless accomplishing much in terms of sabotage, mayhem against the enemy, and excellent field intelligence, also had a downside, one that alas probably never occurred to Churchill or indeed any of those who established SOE in the first place.

This is that the Nazis committed revenge atrocities on a scale hitherto unimaginable but entirely in character with their brutal behavior. One sees this in their reprisal for the SOE's assassination of Reinhardt Heydrich, the SS leader who organized the infamous Wannsee conference in 1942 that formalized the Holocaust, but who was also in charge of suppressing the Protectorate of Bohemia and Moravia. The assassins were Czechs working for SOE, and they were captured and killed. But then the Germans decided to wipe out the entire town of Lidice, slaughtering the entire male population and sending the women and children to concentration camps, where many of them died.

Thankfully similar atrocities on that scale did not take place in, for example, Norway, where brave British agents parachuted in and were able to destroy the "heavy water" experiments that might otherwise have led to the Nazis' successful acquisition of an atomic bomb.

Nonetheless, one does need to wonder whether it was all worthwhile, especially in the light of how many innocent people were butchered by Nazis in revenge. As John Keegan, a strong sympathizer with Churchill, puts it:

> The result was that in urbanized, law-abiding Western Europe most citizens were, understandably, too frightened to resist... The brave minority who did choose to sustain the national honour by cooperating with SOE did so chiefly by passing intelligence, printing illegal newspapers, succouring downed airmen, and com-

mitting sabotage.... The suppression of resistance diverted little German military strength from the main war effort; of the sixty-six German divisions in France on D-Day, none was committed to internal security.[19]

Keegan is also right to say that in southern Europe things were far worse:

Greece and Yugoslavia were ravaged by reprisals, and by the civil wars that resistance provoked... The consequences of encouraging resistance in Yugoslavia and Greece were socially and politically disastrous; they persist to this day.[20]

Another point made to me by veterans of this period is that many outstanding officers were living in mountain caves rather than leading their men in the field against the enemy. A great deal of considerable talent was thus taken away from the battlefield and into raids that took months to prepare, and even if then successful often resulted in atrocities against the local inhabitants.

What is strange is that Churchill hardly mentions the SOE itself throughout his war memoirs, despite it being his brainchild. As David Reynolds puts it in his book on Churchill's books:

As for the Special Operations Executive, this is completely absent from *Their Finest Hour*, even though Churchill spent a good deal of July 1940...[setting it up]. In fact SOE is mentioned only once in Churchill's six volumes, in a 1943 minute in the appendix to *The Hinge of Fate*...Historian David Stafford has called the omission "a classic case, conscious or not, of selective memory."[21]

In the light of our theme—the two years that it took the United States to persuade Churchill to launch D-day at all, Reynolds's reason for this strange omission is significant:

> The root explanation is presumably Churchill's decision to prove his early and consistent support for a cross-Channel invasion.... "Setting Europe ablaze" had proved a damp squib...So Churchill rewrote his strategy in the light of D-Day and postwar American criticism. In so doing, he tried to deceive his readers (and perhaps himself) on an issue of central importance.[22]

In addition, many of the SOE operatives in the field were Communist or strongly socialist, and it is certainly true that Communists did well out of the resistance. This was not to say that Britain supported, say, the Partisans in Yugoslavia because of Communist influence—Churchill's reason was because they were killing far more Germans than the Royalist Chetnik troops in the region—but he was not unaware of the ideological nature of many of the operatives, British and local alike. As Richard Holmes has observed:

> Winston was not prepared to arm the Communists, who only sprang to life after Hitler invaded the Soviet Union, unless they were prepared to do serious damage to the Germans in return.[23]

The omission from his history is a shame, especially because the story has become so popular after the war. But, as we shall see, David Reynolds's interpretation is surely the right one—Churchill's memoirs had a lot to hide, especially when it came to working out how to win in collaboration with the United States.

So we can say that SOE wonderfully shows Churchill's flawed

genius—only a genius would concoct something so daring and unusual, but it was a plan that had as many minuses against it as pluses, and therefore, however brilliant, was ultimately flawed.

The other Churchillian way of taking the battle direct to the enemy was to fight the Axis away from European soil, something that became an option when Italy entered the war, rather opportunistically, after the fall of France in June 1940. Italian territory in North Africa bordered upon theoretically independent but actually British-occupied Egypt, and beyond the Suez Canal were, of course, the oil riches of the Middle East. This too we shall look at in considerable detail, because it is the disasters that befell British (and Empire) forces there, especially in 1941, that made all the difference on when D-day could be launched, and thus elongated the war by a terrible extra year or more.

One other option did, however, remain, and this proved to be the winning decision—the entry into the war of the United States as a cobelligerent.

In June 1940 this still looked like a fantasy, every bit as unlikely as bombing alone being able to defeat Hitler, or blockades starving Germany into submission.

Yet there is no question: it was Churchill's belief that, however discouraging the signals from the United States, one day America would *have* to enter the war that kept his morale alive, and that of the British people along with him. It took a long time—eighteen months from the fall of France to Pearl Harbor—but Churchill was proved right: the United States *did* enter the war, and it was that entry that enabled Britain to be on the winning side come 1945.

Remember, for Chamberlain the United States of America was nothing but words.[24] For Churchill it was the great democracy, the knight in shining armor, as it were, that would rescue the British damsel in distress from the dragon of Nazi tyranny. And, as we know, in this it was Churchill who knew the truth.

In fact, the United States would be to Britain what France should have been but failed to be in 1940: the key ally, without whom war on the Continent could not be fought. In that sense, Churchill's traditional view was vindicated—Britain was, historically, always *primarily* a naval power, but in conjunction with an ally possessed of a strong land army, one that could win the war. This is what happened with the great Duke of Marlborough, and if one wishes to pursue such an analogy (if one can, since we might be stretching it), Eisenhower was to be the 1940s equivalent of John Churchill's illustrious cohort, Prince Eugene of Savoy.

However, there was one major difference, one that Churchill, for all his historical genius, failed to spot, and tragically at the cost of elongating the war, ultimately to the Soviet advantage.

Whereas in previous wars, Britain was always the equal, if not actually the superior in terms of power, with its key continental ally, now in the Second World War the balance of power was to be changed, and drastically so, for the first time in British history. For there was no way in which the United Kingdom, and its Commonwealth associates (such as Canada and Australia) could even possibly have been counted the equal of the United States. As we shall see, by 1943–44, American power was already considerably greater than that of all the forces of Britain and its empire, and was overwhelmingly the predominant partner in the alliance, as the United States has been in all its similar relationships since then.

Nor was the United States a *continental* power, in terms of a major political/military player on the continent of Europe. Indeed, with due deference to the Canadians, it was and is a transcontinental power all by itself, able to project itself both in the Atlantic and the Pacific, as happened in 1941–45.

Churchill, the half-American and historian of "the English Speaking Peoples," knew part of this to be true and that without the United States victory was impossible. But it will be a major argument of this book that, being a romantic imperialist wedded to the "island story" of Britain, he completely failed to grasp that America was a power and military ally of altogether a different and far higher order of magnitude than any of the old-fashioned European allies, from the Dutch republic onwards, on whom the British had relied in the past.

The strategic implications, the fact that the ages-old British policy of the "indirect approach" was now defunct thanks to American might, and that the main enemy could be attacked both swiftly and directly, all these vital things sadly eluded Churchill, the politician whose own fighting past and in-depth knowledge of history now in fact was to mislead him after 1941, rather than, as with the period 1940–41, being one of his most important sources of strength.

But from May 1940 to December 1941 he was right: America would soon be action not words, and with someone in the White House who finally had a British statesman who trusted the United States, there would be Lend-Lease and other tangible proofs that the Americans wanted to do as much as possible to ensure that Britain survived.

Churchill's most famous and defiant wartime speech was delivered to the House of Commons on June 4, 1940, and is revered for what are, in fact, only its last few lines. One can easily understand how the great American journalist and Anglophile Edward R. Murrow (best known in the United States for his opposition to McCarthy in the 1950s, but loved in Britain for his telling the American people how England survived the Blitz) was able to say that Churchill mobilized the English language and turned it into an instrument of war.

> Even though large tracts of Europe and many old and famous states have fallen or may fall into the grip of the Gestapo and all the odious apparatus of Nazi rule, we shall not flag or fail. We shall go on to the end, we shall fight in France, we shall fight on the seas and oceans, we shall fight with growing confidence and growing strength in the air, we shall defend our Island, whatever the cost may be, we shall fight on the beaches, we shall fight on the landing grounds, we shall fight in the fields and in the streets, we shall fight in the hills; we shall never surrender.

Not many people know an unofficial part of this speech that, during the cheers, Churchill whispered to his new deputy, the Labour leader Clement Attlee: "We'll fight them with the butt end of broken beer bottles because that's all we've bloody got."[25]

How true that last statement was! One of the most popular TV shows in Britain has for years been *Dad's Army*, a now oft-repeated series of how a group of Home Guard volunteers met each week in the fictional town of Warmington on Sea to drill and practice against a German invasion that thankfully never came. The part-time soldiers certainly had enthusiasm and patriotic zeal, in real life as well as in drama, but how brave but incredibly amateur fighters would have survived with pitchforks and little else against the combined might of the Wehrmacht and Luftwaffe if it had ever come is a story to which we can be glad we shall never need to know the answer. There is little doubt that most of them would have fought in hills, beaches, fields, and streets but the likelihood that many of the now smaller British army would have survived is, alas, slender.

In fact, Churchill knew from where aid could come, and this is how he finished his speech that day:

And even if we do [i.e., surrender] which I do not for a moment believe, this Island or a large part of it were subjugated and starving, then our Empire beyond the seas, armed and guarded by the British Fleet, would carry on the struggle, until, in God's good time, the New World, with all its power and might, steps forth to the rescue and liberation of the old.

This was of course a monumental gamble on Churchill's part, one that if it had failed, Britain would have been truly ruined and almost certainly defeated by the juggernaut of the Third Reich.

However, in the end he was proved correct, but not by any means that could have been foreseen then: by Hitler's declaration of war against the United States following the American declaration against Japan following Pearl Harbor.

Roosevelt had to walk a careful tightrope, since most American opinion (despite Murrow's legendary broadcasts from London) continued to be actively isolationist. Even as Churchill uttered his majestic words in the House of Commons, the president found it politically necessary, in an election year, to reassure Americans that he would not take them into war. Indeed one could say that it was only the suicidal folly of Japan and Germany that enabled the West to win at all, since the United States would have found it remarkably difficult to manufacture an excuse to intervene on the side of the democracies without being attacked first. So while Churchill's faith in the arsenal of democracy was truly vindicated, it was, to use the analogy of the great British commander of the Napoleonic Wars, the Duke of Wellington, about the final victory at Waterloo, a *very* close run thing.

However, he was right, and therefore one can say that perhaps his most wonderful achievement during the May 1940–December 1941 period was to keep Britain independent and in the war at all. As we shall see later on, this was by no means anything that could be taken for granted, since the United Kingdom could have been invaded and flattened by the Third Reich at any time during that period. It was amazing in itself that 338,000 British soldiers (and some French) had escaped from Dunkirk at all—thousands of others were captured and suffered in prison camps for the rest of the war.

Not only that but for the rest of 1940 Operation Sea Lion, the Nazi plan to invade and conquer Britain, could have taken place, with the dire results on which we just commented.

What saved Britain, Churchill's morale-boosting oratory apart, were two things: its island status, to which he referred often in his speeches, and the Battle of Britain, which now began not on the beaches or hedgerows, but in the skies.

The Germans possessed what was probably then the best *land* army in the world. The doctrine of blitzkreig had created a massive *land-based* empire, with the panzers blasting all before them and defeating easily what was on paper at least a far larger and supposedly better French army, all within the space of a few weeks.

But Britain, thankfully for its inhabitants, could not be invaded by *land* until it had first been conquered by *air* (and, naval enthusiasts would no doubt remind us, also by *sea*).

However, this proved well beyond the capabilities even of the Luftwaffe, despite the German air force's easy conquests elsewhere, in Poland in 1939, for example, and the Netherlands in 1940.

It is miraculous that they failed over Britain as well.

As Churchill so famously put it in his speech to the House of Commons on June 18, 1940:

What General Weygand called the Battle of France is over. I expect that the Battle of Britain is about to begin. Upon this battle depends the survival of Christian civilization. Upon it depends our own British life, and the long continuity of our institutions and our Empire. The whole fury and might of the enemy must very soon be turned on us. Hitler knows that he will have to break us in this Island or lose the war. If we can stand up to him, all Europe may be free and the life of the world may move forward into broad, sunlit uplands. But if we fail, then the whole world, including the United States, including all that we have known and cared for, will sink into the abyss of a new Dark Age made more sinister, and perhaps more protracted, by the lights of perverted science. Let us brace ourselves to our duties, and bear ourselves that, if the British Empire and its Commonwealth last for a thousand years, men will still say, "This was their finest hour."

There is hyperbole in this speech. Earlier in it Churchill was very sanguine about the ability of Fighter Command to survive—which, in a sense, and in a public speech, he had to be, as the truth of the narrowness of British reserves would have been of enormous damage to British morale and of considerable benefit to the enemy.

(Note too the appeal again to the United States, and the reminder to Americans of the disaster that would befall them were Britain to fall: Churchill wisely never forgot that he had an audience across the Atlantic as well as at home.)

The issue of the number of fighter squadrons is also vital to the story of the Battle of Britain itself. Up until then—and in fact, as a major doctrine throughout the war itself—the Royal Air Force had been obsessed with bombers, not the fighters needed to defend the British Isles against external aggression. So it is amazing that there were enough fighters to combat the Germans at all.

In fact, while the battle was at its height in the autumn, Churchill paid one of his many visits to the headquarters of RAF 11 Group of Fighter Command. Seeing how dire the situation was, he naturally asked if there were any reserves—to which the terrifying answer was "no." There were *no* reserves, and all available planes were in the air.

As military historian Richard Holmes has argued, what actually saved Britain was two mistakes, one accidental, the other made by a wrathful Hitler.[26] On August 24, 1940, a German bomber crew accidentally hit London—until now their main targets had obviously been RAF bases, where they could hit fighter squadrons on the ground and prevent them from flying. Churchill in retaliation ordered Bomber Command to hit Berlin, which they then proceeded to do. This enraged Hitler into making a fatal mistake—he ordered London and other British cities to be the targets, rather than the RAF bases where the fighters were stationed. This enabled Fighter Command to survive, and thus saved the day: the Battle of Britain was won not by the Luftwaffe but by the Royal Air Force, and the United Kingdom was safe.

However, the human cost of what is called "the Blitz," the continuous bombing raids on London and major British cities, was catastrophic.[27] Now most people have forgotten what something so truly scary was like—perhaps only the opening scene in the recent movie *The Lion, the Witch and the Wardrobe*, which shows the Pevensie children diving into their garden shelter from German bombs—has given twenty-first-century people an impression of what it was like. Unlike 9/11 in the United States, which were terrible but one-off attacks, the main part of the Blitz, from September 7, 1940, onwards, was fifty-seven days of *continuous* bombardment, and of primarily civilian, not military, targets. No fewer than 43,000 *civilians* were killed, over

139,000 injured, and a staggering two and a half million left homeless—and all this in the space of just a few weeks.

During this time Churchill, who did not flinch away from physical danger, visited numerous bombed sites, as parts of London and other cities resembled ruins of long-departed medieval cities, so widespread was the damage. The period of Blitz may not have been long, but along with the evacuation from Dunkirk it has become iconic in British life. The "Blitz spirit" has entered national consciousness as one of indomitable resistance in the face of an unseen yet evil and deadly foe, of keeping on keeping on, even though, to any rational mind, the situation was entirely hopeless.

(One of the points that the anti-Churchill revisionists make at this point is a fair one, depending upon one's politics. Britain was alone in 1940—with its nearest allies, such as Canada, thousands of miles away across the ocean. The mentality of being "alone" has twenty-first-century repercussions, with many British people today feeling that even decades later the United Kingdom can still survive in the international global economy on its own without membership in institutions such as the European Union. American isolationism is better known but the British equivalent is equally strong, and to such folk Churchill in 1940 remains an iconic figure of the kind of country they would still like to see. Some of his critics, of a more Europhile frame of mind, see this as continuing, decades later, to damage Britain's relationships with her closest neighbors just twenty miles across the Channel.)

It is now that Churchill as national treasure, the heroic leader, with his famous V sign and his legendary cigars (more waved than smoked), comes sharply into the historic imagination of what he loved to describe as the English Speaking Peoples. This is how he is best remembered, and surely deservedly so, since he gave his nation hope when all logic led only to despair.

Furthermore, as we saw in the Finest Hour speech, he realized that he was defending not just Britain but a way of life, democracy against tyranny and freedom against oppression. Because he was such a British nationalist, we forget that, in the West, there was a powerful ideological element in the war as well. There were issues far larger than if the British Isles were conquered. Democracy, freedom, the rule of law, above all, perhaps, human rights, and for Jews, Slavs, socialists, and numerous other kinds or categories of people, the right to be alive at all. This was not a traditional war of the kind that had been fought before, but a new and altogether more terrifying conflict, one in which more civilians would die than soldiers, and whole races would face annihilation. Churchill and Roosevelt, especially the latter, were later to be criticized for the doctrine of unconditional surrender. But one could say that in the Nazi way of warfare, with millions of people destroyed without mercy, *total war* could have no other ending. So, yes, the United Kingdom needed to survive, but so too did all the values of civilization itself. Churchill did all he could to ensure these continued. It is for this as much as anything else that we owe him so much in 1940, and why any other option is surely unthinkable.

Churchill Loses the Plot: The Greek Disaster of 1941 and Its Long-Term Effects

One of Churchill's closest friends was Max Aitken, Lord Beaverbrook, Canadian press magnate and owner of the *Daily Express* newspaper, and a man who, through his friendship with most of the key politicians who counted from around 1915 to 1945, was at the very heart of British politics over that crucial thirty-year period. He and Churchill were the only two people to hold high government office in both world wars, and in our tale he is also important as a man who strongly supported the idea of an early rather than later second front, the better to help the USSR in its struggle against the Third Reich.

Aitken, being a journalist, had an especial eye for the unusual angle, and in his memoirs of the fall of the great Lloyd George coalition in 1922 (of which Churchill was a senior member), Aitken shows that it was a series of bizarre coincidences that led to the political overthrow of Lloyd George, the prime minister and victor of the First World War.

In essence, what we get is a "Cleopatra's nose" version of history—great events shaped not by anonymous economic or social forces, but by a series of seemingly unrelated incidents that seem unimportant at the time but cumulatively have a devastating impact on events.

("If Cleopatra's nose had been shorter" the history of the world would have turned out very differently—this is an aphorism that goes back to the famous seventeenth-century French thinker and philosopher Blaise Pascal. In a nutshell had she not been so beautiful then Mark Anthony and Julius Caesar would never have fancied her, with all the major consequences for subsequent Roman—and global—history that ensued from that. The eminent American historian Daniel Boorstin wrote a book entitled *Cleopatra's Nose* to show how such seemingly small things can lead to the most unexpected of eventual outcomes.)

Aitken's version of all this was that a monkey bite in 1920 set off a chain of events that led to the downfall of Lloyd George in 1922. Since this chapter is about the Greek disaster of 1941 and how it subsequently altered Allied policy beyond repair once Roosevelt and Churchill met later in that year, I will use it as an example of precisely how such things happen.

In 1920 Greece had a young king, Alexander, who sat on the throne because his pro-German father, Constantine, had been deposed not long before. But that year a monkey bit the king, who tragically died of poisoning a short while later. As a result, the strongly pro-Allied Greek prime minister, Venizelos, who was regarded as "the greatest Greek since Pericles," lost power and was sent into exile. This in turn led to the decision of the French government, which had been supporting Greece in its war with Turkey, to drop the Greeks and switch to a more Turkish-friendly position. Thus by 1922 the Greeks were losing, and their only friend left was the British government of David Lloyd George. But Lloyd George's government (of which Churchill was a part, as colonial secretary) was a coalition. The idea of Britain having to go to war again—to help the Greeks from being massacred by the Turks—was anathema to the Conservatives in the coalition, and Lloyd George was deposed in favor of a Conservative prime minister, Andrew Bonar Law. The coalition that had won World War I was no more.

Aitken then goes on to quote the famous nursery rhyme "For the Want of a Nail," about how a missing horseshoe nail cost a king his kingdom, a poem that also appealed to Benjamin Franklin, and many since.

(Alternative history enthusiasts will also know it as the title of Robert Sobel's groundbreaking book of the same name, in which he postulates that if one key battle had gone differently, the Americans would have lost the War of Independence, and the next two centuries would have been radically altered, not only in northern America but in the rest of the world as well.)

A missing nail, a longer nose—all these are the "what-ifs" of what used to be called alternative history for science fiction fans, but is now called counterfactual history by serious historians (such as Harvard's Niall Fergusson, a major practitioner of the genre).

There is a case, made eloquently by Cambridge professor (and authority on the Third Reich) Richard Evans, that all this is just fun and not to be taken too seriously. There is much to be said for this view—history is what *did* happen rather than what *might have happened*. But as it turns out, Churchill was himself an alternative historian, or what would now be called a counterfactualist.

We see this in his own chapter, "If Lee Had Not Won the Battle of Gettysburg," published in 1932 in a book entitled *If It Had Happened Otherwise*. (Other chapters consider history if the French Revolution had not occurred or if Napoleon had won instead of Wellington at Waterloo, two staples of the imaginary history genre.)

Clearly of course the South lost the Civil War. But the one merit of counterfactual history is that it shows that what happened was not inevitable, that things could have turned out radically differently had other strategies been followed, and that one can judge people's actions by what *might* have happened otherwise rather than simply by what did take place. In other words, in determining what happened, it is as important to look at sins of omission as it is to examine what people actually did do. *Should X have done A, B, or C?* is a question we need to ask as well as *X carried out D and E: was that a good choice?*

Churchill in his memoirs also realized that things could or perhaps should have turned out differently when, as we shall see, he understood the criticisms of those who felt that he should have stood up more to Stalin (and, thus to some extent, also Roosevelt) over Poland. Might the entire Cold War, which was just emerging as Churchill wrote his *History of the Second World War*, in fact not needed to have erupted at all?

So I think that, Evans's objections notwithstanding, Churchill's own delving into counterfactual history does show that the genre does have some serious merit to it after all, even if stories such as the South winning the Civil War more properly belong on the fiction shelves rather than in the history section of your local bookstore.

One of the reasons why Britain's failure to adopt Marshall's plan for victory was so serious in its long-term outcome is precisely because of the battle that has raged among historians, generals, journalists, and all assorted kind of commentator and pundit as to whether or not we lost the peace in 1945. General Wedemeyer was saying this in 1958 in his book *Wedemeyer Reports!* But the key place in which it was raised was the book I have referred to elsewhere, Chester Wilmot's famous tome *The Struggle for Europe*.

The fact that the Allies won the war, only to lose the peace to Stalin is one of the most important themes of this deservedly legendary book, and in my own work here I am consciously following in Wilmot's footsteps, since my basic conclusions are the same. But where I would disagree strongly with what historians call, with due reverence, the "Wilmot thesis" is on *how this happened.*

We will see shortly in the chapter on Marshall's plan to win victory in 1943 that in fact the generals, rather than being politically naïve, as both Wedemeyer (who was one himself) and Wilmot claim, actually had the blueprint for an early victory that would have ended with the *Western* Allies—Britain and the United States—winning both the peace and the war. In addition, the Wilmot thesis and most British historians, even those critical of Churchill's mistakes, tend to put much blame on Roosevelt, especially his complete naïveté over Stalin and Soviet long-term intentions. While I can understand such a view, I would want to say that by 1944 it was already far too late, and that even had Roosevelt seen through Stalin, there was, by then, very little else that the Allies could have done to stop the Soviet juggernaut from capturing all of Central and Eastern Europe.

So whose fault was it? Ironically, in view of his famous anti-Soviet rhetoric pre-1938 and his grave concerns about Stalin after 1943, the answer is, alas, Winston Churchill himself. The reason was not blindness on his part, but a classic example of Cleopatra's Nose / the Missing Nail in operation.

This in essence is therefore my argument:

a. In 1941 Britain was beating the daylights out of the Italians in North Africa.

b. By early 1941 General O'Connor could in fact have beaten them altogether, thereby preventing Rommel and his army (later called the Afrika Korps) from even landing.

c. The reason we snatched defeat from victory in North Africa in 1941 is that many key British and Commonwealth divisions were switched from there to Greece, to defend that country from German invasion.

d. We had nowhere near enough men to win against the Germans in Greece, let alone prevent the Greeks from being conquered.

e. As could have easily been predicted, the Greek campaign was lost, thousands of Allied troops were killed or captured (in Crete as well as in mainland Greece), and enormous amounts of equipment lost.

f. Stopping O'Connor's victorious roll in North Africa enabled Rommel to land, and so good were his troops that it took until 1943, two years later, finally to drive him out of Africa. Rommel, in fact, came within a hairsbreadth of capturing Egypt and from that the route to all the Middle Eastern oil that would have made enormous difference to the Third Reich had it been captured.

So why is all this so important?

The answer is that it enabled Churchill easily to persuade an already open Roosevelt, massively to the detriment of Marshall's winning plan to end the war in 1943. We can therefore continue:

a. Roosevelt wanted US forces to engage with the Germans *immediately* in order to be able to grant victory to those who wanted to put war on Germany ahead of war against Japan.

b. The buildup Marshall's victory plan—Bolero—needed would have taken some months to complete (as we shall see) so no *instant* plan was available except Churchill's plea to Roosevelt to send troops to help the British in North Africa (Gymnast until its name was changed to Torch).

c. So Roosevelt went with Churchill rather than with Marshall—the short-term need won over the long-term guarantee of early victory.

d. We did not push the Germans out of North Africa until 1943, and so, as Marshall realized, sending American troops to that front effectively delayed Bolero and thus the liberation of Europe until 1944.

e. As a result, by the time the Allies landed, Soviet troops were far further west than they would have been in 1943; millions of civilians—Jewish, Russian, Polish, German, and otherwise—died who might have lived; and, as writers from Chester Wilmot in the 1950s to Norman Davies in recent years have shown, Stalin was the real victor in 1945.

f. Finally, and ironically, the man who made famous the term "Iron Curtain," Winston Churchill, was the person who guaranteed its full extent and its continued existence, in a forty-four-year cold war, until 1989, with all the immense suffering to the oppressed peoples of the Soviet bloc during that time.

It goes without saying that Churchill's decision to save Greece in 1941, against completely impossible odds, could not even remotely at the time be seen to lead to the eventual results I have just outlined. Apart from anything else, the United States was months away from joining the war—Britain's key requisite for victory—and while Hitler was honing Barbarossa, his attack on the USSR, Stalin was still actively in denial about German plans and still keeping to his side of the Faustian pact he had made with Hitler in 1939.

Nonetheless, the eventual outcome—the Cleopatra's Nose effect, if you like—of the decision to postpone a virtually guaranteed victory against Italy in 1941 in order to send what could be no more than a token force against the German juggernaut, a heroic but guaranteed-to-fail gesture, was the postponement of Allied victory in Europe, as Marshall realized when he came to Britain a year or so after the fall of Greece to the Axis. But, as we shall see in this chapter, the die had been cast long before he came, in the light of Churchill's ability to persuade Roosevelt to send American forces into battle straight away.

Bolero—the plan to bring over a fully battle-trained and equipped American army ready to take on the direct might of the German army in Europe itself—and sending an American army to keep the British from being wiped out and defeated in North Africa, were, as Marshall knew, incompatible, and so it proved. But had O'Connor been given all the forces he needed in North Africa in 1941, instead of losing key troops to Greece (and to Ethiopia, where the Allies won), there would have been no Afrika Korps in North Africa to defeat, and the American troops sent as part of Torch would never have been needed.

So, I would argue, Greece really did in the end make all the difference. It is the best example in World War II of the laws of unintended consequences, of how Churchill, the savior of his nation in 1940, was increasingly losing the plot.

John Keegan, a military historian who is strongly sympathetic to Churchill, does not disguise the scale of the defeat in Greece:

> His expedition to Greece, mounted with troops withdrawn from the Western Desert, resulted in a second Dunkirk. Regiments that had lost all their equipment in France a year earlier now lost it a second time.... In the absence of British troops sent to Greece, Rommel mounted a desert offensive that reversed the results of their victory over the Italians.[28]

(In terms of the wider war, this was still all a sideshow, a point we saw in our introduction. As Keegan goes on to remind us:

> The desert war, important though it seemed to the British public, was, in any case, too peripheral and small-scale to influence the outcome of the titanic struggle between the Wehrmacht and the Red Army.[29]

Keegan is entirely right—and one of the major tragedies of the war is that Churchill, for all his genius, never got this point, as we shall see.)

It is also possible to say, as Israeli historian Tuvia Ben-Moshe showed all the way back in 1992 in his book *Churchill: Strategy and History*, that the die was cast as long ago as the 1890s, and Churchill's admiration for what historians have given names such as the "Mediterranean strategy," or Churchill himself called attacking the "soft belly"—what American strategists call the "indirect approach." We shall examine this in much more detail when we consider how Marshall's plan, put before the British in 1942, would have won the war far earlier, the American "direct approach." But we need to refer to it here in relation to Churchill himself, since war in the Mediterranean and through indirect places such as Greece, or the Dardanelles, or, later on, through the Ljubljana Gap (in today's Slovenia) was the place to win.

On January 7, 1941, Churchill told the Chiefs of Staff, via General Ismay, that the "speedy destruction of the Italian Armed Forces in North East Africa must be our prime overseas objection in the opening months of 1941."[30] As usual with Churchill, he was keen to micromanage the attack, giving target details (principally Tobruk), and, as always, he insisted that "the need for haste is obvious."

If only things had stayed there. For it was obvious that the wind was in the sails so far as British success in driving the Italians out of Africa was concerned, and that a real victory was imminent.

But life was not that simple. Churchill was under the illusion that the Greeks were capable of holding their own in the Balkans, despite their failure at Valona. However, he realized—correctly as it soon turned out—that the situation could change for the worse. As he advised the Chiefs of Staff, Britain might have to "give quickly...four or five more squadrons from the Middle East...and some or all of the tanks of the Second Armoured Division" that had just arrived in Egypt.

Churchill continued:

It may be possible for General Wavell, with no more than the forces he is using in the Western Desert, and in spite of some reduction in his Air Force, to conquer the Cyrenaica province [of Italian-ruled Libya] and establish himself at Benghazi; but it would not be right for the sake of Benghazi to lose the chance of the Greeks taking Valona and thus to dispirit and anger them, and perhaps make them in the mood for a separate peace with Italy. Therefore the prospect must be faced that after Tobruk the further Westward advance of the Army of the Nile must be seriously cramped. It is quite clear to me that supporting Greece must have priority after the Western flank of Egypt has been made secure.

The way things turned out, a Greek surrender to the Italians would have been by far the least bad of the options. For this was to be the truly fatal decision that was in turn to lead on to all the other mistakes that led to victory in 1945, not two years earlier in 1943, and to the USSR being the real victors of World War II in Europe, not the Western Allies, Britain, and the United States.

Why is this? Let us play consequences:

a. British troops under General O'Connor did indeed beat the Italians: good news!

b. But they could not follow up on their victory because by the time they won, the troops were exhausted and needed replacements.

c. And the replacements that would have worked had all been sent to Greece.

d. The Greek campaign became so messy that Hitler sent in German troops to help his Italian allies.

e. This led to one of Churchill's fears of April 7, 1941, being fulfilled: a German invasion of Yugoslavia as well as Greece, and the conquest of both countries.

f. Rommel, the "Desert Fox," was able to land his panzer divisions in northern Africa, and, unlike the easily defeated Italian troops there, it took the British and then the Americans nearly two and a half years to drive him out.

This would not have mattered in and of itself, but for the way it played into Churchill's hands in his discussions with Roosevelt, and to America's grave disadvantage, along with any hope of an earlier end to the war. For when Marshall had persuaded Roosevelt of the need to hit the main enemy, Germany, directly in the place it hurt most, northwestern Europe, Churchill used Roosevelt's desire to see American troops in action *immediately* to send them off to a two-year detour in northern Africa, a campaign that only happened because the British had failed to win there when they could have done so easily in early 1941.

Three days later, the news from Greece was getting worse. The Greeks realized that German troop movements in Romania were a signal of the Third Reich's readiness for future action. It was no longer a question simply of Greek vs. Italian, but of a full-fledged German invasion, a proper army against what was a far inferior force.

Churchill therefore told both General Wavell and Air Chief Marshal Longmore, the Royal Air Force commander in the region, to go to Athens forthwith to begin negotiations with the Greeks. Churchill was stark:

Nothing must hamper capture of Tobruk, but thereafter all operations in Libya are subordinated to aiding Greece, and all preparations must be made from the receipt of this telegram for the
immediate succour of Greece.[31]

The die was cast, and the hard-won British victory in northern
Africa thrown away.

It is fascinating to see Churchill at work, though. Take this terse
telegram he sent the next day to the Royal Air Force chiefs:

Must the operational reports from the Middle East be at their
present inordinate length and detail? It is surely not necessary to
describe minutely what happened in every individual raid.[32]

Of course Churchill himself was exempt from such strictures!
The same day he was asking in minute detail about yeomanry regi-
ments in the area, now that horses were no longer needed.[33] He also
stuck to the imperial names of his youth, as he reminded the foreign
secretary:

If you approve I should like Livorno to be called in the English—
Leghorn; and Istanbul in English—Constantinople... And why is
Siam buried under the name Thailand?[34]

Churchill did concede though that in writing to the Turks, their
own name for their former capital city, Istanbul, was the one to use!

But on what really mattered—the conduct of the war—Churchill
still made clear that "once Tobruk was taken the Greek-Turkish situation must have priority."[35]

The reference to Turkey was, as things turned out, a chimera:

Churchill was desperate to get the Turks into the war on the Allied side (a topic I have addressed at great length in another book).[36]

The Turks realized—surely correctly—that the Germans would sweep through Anatolia like a hot knife through butter, and, while always as friendly as possible to Churchill as neutrality allowed, nonetheless spurned his offers until just before the Allied victory in 1945. But to get them onside, Churchill was willing to sacrifice RAF planes urgently needed in North Africa, if it made Turkey feel even a little bit safer.

Worse still, as Churchill did not realize fully until April, when it was getting rather late in the day, the victorious British captors of Benghazi, the Seventh Armored Division, were sent back on February 6 to Cairo for a refit. So there were not even frontline and experienced troops there to hold the fort, which Rommel quickly saw to his considerable advantage.[37]

On February 12, 1941, the foreign secretary and the Chief of the Imperial General Staff, Sir John Dill, set out for their trip to the Balkans, one that took them longer than expected because of the dangers of Axis air forces.

Churchill's instructions to Eden were quite explicit.

His principal object will be the sending of speedy succour to Greece. For this purpose he will initiate any action as he may think necessary with the C in C of the Middle East…and with the Governments of Greece, Yugoslavia and Turkey.[38]

Churchill did understand though that there would be ramifications in Africa. What, he asked, was the "minimum garrison that can hold the frontier of Libya"? This was because, of the forces in Egypt, "the strongest and best equipped force" should be "despatched to

Greece at the earliest possible moment." It was, Eden should remember, "our duty to fight, and, if need be, suffer with Greece."[39]

Churchill, as we shall soon see, was resolute at this stage, and then wobbled at the last hurdle, only to be persuaded in his resolve by Eden, who determined that British aid to Greece should go ahead regardless.

The effects in the Middle East now became woeful. Churchill realized in writing to the Chiefs of Staff the next day that the situation was tight. But rather than consolidate his gains, he continued to opt for Greece:

> It must be remembered that the whole character of the problem is altered by the fall of Benghazi and the almost certain decision not to advance into Tripoli. The Services which have hitherto borne the strain of the desert fighting can in the large part now be diverted to operations elsewhere.[40]

This was a colossal error, since it was to give Rommel exactly the space he needed in which to land the panzer divisions in North Africa, stop the Allied momentum, and keep them bogged down there the next two years.

Churchill explained his position to Sir Alec Cadogan:

> It is impossible to make a serious advance upon Tripoli across 300 miles of desert without drawing our air and naval forces in such a way as to render it impossible for us to offer any effective aid to Greece or Turkey...All the points you have made have been considered by the Chiefs of Staff and their force is not denied.[41]

Churchill admitted that any troops the British could send Greece would "not, I fear, be very numerous." But to Churchill the real disaster would be an Axis conquest of Greece, with all Greek airfields in Hitler's hands, which is, alas, precisely what happened.

(Cadogan's diaries reveal that he oscillated in being against the Greek intervention and then for it—alas for him his first instincts were correct.)

By February, as Churchill heard from the Royal Navy, the Germans were (as a result, I would argue, of his negligence) now able to land troops in Libya. Churchill was wont to blame the navy, which was surely unfair.[42] He admitted by April, when Rommel's armies were storming ashore and pushing back the British (and other Empire forces), that in preventing Rommel from getting too far inland, "losses must be faced" and the "urgency was extreme."

But British superiority had been thrown away, and so Churchill was pursuing a will o' the wisp.

Now things were getting worse. Without vital supplies, it seemed that even the Suez Canal[43] would fall to Rommel's desert blitzkrieg and, just to add to British woes, Rashid Ali, a pro-Nazi Iraqi officer, had launched a coup in Baghdad, which had urgently to be suppressed by British troops if Iraq and all its oil were not to fall effortlessly into Axis hands.[44]

By the end of April it looked very much as if Cairo itself could fall—plans for evacuation were already under way. This would, Churchill realized, be "a disaster of first magnitude," second only, he wrote, to Britain itself being conquered.[45] But there were, he ordered, to be no surrenders until at least 50 percent of a unit had been destroyed, and even the injured were ordered to fight. Things really had become *that* dire.

In the end, although Rommel was easily able to recapture most of Libya, he did not manage to get all the way to Cairo itself. Tobruk was besieged, but did not fall until June 1942 (a 240-day siege), although all valiant Allied attempts to lift the siege were to fail. The mess cost Wavell his job, being replaced by General Sir Claude Auchinleck ("the Auk" to his devoted soldiers), and he was transferred to India, where he ended up, ironically in view of his desert failures, in the top job, that of viceroy.

By June 21 Churchill was becoming despondent in the Middle East—so far as he was concerned, Wavell was simply sitting "on the defensive,"[46] when he could be mounting a tank offensive. Churchill was keen to know precisely how many tanks and of what kind were on their way to the Middle East. It was, he told them in a separate memo by September, time for some "serious fighting."[47] It was, for him, a moral issue, because were Britain not to be on the offensive, there would be the just accusation that the Russians would be spilling their blood to fight Germany, and we were not—and, Churchill added, it would look bad to Roosevelt if we were not engaged against the enemy.

Historians differ on how much Wavell was to blame, if at all. His most recent and definitive biographer, Victoria Schofield, is careful not to let him off the hook, and as she shows, he always took his full share of responsibility for the disastrous decision to throw victory away and send the troops so urgently needed in North Africa to defeat and ruin in Greece and Crete.[48] The official historian, J.R.M. Butler, in his *Grand Strategy* is ambivalent,[49] and it is, in some ways, a hard call to make.

Soldiers differ as well. General John Strawson, in his 1969 book, *The Battle for North Africa*, is inclined to say that while Churchill always gave himself the benefit of the doubt, nonetheless on this issue Churchill really was correct, and he repeats the oft-given excuse that had Hitler not invaded the Balkans in spring 1941, he could have successfully conquered the USSR later that year.[50]

Since the latter is a view that is also held by someone as authoritative and knowledgeable as Professor Paul Kennedy at Yale, who, his later works apart, began his career as a researcher for Sir Basil Liddell Hart, it is not a view one can dismiss lightly. Yes, we threw away victory in North Africa and we lost spectacularly in Greece, but in delaying Barbarossa, the invasion of the USSR—the biggest and most bloodthirsty campaign of World War II—even by a short while, we made the crucial difference between Soviet defeat and the miraculous defense of Moscow that actually occurred in December 1941, enabling Stalin to hang in by his fingernails, and thus survive to destroy Hitler in 1945.

However, as Strawson admits, not only was O'Connor a genius who won against all the odds:

> But had O'Connor won the battle for North Africa in February 1941, there might have been no Rommel, or no Desert Fox at least . . . Rommel made one . . . revealing comment about O'Connor's campaign. "When, after a great victory which has brought about the destruction of the enemy, the pursuit is abandoned . . . history almost invariably finds the decision to be wrong and points to the tremendous chances which have been missed."[51]

Rommel was right, and so too, I would argue, were both the most famous historian of the desert war, Correlli Barnett, and one of the most senior wartime generals, Sir John Kennedy, who was Director of Military Operations at the War Office 1940–43 and then Assistant Chief of the Imperial General Staff for Intelligence for the rest of the war.

We can start with Kennedy, whose book (edited by another illustrious British veteran, Sir Bernard Fergusson, who served during the war on Wavell's staff), *The Business of War*, appeared in 1957. As Fergusson points out in the preface, over "and over again throughout the war we see military appreciations being distorted by political considerations," and that on Greece, to make matters worse, "no strictly *military* appreciation" was given by Wavell to Churchill.[52]

As Kennedy himself puts it:

> It can of course be argued that we gained a great moral advantage in the eyes of America and the world when we went to the rescue of the Greeks. It is arguable, too, that it would have been wise policy to send our forces to Greece even on a forlorn hope against military advice. But these were not the grounds on which the enterprise went forward. The military opinion tendered to the Cabinet by the Chiefs of Staff and Wavell was proved wrong in every respect. Nor is there any truth in the belief, at one time widely held, that our intervention delayed the German attack on Russia, and helped to save the Red Army by shortening what remained of the campaigning season, before the winter set in. It is clear from German documents that Hitler confirmed the 22nd June as the date for the offensive as early as 30th April, and that our operations in Greece caused no postponement.[53]

Kennedy, the main British planner for much of the war, is surely correct when he argues this. As he told both the Chiefs of Staff and, through them, Churchill himself, before the crucial decision was taken:

> With regard to the threat in the centre of the Mediterranean [the war against Italy] what we should do is to push on to Tripoli before the opportunity to do so has disappeared...Nothing we can do

can make the Greek business a sound military proposition...Anything we put into Greece on account of the very important political aspect we should be prepared to lose. We must not lose so much that our power of offensive action in the Middle East is killed, nor so much that our power of defence in the vital Egyptian centre is impaired.[54]

But this is precisely what happened. As Correlli Barnett puts it in the book that made him a household name in Britain in the 1960s, *The Desert Generals*, O'Connor deserves to be called the forgotten victor, wrongly deprived of what should have been the first major British victory of World War II.[55] To Barnett, the "Greek episode lengthened the campaign in North Africa by two years," and in going to help the Greeks, Churchill not only threw away O'Connor's achievements but showed that he might be descended from the great John Churchill, but was no Marlborough himself! While the generals advising Churchill bore their fair share of the blame, the "principal responsibility" lay with Churchill himself.

This was also the view of someone who was then simply a British military planner, but who was to go on to be famous as Montgomery's endlessly patient and highly effective Chief of Staff, General (at this time Colonel) Francis de Guigand.

In two books he shows beyond doubt that the war in Greece and the failure to proceed to victory in 1941 was an act of considerable folly.[56]

While this has clearly all been said before, I do think that the book you are reading is new in saying that all this delayed not merely the liberation of North Africa from the Axis until 1943, but also the conclusion of the whole war itself. Kennedy, the director of planning, had suggested that invading Sicily would be a better idea than a quixotic attempt, for political reasons, to help the Greeks. In 1943 the Allies did exactly that. But had O'Connor's victories been consolidated, as they should have been, rather than thrown away, then there is no reason why the invasion of Sicily could not have happened far earlier, with dramatic consequences in knocking Italy out of the war sooner than proved to be the case.

This is not to say that the British (and Empire troops) could have done this all by themselves—in fact far from it! It would take US entry into the war, in December 1941, to do that. But a safely secured North Africa would have been an excellent base for a much earlier invasion, one with considerable consequences for the better.

However, all that is to presume that invading Italy was a good idea at all, at least as far, say, as Rome, or what became later on known to its north as the Gothic Line. For there is a very good argument for saying that the entire Mediterranean strategy, once America was onside and in the war, was a complete diversion in itself, and that what *really* mattered was the defeat of the *main* enemy, Nazi Germany.

This was something in which the Americans, especially General Marshall, the Chief of Staff for the US Army, believed strongly, and for the next two years what to do in the Mediterranean was to be one of the longest-running arguments between Britain and her post–December 1941 ally, the United States. As we shall discover, it was Roosevelt's decision to overrule Marshall, his principal military adviser, and agree with Churchill that was to end up doing more than anything else to elongate the war, with the millions of casualties that happened as a result.

How was this? The answer is at the heart of our book: the unnecessary postponement of D-day by over a year, from April 1943 to June 1944. What was Churchill's problem? Historians have argued over this for decades, but I think it was the defeat in Greece, followed by the fall of Singapore to the Japanese, that convinced Churchill that British troops simply did not have what was required to win. This is the thesis of the Israeli historian Tuvia Ben-Moshe, and I think it is convincing. As he puts it, after the fall of Greece, and then of Crete, "something broke Churchill."[57] He simply no longer felt that British troops were up to a direct frontal assault on the Third Reich. The Germans were better fighters. And, as an automatic follow-on from that, if British troops were no good, then Americans would not be either: "the roots of British denigration of the Americans ran too deep."[58]

These two legends—German invincibility and American hopelessness—are ones that have sadly prevailed, despite the attempts of historians like Ben-Moshe to show that they are both groundless.[59] Although it is true that the average killing ratio of an individual German soldier was indeed 50 percent higher than those of Western soldiers, the fact remains that after D-day the Wehrmacht collapse in the West was fairly swift, ratios notwithstanding, and that the soldiers doing the bulk of killing the Germans were American, not out of any superiority over the British but by sheer force of numbers.

But as Ben-Moshe then goes on to say:

Churchill, of course, found it hard to inform the Americans during the war and the readers of *The Second World War* thereafter, that the principal source of his opposition to a grand invasion of Western Europe lay in the fact that he had lost confidence in the ability of the Anglo-American ground forces to confront the Wehrmacht on the plains of Western Europe. Instead, what were presented were secondary reasons and operational and strategic excuses.[60]

To me this is convincing on Churchill,[61] but what makes it all the more tragic is what we have seen in this chapter—*but for Churchill*

the war in North Africa would have been won in 1941 instead of by 1943.
British troops under O'Connor *were* winning and Germany would
have been seriously disadvantaged had the British been able to wipe
the Axis from the southern shores of the Mediterranean. Likewise,
US and British troops were to be powerfully successful precisely on
those plains of Western Europe after 1944, and there is therefore no
reason to assume that they would have been any less effective if Marshall's plan, the central theme of this book, had prevailed with D-day
in 1943. Yes, the German war machine was a most powerful one, but
no, it was far from invincible, as its defeat in 1945 shows us. So as
we look now in more detail at the Anglo-American relationship as it
unfolds, let us bear all this in mind.

CHAPTER THREE

Getting to Know One Another

IN DECEMBER 1941, just before he went to Washington DC for his first visit with Roosevelt, Churchill outlined his views on the future strategy of the war.[1]

Churchill was remarkably sanguine—by the start of 1943 he envisaged Allied control of North Africa and the Middle East from Dakar to the Turkish border and Allied naval superiority in the Pacific, with Japan on the run. There might even be Allied forces in Italy.

But this, he realized, correctly, would not mean that the war was over. The great chimera that had bewitched Chamberlain—that of an internal German collapse—was something, Churchill understood, that could not be relied upon (and, as we know, never happened). So however glowing things *might* be by early 1943, just over a year hence, the war against Germany would still be on.[2]

But the obvious means of winning—a full, frontal assault on

Germany—may have been clear to the American military planners, but not so to Churchill. It was the scatter approach personified, the very kind that drove military experts such as Marshall and Wedemeyer to despair.

> We have, therefore, to prepare for the liberation of the captive countries of Western and Southern Europe by the landing at suitable points, successively or simultaneously, of British and American armies strong enough to enable the conquered populations to revolt. By themselves they will never be able to revolt owing to the ruthless counter-measures that will be employed; but if adequate and suitably equipped forces were landed in several of the following countries, namely, Norway, Denmark, Holland, Belgium, the French Channel coasts and the French Atlantic coasts, as well as Italy and possibly the Balkans, the German garrisons would prove insufficient to cope both with the strength of the liberating forces and with the fury of the revolting peoples.

This is Churchill at his romantic best, but as military reality, with the precious Allied forces being dispersed from Norway to Italy and from France to the Balkans, it is, alas, a fantasy. Churchill hoped that by this means, and by effective Allied aerial bombing, it would be possible to "win the war at the end of 1943 or 1944."

On January 4 Churchill decided to take "a few days quiet and seclusion to review the salients of war as they appear after my discussions here."[3]

He grasped that the United States would not be able to have significant forces during 1942, but that, shipping permitting, 1943 offered real possibilities for "large offensive operations."

Churchill remained concerned that a German invasion of Britain "in 1942 [was] the only supreme means of escape and victory open to Hitler." Since the overwhelming majority of the German armed forces were now in the epic conflict on the Eastern Front against the USSR, this is somewhat surprising, but it showed that the defense of the United Kingdom itself, and the need for troops to remain on British soil, was clearly vital for Churchill. (He was still hoping too for Auchinleck to achieve a major breakthrough in North Africa—sadly, things on this front were soon to get far worse, as we shall see.)

In addition, the situation in Russia was still far from clear. We must not think of early 1942 in the hindsight of the Soviet Union's eventual victory against Nazism. As Churchill lay recuperating from illness in the United States, the possibility of German victory against the Red Army—and in particular a successful thrust through the Caucasus to the oil fields of Baku, and from there to the Middle East (and the huge oil fields of Iraq)—remained for all the Allies (not just for Churchill) a real nightmare that would have made a hideous difference to the eventual winning of the war.

(Churchill even wondered if the United States should not send a fifteen-division army to defend the Persian Gulf, which in the light of twenty-first-century developments is interesting, to say the least. But the plan clearly cut no ice in Washington, as it never materialized.)

Back in Britain, Churchill's fertile mind continued to ponder on the fate of the fighting.

CHAPTER FOUR

Churchill and the War's Wrong Turn

APRIL TO JULY 1942 were the key months in the decision-making process of the Second World War, the days during which the fatal decision was taken to postpone the victorious invasion of north-western Europe from a definite date in 1943 into a time that prolonged the fighting, enabled Stalin to win the struggle for much of Europe, and allowed over a million extra Jews to die in the Holocaust. We should also recall that none of the key decision makers in the West knew that that would be the consequences of their discussions. However, those were the results, and what we will see in this chapter is how the fatal blunders, with such devastatingly unintended consequences, came to be made.

At the heart of all the talking was Winston Churchill, a leader who was far more involved in the day-to-day running of the war than was ever the case with Roosevelt, and who had, as the result of years of writing, thinking, and in his own youth, actual fighting, the perception of himself as a strategist. This is something to bear in mind as this part of our story unfolds and we examine our theme, the tragically flawed genius who knew that victory was impossible without the Americans but who failed to see how the United States would transform war in a way that Churchill and centuries of British military tradition never matched.

Before we go on, it might be helpful to have a list of the various code names for operations that are the source of all the Anglo-American arguments in the next few chapters, since otherwise it is possible for most nonspecialist readers to get easily confused. (So too did Churchill and Roosevelt!)[1]

So here they are:

BOLERO: the American plan to build up enough US troops in Britain to launch an invasion of the Continent, on what we now call D-day

SLEDGEHAMMER: Marshall's idea of an emergency invasion of northern France in 1942, should the USSR collapse suddenly in the face of the Nazi invasion

ROUNDUP: later on familiar to us as Overlord, the invasion of northwestern Europe, but, in 1942, recommended by Marshall (and Eisenhower) as something that should take place in *1943*

JUPITER: Churchill's own rather quixotic plan to invade Norway, which never actually happened

GYMNAST (later known as Torch): the plan of Churchill's which Roosevelt backed over Marshall's plan to invade Europe in 1943: this was the invasion by American troops in North Africa to help the British who were already there to fight Rommel

Let us now see what happened over these next vital few months, and how they so altered the long-term fate of the war, starting off with Churchill's own account of the meetings in his book *The Hinge of Fate.*[2]

The Hinge of Fate

The Hinge of Fate has been described by BBC history presenter David Reynolds as the "messiest" of Churchill's six history volumes.[3] Part of that is for reasons extraneous to our own book, such as where Churchill and his team placed which incident, sometimes in the wrong volume.

But one can argue it is also a mess because Churchill's own strategic thoughts were a mess.

One of the main arguments of this book is that Churchill delayed Overlord by a crucial year, to the overwhelming detriment of both Britain and the United States. In the period we are dealing with here, it is clear that the prime minister had no idea he was doing this, and I think we can say that he was entirely genuine in his delusion: *he really thought that invading France in* 1943 *was compatible with all the other many things that he wanted to do.*

This is important because, whereas one can claim with some degree of fairness that the British Chiefs of Staff were opposed to landing in France in 1943 (and emphatically, with good cause in 1942), Churchill was not, but he wanted to do so many other things at once, from Torch in North Africa (which actually happened) to Jupiter in Norway (which to the great relief of Sir Alan Brooke did not), that he would have scattered British and American troops in so many places simultaneously that the landings in Normandy, when they did take place, would have been a disaster in whatever year they had happened.

As Paul Kennedy and Richard Holmes are both surely right to say,[4] throughout his life Churchill was a total enthusiast for whatever he did. Nor, I would add, is there any question but that in 1940–41 this was a thoroughly good thing, as without his self-belief, his enthusiastic patriotism, his indefatigability, and much else besides, we would have sunk beneath the Nazi hordes.

But it also goes without saying that large-scale enthusiasm for the impossible or even the dangerously reckless is a liability, not an asset, and as we shall see throughout the rest of the book it was the solemn duty of his Chiefs of Staff to prevent him taking Britain, with enormous gusto, excitement, and reckless enthusiasm, over the edge of the cliff.

Churchill therefore wanted to be in several places at once. He was also a profoundly old-fashioned imperialist, as made evident by his years in vigorous opposition to even the mildest form of self-rule for India in the 1930s. It is precisely these archaic views that now also so derailed his strategic grasp. For while it was of paramount importance to *Britain* that the United States had decided to put Europe first, Churchill was equally perturbed about the *British Empire*, thousands of miles away, and about the Pacific, the region that the US Navy, and probably also American public opinion in general, thought was the more important place to fight an enemy.

So in discussing the Marshall/Hopkins visit of April 1942 in his memoirs (written, as David Reynolds helpfully reminds us, in 1950),[5] Churchill is more than revealing of his own underlying attitudes.

"Let me now set out my own view," he begins, "which was persistent, of what had so far been decided and of what I thought should be done."[6]

He continues:

In planning the gigantic enterprise of 1943 it was not possible for us to lay aside all other duties. Our first Imperial obligation was to defend India against the Japanese invasion, by which it seemed it was already menaced. Moreover, this task bore a decisive relation to the whole war. To leave four hundred millions of His Majesty's Indian subjects, to whom we were bound in honour, to be ravaged and overrun, as China had been, would have been a deed of shame. But also to allow the Germans and Japanese to join hands in India or the Middle East involved a measureless disaster to the Allied cause. It ranked in my mind almost as the equal of the retirement of Soviet Russia behind the Urals, or even of their making a separate peace with Germany. At this date I did not deem either of these contingencies likely. I had faith in the power of the Russian armies and nation fighting in defence of their native soil. Our Indian Empire, however, with all its glories, might fall an easy prey. I had to place this point of view before the American envoys. Without British aid, India might be conquered in a few months. Hitler's subjugation of Soviet Russia would be a much longer, and to him more costly, task. Before it was accomplished the Anglo-American command of the air would have been established beyond challenge. Even if all else failed this would be finally decisive.[7]

The contrast between this and the far simpler strategic vision of a George C. Marshall could not be more marked. Britain had come close to defeat by Nazi Germany. The Americans and British had agreed in Washington DC only weeks earlier that *the* decisive enemy for both of them was Germany, and thus, to the sorrow of the US

Navy, by definition not Japan. So what did Marshall do? He drew up an excellent plan that would use the full might of the United States to defeat Germany, *the main enemy*, and to do so directly where this could best be accomplished, in northwestern Europe.

As Field Marshal Dill wrote from DC to the prime minister:

> There is no doubt that Marshall is true to his first love, but he is convinced that there has been no real drive behind the European project [i.e., Roundup]. Meetings are held, decisions take place, and time slips by. Germany will never again be so occupied in the East [i.e., Russia] as she is today, and if we do not take advantage of her present preoccupation we shall find ourselves with a Germany so strong in the West that no invasion of the Continent will be possible. We can then go on pummelling each other by air, but the possibility of a decision will have gone. Marshall feels, I believe, that if a great business man [*sic*] were faced with pulling off this *coup* or going bankrupt he would strain every nerve to pull off the *coup* and would probably succeed.[8]

Marshall was entirely right—and France was to be far more heavily guarded in 1944 than it was in 1943.

So here we have the Americans, with all the might of the greatest industrial power in the world and, crucially, a population far larger than that of the United Kingdom, offering on a plate the plan needed for ending the war. Japan could be defeated later.

But about what does Churchill worry? *India...*

Apart from the fact that India should not have been conquered by the British at all in the eighteenth and nineteenth centuries—we in the twenty-first must remember that people thought very differently then—it should certainly have been independent by 1942, as we shall see later. It had a huge army, with, by this time, a rapidly growing number of Indian, as opposed to British, officers, as well as ordinary soldiers. It was perfectly capable of defending itself and, as proved later in the war, it had, in General Sir William Slim, someone reckoned as perhaps the best British commander of the whole war.[9]

The other point Churchill makes turned out to be critical—it can be said to be the key decision that turned Roosevelt against his own Chief of Staff, George C. Marshall, and in favor of what turned out to be the great delaying tactic in North Africa that finished off any chance of a speedy end to the war.

For as Churchill wrote, eight years later in 1950, if the main invasion of Europe was going to be in 1943:

But what was to be done in the interval? The main armies could not simply be preparing all the time. Here there was a wide diversity of opinion.[10]

As Churchill realized:

It was impossible for the United States & Britain to stand idle all that time without fighting, except in the desert. The President was determined that the Americans should fight the Germans on the largest possible scale *during 1942*. Where then could this be achieved? Where else but in French North Africa, upon which the President had always smiled? Out of many plans the fittest must survive.[11]

This was, as we shall soon discover, to be *the* clinching argument with Roosevelt. It was, in that sense, the fatal flaw with Marshall's plan—the time to build up the invading army (Bolero), so as to have

Roundup at the most opportune moment (April 1943), had, inevitably, a fallow period built in, while US troops and equipment poured across the Atlantic to the United Kingdom.

I think it is right to say[12] that this played well with Roosevelt because of the *political* need in the United States to be seen fighting the Germans straight away, which opportunity Churchill gave the president, with all the results that followed.

Since we will examine this in more detail when we get to discussing the later conferences between the two leaders and their Chiefs of Staff, one point does need to be made here. Churchill concentrated both at the time and in his memoirs on the dangers, if not the actual desirability, of Sledgehammer. As we have seen, this was only ever an interim operation, based upon the premise of a Russian collapse. Here, as David Reynolds is right to argue,[13] this was not the main proposal but a contingency plan.

But in conflating the two, as Churchill does, it looks as if what the Americans were suggesting was an essentially *British-Canadian* invasion, in 1942, with, as the prime minister puts it, "two-thirds of the troops...provided by us."

It was only in July 1944 that the majority of troops actually fighting were American, and I shall show later that Churchill's failure to realize the impact of the sheer size of the contribution until then was a gigantic flaw in his strategic thinking. For while it was indeed true that in *1942* most *Western* troops fighting the Germans were either British or from some part of the empire (Canada, Australia, India, etc.) that was not even remotely true of the war as a whole; most of the Allied troops were Soviet, not Western, and certainly not so far as the war against not Italy but the main enemy, Germany, was concerned. The major war was on the Soviet-German *Eastern* Front, something that was to remain true throughout the war. Historians have correctly

pointed out that Churchill virtually ignores that part of the war altogether,[14] giving considerably less space to the titanic Russian struggles
and far more to the far less important battles in North Africa: the
Axis, for instance, lost 13,000 at El Alamein but *half a million* in the
battles and siege for Stalingrad.

(Since *The Hinge of Fate* does give much prominence to the epic
battles fought between the US Navy and the Japanese that year, which
in terms of the Pacific war were absolutely crucial, it is surely right to
say that his omission of the Eastern Front is therefore very strange,[15]
and does, I would think, point out a fundamental weakness in his
very strategic concept of the war.)

Had Bolero continued at the pace Marshall wanted, this imbal-
ance in Europe would never have been fully equaled—America was
fighting the Japanese, and regarding the USSR the whole nation was
fighting a battle for survival itself—but the disproportional nature
of the European struggle would have been far less much earlier on.
Churchill might well have understood earlier in the war than proved
to be the case that Britain was now only a comparatively minor partner in a much greater confrontation, of which the United States and
the USSR were by a very long way the biggest Allied contributors.

But while it was the decision to go for Torch (or Gymnast) that
created the mess, there is no doubt that had Sir Alan Brooke not been
able to rein in the prime minister things could have been much worse.
In his memoirs Churchill still lauds the idea of Jupiter, which we saw
was the idea of invading Norway to gain a direct foothold on the Continent to aid the northern convoys taking aid to Russia. As Churchill
put it:

Here was direct aid to Russia. Here was the only method of direct
combined military action with Russian troops, ships and air. Here

was the means, by securing the northern tip of Europe, of opening the broadest flood of supplies to Russia. Here was an enterprise which, as it had to be fought in Arctic regions, involved neither large numbers of men nor heavy expenditure of supplies and munitions. The Germans had got these vital strategic points by the North Cape very cheaply. They might also be regained at a small cost compared with the scale which the war had now attained. My own choice was for "Torch", and if I could have had my full way I should have tried "Jupiter" also in 1942.[16]

This is beyond question Churchill at his most brilliant but also utterly quixotic. A genius who comes up with ideas that sound wonderful but which are in reality entirely flawed is a mixed blessing, and Churchill was surely that throughout the war. The logistics of landing in Norway would have been considerably more difficult than in Normandy, especially in view of the much greater distances and the need for even greater air cover as well as naval success. The *concept* of helping the Soviet Union—it is possibly significant that Churchill always calls it the USSR, not Russia, its old imperial name—and as a by-product liberating an occupied country, Norway, is a great one. But taking Norway would not launch Allied forces into the heart of the Reich, which was Marshall's option. Churchill never revealed just why he felt—in 1942, before most American troops had arrived under any plan, his or Marshall's—that the limited amount of British and Empire troops could, with small American additions, have fought successfully on two fronts thousands of miles apart (from Norway in the north down to Tunis in the south). Not only that but the Germans would surely have sent thousands of troops and planes to eject the Allies—even presuming that British and US forces could have landed in Norway at all—and the tiny amount of forces on both sides, German and Allied, up in the Arctic that Churchill presumes would soon have evolved into major armies, especially on the German side.

But as we saw when we looked at the consequences of the fall of Norway in early 1940, there was a silver lining. Thousands of German troops were stuck in that country, awaiting an invasion that never came, and thereby robbing both the Eastern and Western Fronts of divisions that would otherwise have been used to fight the Allies in either or both places. Churchill's idea might have been flawed genius, but Hitler's fear of what Britain *might* do there had nothing but a beneficial effect.[17]

Let us now look in detail on the plan Marshall presented and the difference it could have made.

Marshall's Victory Plan: How He Could Have Won the War in 1943

In the immortal phrase of Britain's greatest ever admiral, Horatio Nelson, who beat the French at the battle of Trafalgar in 1805, "engage the enemy more closely."

As we saw in the last chapter on the war in North Africa, if only we had done so in 1941, the outcome of World War II would have been drastically different, with victory possibly (if not probably) as early as 1943, with millions of Jewish lives saved, not to mention those other millions, civilian and military, who perished in the period 1943–45. Maybe as many as a million Jews would have lived—the extermination part of the Holocaust did not truly get under way until after January 1942—not to mention countless non-Jewish civilians in other parts of Europe who perished in everything from Allied bombing raids (such as on Dresden) to the indiscriminate murder of German women by the Soviets in 1944–45, all that on top of those massacred by the SS and other organs of the Third Reich.

Proving something that never happened is a difficult thing to do, as Marshall's key planning staffer, General Albert Wedemeyer, was the first to admit. In agreeing with Marshall and his key supporters, such as his chief planner, General (later President) Dwight Eisenhower, I am very aware of the unusually hard task I am giving myself in this book. The debate on the second front, as it was called, preoccupied the Western Allies, the United States and the UK, throughout 1941–43, and was a cause of immense bitterness against the West in the USSR, since the Russians under Stalin believed, and not without good cause, that the West was allowing millions of Russians to die— well over twenty million during 1941–45—while refusing to attack the German heartland directly themselves, until D-day in June 1944.

As we have seen, direct engagement with the enemy was not only against everything that Churchill believed in himself, not just because of his fear that British troops were not up to the job or because he feared a repeat of the carnage at the Western Front in 1914–18, in which millions died needlessly in the trenches, but also because that was what British military doctrine had argued for centuries, not to mention his own passionate belief in the "soft underbelly" approach he'd held all his military and political life.

By contrast, as we have also just seen, the United States has always believed in the frontal approach. When we finally did land on continental Europe, in June 1944, we came very close indeed to finishing off the war in Europe that same year, and probably would have done so had Eisenhower's plans prevailed over those of Field Marshal Montgomery, and had an American general such as Patton been allowed his full head of steam. How much earlier still, therefore, might we have concluded the war had Marshall's plan for victory (which Eisenhower and Wedemeyer helped in drawing up) been allowed to prevail back in April 1942?

Roosevelt's main aide, Harry Hopkins, knew that Roosevelt was eager for action, and preferably in 1942. (As we shall see, this became a problem that Churchill was able to exploit, since Roosevelt did not really care *where* the military action was so long as there was direct fighting with the Germans *somewhere*.)

Hopkins thus wrote to his boss on England:

There is nothing to lose. The bridgehead [Sledgehammer; see below] does not need to be established until air superiority is complete. I doubt if any single thing is as important as getting some sort of a front this summer against Germany. This will have to be worked out very carefully between you and Marshall in the first instance, and you and Churchill in the second. I don't think that there is any time to be lost, because if we are going to do it plans need to be made at once.[18]

The plans were agreed between Hopkins, Roosevelt, Marshall, and others in April. From the British viewpoint, and from that of General Marshall, the decision was critical—to attack Germany, not Japan, first. This, British audiences often forget, was sacrificial for Roosevelt, since the anger of the American people was, after Pearl Harbor, naturally turned against Japan not Germany, and the naval lobby, to which Roosevelt, as a former assistant secretary of the navy, was not oblivious, also favored making the war in the Pacific priority over the Atlantic. But as Marshall told the president, Western Europe, and Britain in particular, was:

[T]he only place in which a powerful offensive can be prepared and executed by the United Powers in the near future. In any other locality the building up of the required forces would be much more slowly accomplished due to sea distances... The United States can concentrate and use larger forces in Western Europe than in any other place, due to sea distances and the existence in England of base facilities. The bulk of combat forces of the United States, United Kingdom and Russia can be applied simultaneously only against Germany and then only if we attack on time. We cannot concentrate against Japan.

For Britain this made all the difference. A country fighting for its life, and with no major victories in the Western Desert—except those that we saw Churchill and Wavell throw away in order to send troops to Greece—the British position was truly perilous.

Whatever faults Churchill had—and this book does not disguise them—he did understand more than anyone else that without the full and active military aid of the United States, the United Kingdom and its empire were doomed. So although I am arguing here that Churchill, having finally obtained the US help for which he had, correctly, longed since 1938, now went on to make gigantic errors, it should always be remembered that virtually alone of eminent British statesmen of his era he realized that America and America alone was the key to the very continuation of Britain as a free and independent country. While reputable British historians such as Correlli Barnett and John Charmley might argue that at this point Churchill effectively threw away British hegemony in favor of establishing American global predominance—which was inevitably at British expense— surely the *real* issue, as Churchill saw, was whether Britain survived at all. Without America that would not have happened, and on that the half-American Winston Churchill was triumphantly right.

(Not only that but I would also argue that the United States was correct on other issues, such as Indian independence—as we shall see, Churchill's dogged imperialism, while great for British morale in 1940–42, was positively antediluvian, as Roosevelt was so right to remind him.)

Roosevelt approved the Marshall memorandum in the White House on April 1, 1942, and Marshall and Hopkins duly set out for Britain on the fourth, in a visit code-named Modicum. They arrived, via Bermuda, on the eighth. The memorandum began:

> Western Europe is favored as the theatre in which to stage the first offensive by the United States and Great Britain. By every applicable basis of comparison, it is definitely superior to any other. In point of time required to produce effective results, its selection will save many months. Through France passes our shortest route to the heart of Germany. In no other area can we attain the overwhelming air superiority vital to successful land attack; while here and only here can the bulk of British air and ground forces be employed. In this area the United States can concentrate and maintain a larger force than it can in any other. A British-American attack through Western Europe provides the only feasible method for employing the bulk of the combat power of the United States, the United Kingdom and Russia in a concerted effort against a single enemy.[19]

The case for attacking the Third Reich head-on could not have been better expressed, and the same applies to the US doctrine of going for your main enemy directly, rather than wasting peripheral attacks that fail to address the main object: the military defeat of the principal opponent.[20]

(Not only that, but as we shall see, when the Allies *did* finally land in 1944, in more adverse circumstances, *after* Rommel's creation of an effective "Atlantic Wall" defense system, we came close to winning within a few months, but did not, because of Montgomery's slowness in breaking out of Normandy and his failure to capture the final bridge across the Rhine at Arnhem—the famous "bridge too far.")

The first paragraph set out Marshall's stall. There were two phases: Bolero, the buildup mainly in Britain of US forces, and then Roundup itself, the actual invasion of continental Europe that we now know as D-day.

There was also another plan, just in case the Soviet Union disintegrated in the face of continued German onslaught. We know today that this did not happen, that the Russians held out at Stalingrad and were able to turn the tide. But that was far from clear at the time, and the fall of Russia to the Third Reich was a constant worry through to the turning-point battles on the Eastern Front such as the greatest tank battle of all time, that at Kursk in 1943, which the Soviets won.

As the Marshall memorandum put it:

Finally, successful attack through Western Europe will afford the maximum possible support to Russia, whose continued participation in the war is essential to the defeat of Germany.

So wisely, although Marshall felt that the *main* Allied thrust should take some time to create—Bolero/Roundup—what he and Roosevelt thought might be a sacrificial initial spearhead attack to give the Red Army breathing space should be considered as well.

This was code-named Sledgehammer, and while D-day eventually did take place, albeit a year too late, this other attack, much discussed and debated between Britain and the United States, never happened.

As Marshall suggested:

Another, and most significant consideration is the unique opportunity to establish an active sector on this front this summer [1942], through steadily increasing air-operations and by raids or forays along the coasts. This initial phase will be of some help to Russia and of immediate satisfaction to the public; but what is more important is that it will make experienced veterans of the air and ground units, and it will offset the tendency towards deterioration in morale which threaten the latter due to prolonged inactivity.[21]

Those who condemn the whole idea that the Western Allies could have invaded in *1943* love to use Sledgehammer—the plans for diversionary practice raids upon the Continent in *1942*—as proof of the folly, as they see it, of going to war anytime before we actually did so in *1944*. Sir Basil Liddell Hart, Britain's great tank strategist, and the virtual inventor of modern mechanized warfare, is an example of this, in his writing about Churchill soon after the latter's death in 1965.[22]

As supporters of 1943 would argue, there is a considerable difference between a raid in 1943 and one in 1942—the only one that did take place in 1942, which we will see, was that of Dieppe, and this was one planned not by the Americans but by the British, and it was a total disaster. But Marshall was never advocating a full-scale invasion for 1942, only a major diversion to help Russia should the Germans manage to gain and maintain the upper hand on the Eastern Front. Sledgehammer was never intended to be the real thing; Marshall fully intended the real one to be the following year, 1943, when a massive *American* army would be ready and operational, not just a few brave—and principally British and Canadian—commando raiders as took part in Dieppe.

This is clear from the way in which Marshall's argument continued. As he wrote (with the aid of Eisenhower, Wedemeyer, and the other planners):

> Decision as to the main effort must be made now. This is true even if the invasion cannot be launched during this year [1942]. A major attack must be preceded by a long period of intensive preparation. Basic decision is necessary so that all production, special construction, training, troop movements and allocations can be co-ordinated to a single end.

(Churchill's generals were always complaining that the prime minister did not understand modern twentieth-century logistics. Mentally, as even his great defender, cohort, and cheerleader Brendan Bracken put it, "Winston always remains the 4th Hussar," referring to the mounted horseback cavalry regiment in which Churchill served as a young man back in the nineteenth century. In Basil Liddell Hart's words, his view of the new kind of fighting, of the kind the world saw post-1939, was "made all the worse by his misunderstanding of modern mechanized warfare.")

Unlike Churchill, Marshall and his planners fully understood the need for getting going in plenty of time. As he (and they) therefore continued:

> Until this process of co-ordinated and intensified effort is initiated, it is difficult even to calculate even the approximate date at which a

Churchill at Chartwell

Churchill, Gamelin, and Gort

Churchill leaving No. 10

Churchill and Clementine on board ship

Churchill inspecting the Home Guard

Churchill visiting blitz victims

Churchill and a snake

Churchill making a speech

Churchill shooting

Churchill and Roosevelt in 1941

Churchill and Roosevelt

Churchill making a speech to Congress

Churchill smoking a cigar

Churchill, Clementine, and Eden

Churchill's return from Moscow

General George Marshall

Churchill, Roosevelt, Marshall, and Brooke

Churchill on board ship

Churchill inspecting French soldiers

Churchill in one of his finest hours

major offensive can be undertaken. Decision now will stop continued dispersion of means.

This last sentence proved to be an understatement!

For this is what the British were now doing on a major scale, for reasons fully in tune with centuries-old British strategy, as we have seen, but to immense cost in delaying what the Americans knew to be the only way of winning: the landing of Allied troops in France. For not only were Churchill and his Chiefs of Staff wanting to have a major British/American force in North Africa, but also for it to fight in other parts of the Mediterranean, in Italy, and, if Churchill had his way, in the Balkans as well.

Not only that but Churchill (unlike Sir Alan Brooke, his main military adviser) wanted to invade Norway as well, through Operation Jupiter—which was a rerun of an idea Churchill had had as First Lord of the Admiralty back in 1914, to seize the Baltic island of Borkum.[23] All these schemes, harebrained and otherwise, were, as Marshall, Eisenhower, and others fully understood, a *massive* dispersion of Allied means, and a total distraction (what Marshall was later to call a "suction pump") from the main objective of attacking Germany directly, through France.

(In addition, the Allies did not know what would happen with several countries that were then neutral, but which could be overrun by Hitler at any time: attacking Hitler before the Axis could attack these countries was vitally important to Marshall.)

Therefore, the American plan was this:

Our proposal…provides for an attack, by combined forces of approximately 5800 combat airplanes and 48 divisions against

Western Europe as soon as the necessary means can be accumulated in England—estimated at 1 April 1943, provided decision is made *now* [Marshall's italics] and men, material and shipping are conserved for this purpose.

Marshall then outlined the details. The Western allies would need:

(a) Adequate air superiority over the enemy, involving the use by the allies of a minimum of 3000 fighters and 2850 combat planes other than fighters [both British and US]

(b) Sufficient landing-craft to land in the first wave the major combat elements of an infantry and armored force of at least six divisions. At the beginning of the actual invasion, *US* [*sic*] land forces in England or *en route* should approximate 30 divisions. Total US strength in England at that time will approximate 1,000,000 men.

(c) An ability to land on the western coast of Europe behind the leading wave, a weekly increment of at least 100,000 troops, and, after the invasion forces have landed, a continuous flow of reinforcements from the United States at the maximum rate that shipping will permit.

(d) Sufficient naval support to assure freedom from interference by hostile surface and sub-surface craft.

Marshall reckoned that about a million men would be needed for an "invasion of France" between what they then thought would be "Le Havre and Boulogne." The much better idea of landing in Normandy, where D-day actually happened, had not yet emerged. The planners and Marshall realized:

Logistical factors fix the earliest possible attack on this scale at about 1st April 1943. Bottlenecks, as to time, will be shipping and landing-craft, which will not be available in sufficient quantities by the time that aircraft, ground equipment and ammunition can be supplied.

(The amount of landing craft of various descriptions that would be needed has become one of *the* biggest factors in the row between historians who support Churchill in postponing D-day and those, including your author, who think they could in fact have been available and in time if needed—we shall see this in more detail later. But Marshall was certainly well aware of their importance and of the issues involved.)

Marshall's genius sadly failed to impress the most important of the British Chiefs of Staff, Sir Alan Brooke, Chief of the General [i.e., Army] Staff and Churchill's main strategic adviser during the war. Thankfully for us, Brooke kept copious diaries, written in the form of letters to his wife—all against strict military regulations—and then commented on all these when a heavily expurgated version of them came out in the 1950s, edited by the historian Sir Arthur Bryant. These diaries, now in London, have recently been published in full, and they are highly illuminating for the innermost thoughts of Britain's top Second World War army Chief.

On April 9, 1942, Brooke and Marshall met each other for the first time. Brooke confided to his diary:

> I liked what I saw of Marshall, a pleasant and easy man to get on with, rather over-filled with his own importance. But I should not put him down as a great man.[24]

Fifteen years later these diaries were being prepared for partial publication and Brooke had to think again of his first impression.

Brooke then wrote that his initial views were "incomplete" and his plans for a possible invasion as early as September 1942, to create a toehold in France, were "fantastic!"

Hopkins's notes on the initial meeting reveal that Marshall thought equally little of Brooke:

> We dined…as guests of the Prime Minister, but the conversation was in the main social…although General Brooke got into it enough to indicate that he had a great many misgivings about our proposal. Brooke made an unfavourable impression on Marshall, who thinks that although he may be a good fighting man, he hasn't got Dill's brains.

(Significantly, much of Hopkins's own discussions with Churchill were on the India issue; unfortunately, space does not permit us to look at it as much as one would like, as it is a fascinating issue, and one that was very important in determining how the United States saw Churchill as a leader. Even at one of the most critical points of the war, Churchill was arguing with Roosevelt in favor of maintaining the British Raj!)

General Marshall was welcomed to a committee meeting of the Combined Chiefs of Staff on April 9, 1942, in the war cabinet offices in London, with the Chief of the Imperial General Staff, Sir Alan Brooke, in the chair.[25]

Marshall—in minutes written by his British hosts—set out his stall. The "reason for his visit," he told the gathered Anglo-American audience, "was to reach a decision as to what the main British-American effort was to be, and when and where it should be made."[26]

There were, he continued, "two main considerations," the first being Russian resistance, which even at this stage in the war was legitimately still very much a source of grave concern, as is clear from British and American contemporary records.

But the second item is, in the light of the argument of this book, a very important one: "it was essential that the large American army now being built up and trained should become engaged on active operations and gain war experience."

Unfortunately for Marshall, this worked both ways. First, the British, as Wedemeyer noted to his disgust,[27] tended to look down on the Americans and regard them as not very good—rather ironic in the light of the catastrophic *British* military failures in 1942, at Singapore and Tobruk. Second, Roosevelt was, as we shall see, to use the need for *instant* US field warfare experience to delay all that Marshall was trying to achieve in finishing the war early, by going along with Churchill's idea of US troops beginning their war not in Europe, but in North Africa. However, while we must bear this in mind while looking at the April military conversations, we must not get ahead of ourselves.

So Marshall now made what, in retrospect, was his strategic blunder—his willingness to insist not merely on Bolero, the buildup over time of American forces in Britain, in order to enable Roundup, the invasion itself, in April 1943, but what the British regarded as a sacrifice operation, Sledgehammer, what we saw earlier was designed to be a holding operation in Europe in the eventuality that, as Marshall put it to Brooke and the others, "the Russian situation developed unfavourably."

Marshall saw this as what he called an "emergency operation." This is in reality all it was intended to be. But unfortunately for his campaign to win the war effectively and quickly—and for all those who lost out because of the one-year delay of D-day—he clung as much to Sledgehammer as to Bolero and Roundup. This was to prove a major tactical blunder on his part, as it would enable Roosevelt, as well as Churchill, to delay what should have been an open and shut case.

In fact Lord Louis Mountbatten, King George VI's cousin came in immediately with reservations. (It is ironic in the extreme that the US Chiefs of Staff all liked Mountbatten, the embodiment of the arrogant aristocrat, as opposed to his far more down-to-earth and, one could argue, far abler colleagues such as Brooke. Personal chemistry between leaders is sometimes a strange thing.)

Mountbatten immediately pointed out the logistical problems of supply, something which, in fact, was to be solved (ironically in the light of his prevarications over launching D-day) by Churchill himself, in the form of the Mulberry harbors that enabled the Allies to maintain effective logistics after the initial invasion. Nor did Mountbatten think that any invasion of Europe could be kept secret—again this was something brilliantly solved by the deception operation in 1944 that convinced Hitler and the German high command that the invasion was to take place near Calais and not on the Normandy beaches. But this was still two years and more into the future.

Sir Charles Portal, Chief of the Air Staff, and the British Chief most admired (if that is the right word) by his American counterparts, also concentrated on the pitfalls of 1942 rather than on the more important point that Marshall (and, at this time, still Roosevelt) was making, about getting ready for 1943.

So Marshall was already being hard-pressed about Sledgehammer. As he replied, when it came to 1942, he realized he "could not press" for what he described as an "emergency operation" before September that year "as American assistance could not be given before that date on any scale."

This was, of course, to play into the hands of Brooke, Portal, Mountbatten, and the others; and ever since, British writers have argued that what Marshall was suggesting was an American initiative that would mainly use up British lives, since, as Churchill himself realized, it was not until after D-day in 1944 that there were more US troops engaged in combat than British (and Empire, including Canadians). Had an operation been necessary in 1942, this would indeed have been the case, although one could argue that, while it was not until 1943, with major Soviet victories at battles such as Kursk, that the Eastern Front really turned around against the Germans, the siege of Stalingrad in 1942 at least showed that beating the Soviets was beyond the capabilities of the German army, as we have shown elsewhere, in looking at Operation Barbarossa when it was launched in 1941.

But, with all that aside, Marshall now tried to get back to his main point:

> He again emphasized the great value to American troops of battle experience and said that they were ready to take their part in any operation. He realized that even with good judgment, losses might be sustained and these they were ready to accept.

This last argument, while something in which the Americans believed, is naturally a hard one to make! It was something of which Churchill despaired—that German troops, infused with Nazi propaganda, were prepared to take far higher casualties, and as Norman Davies and Max Hastings, in their books on the Second World War have shown, so too were the Soviets, who had, in any case, "punishment battalions" behind the front lines to shoot anyone who dared to try to escape or retreat. Thankfully American troops in Europe, after their initial glitches in 1943, were to show that any GI was a full match for the Wehrmacht, and the Marines were demonstrating the same martial qualities against the Japanese in the Pacific.

On April 11, 1942, Colonel Wedemeyer met with a British-American committee under the chairmanship of Oliver Stanley, a traditional Conservative who had never quite summoned the courage pre-1939 to have resigned over Chamberlain's appeasement policy, and a scion of the great aristocratic family of Lancashire landowners.

Stanley argued for the British viewpoint—even Roundup would imply that German morale was on the collapse,[28] which showed a degree of caution about invading the Continent that even Churchill did not begin to match.

Wedemeyer disagreed, and made it as clear as he could to the British that the American plans—the "Marshall Memorandum" that had in fact been written by himself and Eisenhower—presumed several things. First, the bulk of the German forces were presumed to be fighting the Soviet Union. Next, it was as vital as possible for American troops to have combat experience and for them to be substantial in number. Not only that, but:

> Finally he emphasized that the United Nations [the phrase they used for Britain and the United States] must adhere to the broad concept of strategy, viz. that Germany is our principal enemy and Central Europe our main theater of operations, while the dissipation of our combined resources in other theaters should be discontinued or at least held to the minimum, on consonance with the accepted strategy of concentration on offensive operations in the European theater, with current defensive operations in all others.

This should have been manna from heaven to the British, since it was clear that even an Anglophobe such as Wedemeyer believed in the Europe-first strategy, the one policy guaranteed best to help the United Kingdom in its life-and-death struggle with Nazi Germany.

But at both the first meeting and the next one, on the twelfth, the main British concern seems to have been over a lack of landing craft and other vital necessities, not so much for the potential fight against Germany in northwestern Europe, but in those very peripheral areas of which the Americans despaired—India and the Middle East.[29] As we have seen, the United States was determined to protect Britain itself, but as for the British Empire, that was another matter altogether, and yet it was in these—to the Americans—peripheral areas that the United Kingdom representatives on the committee seemed most anxious.

On April 13, the British Chiefs of Staff gave their initial written reply. As the British later confessed, they decided not to reveal quite *how much* they disagreed with the American Chiefs of Staff, simply because they were so relieved that the United States had decided to give Germany priority over Japan. Naturally this was strongly in Britain's interest, and Churchill and his generals were more than keen not to upset any possible applecarts at this early stage in the proceedings—something that Churchill's personal Chief of Staff, General Hastings Ismay, was later much to regret.[30]

So, in essence, they pretended to go along with Roundup—an invasion of the Continent in April *1943*:

> As regards the long term view, we agree entirely that plans should
> be prepared for major operations on the Continent by British and
> American forces in 1943 on the lines prepared in your [i.e., Mar-
> shall's] paper.[31]

This was entirely disingenuous, because it was, to put it bluntly, not the view of the British Chiefs of Staff at all. Churchill, as we shall see, did not understand what the Chiefs of Staff of both countries knew fully: namely that an Allied expedition to North Africa (at this stage called Gymnast, and later by its more famous final name of Torch), to rescue the beleaguered British in the Middle East, made landing in northwestern Europe entirely impossible. We can therefore forgive Churchill, who, it appears, genuinely seemed to think that military operations in both the Middle East and northwestern Europe were *simultaneously* possible. But when it comes to Brooke and the other British military leaders, who did grasp the strategic/logistical realities, being forgiving is a harder thing to do.

In addition, the British were also drastically overstretched for a country of such finite resources. As the military leaders put it, they were obliged to "point out that action against Germany as outlined...may be entirely vitiated unless we take the necessary steps to hold Japan in the meantime....We do not possess enough naval forces, even leaving the barest minimum for our vital commitments in Home Waters [i.e., Britain itself] to meet the Japanese forces already operating in the Indian Ocean, not to mention those which may be added to them. We are also very short of aircraft in this theatre."[32]

Historians such as Correlli Barnett have argued, one could say correctly, that British obsession over the Middle East caused the fall of Singapore to the Japanese, since one part of the world was denuded of troops in order to fight a war elsewhere. The simple fact of the matter was, of course, that the British Empire was now stretched a very long way indeed beyond any resources it might ever have had, and that in being scared of fighting simultaneously with Germany, Japan, and Italy the prewar Chiefs of Staff were entirely correct—*were Britain fighting on her own*. However, as I shall argue later on, this was entirely to neglect the overwhelming difference that American involvement in the war now made to Britain and the British/Empire ability successfully to wage war. Britain no longer had to go it alone!

Meanwhile, Marshall continued to get bogged down in what might be possible in September 1942: the well-meant but unfortunately impossible Sledgehammer continued to divert attention from the real war-winning strategy he had for delivering victory. Soon he was discussing the likely autumn weather,[33] and trying to persuade the skeptical British Chiefs of Staff that he really could deliver Bolero, and have enough US forces in place by the requisite time frame. When Portal tried to talk about the need to send air forces to the Middle East and to India, the meeting minutes describe Marshall's riposte:

> There was no doubt that once we had our view firmly centred on
> a project problems became greatly eased. Within the last few days,
> he had already had satisfactory examples of this.

The minutes continue with Marshall putting the issue in a nutshell:

> Finally he said he was anxious that the dispersion of forces should
> be reduced to a minimum. To what extent might it be necessary
> to send more forces to the Middle East and India? He thought it
> essential that our main project, i.e. operations on the Continent,
> should not be reduced to the status of a "residuary legatee" for
> whom nothing was left.

Marshall could not have put it better. But in effect the British and American Chiefs of Staff were, as one wag once put it, two peoples separated by a common language.[34] But in fact one could argue that even if they really were both speaking English, they were in practice speaking entirely different languages altogether. Here were the direct-approach Americans, and the indirect-approach British, both steeped in the history and ways of doing things of their own cultures, traditions, and backgrounds.

It is not surprising therefore that a genuine meeting of minds was not taking place.

Consequently, on the fourth meeting, on April 16, US Army colonel J. E. Hull felt it necessary to try to get the British back to some basic realities:

> To achieve the defeat of Germany we must get ashore on the Continent and fight them. Planning for this must start now. The forces for this must be sufficient not only to get ashore, but also to exploit the success thus achieved. The United States proposals had shown the forces that they could provide and the total which they considered necessary to achieve this object.[35]

Yet alas even this did not convince the British to change what, to be fair, was centuries of tradition, and it was perhaps not insignificant that the person to pour cold water on the American plans was a Royal Navy captain, J. E. Hughes Hallett; at the very least, he argued, we could only hope to get a bridgehead on the Continent in 1943 "and to prepare for further advance by 1944," which, as we know, is exactly what finally happened on D-day.

Here it is relevant to look at the interview between Forrest Pogue and Churchill's personal Chief of Staff, General Hastings Ismay (later on, as a civilian, the first ever secretary-general of NATO).[36]

As he admitted, years later, to Pogue:[37]

And that was the time when I thought there was a grave misunderstanding—we were all rather carried away by the idea of millions of Americans falling into England and charging into the [English] Channel, and I thought that the British—Winston was carried away emotionally—[believed in] this great brotherhood in arms. I think that the British were rather in a way not unfair but not straightforward enough. We knew perfectly well that there wasn't a hope in hell of Roundup. We would have had to supply nearly all the stuff of Sledgehammer, but we didn't say so...and I think Marshall and Hopkins went back feeling that we were all sold on it and everything was pretty good.

Not only that, but this was the time when the British were losing heavily in North Africa, and, as even Churchill confessed to his physician, Charles Wilson, whom he now made Lord Moran, there was serious question in ruling circles in the United Kingdom that their own soldiers were simply not up to the job. The British/Empire loss of Tobruk in June 1942 had not yet occurred when these talks began, but the imminent collapse of the garrison there was in everyone's mind. As Ismay revealingly went on to tell Pogue:

We were very, very weak then and the Germans were very strong...Let's face it—we had not got the offensive spirit. We hadn't got a victory to our credit anywhere. Conversely the Germans had had no defeat. They were full of confidence...we should [in talking to the Americans] come clean, much cleaner than we did and said, "We are...honestly frightened of what we have been through in our lifetime—60,000 in a day—the 1st of July 1916...and we have not got a big population. 60,000 in a day—that was the casualties... We who had survived, had got that in our minds, and 'never again' you see..."

From the *solely* British point of view, what Ismay argues was at the back of the minds of all the military (and civilian—Churchill spent time on the Western Front) leadership is precisely this—*never again*. Indeed, any civilian who writes on war who has not himself been in direct combat—your author has been in two civil war zones[38] but not in anything like the harm's way a soldier is in during battle—ought to be very careful indeed in chiding soldiers for not wanting to face the enemy directly.

However, and this is a recurring theme of this book, nonetheless the basic error that Churchill and all the British civilian/military leadership made in World War II is that they continued grossly to underestimate the sheer power and resources for victory that the United States was now offering them, and on a plate. Ismay was correct to remember the carnage of the First World War, which is why the British commanders, notably Field Marshal Montgomery, were so very understandably loath to accept high levels of Allied casualties—the mud of the trenches in Flanders naturally haunted them all. But the phrase when he says "we have not got a big population" is and was true of the United Kingdom, but was not at all true of their new ally, the United States. America could and was now offering to raise armies way beyond the capacity of even the British Empire at full stretch.

Yet Churchill, the Chiefs of Staff, and his fellow politicians continued to think of the conflict as an essentially *British* war, fought according to hallowed British precepts, all of which presumed a comparatively small army, a powerful navy, and, by this time, an air force that could defeat the enemy by aerial bombardment alone. This, to me, is the real tragedy of the April–June 1942 talks, that Churchill and his empire were offered the greatest army the world had ever seen, with Europe as priority over Japan, and yet failed utterly and consistently for the next three years to understand the implications for battle and for eventual victory of that glorious offer. Marshall and his colleagues were offering them the Crown Jewels and all they could see were circus baubles. And, as argued already, this failure was to do the one thing Churchill dreaded by late 1944/early 1945: give effectual victory in Europe not to the Western Allies, but to Stalin.

To revert to our narrative, on April 10, the key British and American leaders all went to see Churchill at Chequers, the official country residence of British prime ministers. Brooke had had to suffer Churchill's incorrigible late-night sessions for some time now, but for Marshall they were a wholly new experience. As Brooke wrote in his diary, "We were kept up till 2AM doing a world survey, but little useful work." Years later he added for the published version:

> I remember being amused at Marshall's reactions to Winston's late hours, he was evidently not used to being kept out of his bed till the small hours of the morning and not enjoying it much! He certainly had a much easier time of it working with Roosevelt, he informed me that he frequently did not see him for a month or six weeks. I was fortunate if I did not see Winston for 6 hours.[39]

On April 15 Brooke met Marshall again. Brooke positively dripped with condescension. Commenting on the visit that night, he wrote:

> He is, I should think, a good general at raising armies, and providing the necessary links between the military and political worlds.

But his strategical ability does not impress me at all!! [*sic*]. In fact in many respects he is a very dangerous man whilst being a very charming one!

All this was from a British general who had never won a major battle, but who, nonetheless, thought he knew more than a mere American....

Brooke knew about the pressure Marshall was under from Ernest King and Douglas MacArthur to switch priorities to the Pacific. On this, Brooke wrote:

To counter these moves Marshall has started the European offensive plan and is going 100% all out on it! It is a clever move which fits in well with the present political opinion and desire to help Russia. It is also popular with all military men who are fretting for an offensive policy. But, and this is a very large 'but', his plan does not go beyond just landing on the far coast!! Whether we are to play baccarat or chemin de fer at Le Touquet, or possibly bathe at Paris Plage is not stipulated![40]

Marshall's plan did not specify the details of the second day—on that Brooke had a fair point. But in order to invade a country, one first has to land one's troops, and this was certainly something that Marshall had worked out very precisely and in immense detail.

Fifteen years later, Brooke, then Field Marshal Lord Alanbrooke, commented that he did not believe Marshall had worked out the strategic implications of what happened after the troops had landed. In fact:

I saw a good deal of him throughout the rest of the war, and the more I saw of him the more clearly I appreciated that his strategic ability was of the poorest. A great man, a great gentleman and a great organiser, but definitely not a strategist…his stunted strategic outlook made it very difficult to discuss strategic plans with him, for the good reason that he did not understand them personally but backed the briefs prepared by his staff.

As the April 1942 brief was drawn up by Eisenhower, the victorious Supreme Allied Commander in Europe 1944–45, this attitude says more about Brooke than about Marshall, whose strategic genius, and vision of attacking the main enemy directly, Brooke, with his more blinkered, traditional, and overcautious outlook, did not grasp at all.

In fact, Brooke never really had his heart in D-day even when it took place finally in 1944. On the day before, June 5, he confided:

I am very uneasy about the whole operation. At best it will fall so very very far short of the expectation of the bulk of the people, namely all those who know nothing of its difficulties. At the worst it may well be the most ghastly disaster of the whole war. I wish to God it were safely over.[41]

As we know, D-day succeeded, and Eisenhower, the former planner turned Supreme Allied Commander, whom Brooke dismissed earlier in 1944 as merely a "swinger and no real director of thought",[42] nearly led the Allies to victory that year, had Montgomery's tactlessness and failure at Arnhem not prevented it.

Marshall went home thinking that the British were on his side. He was soon to be disabused of this happy notion, since it became clear very soon that the British were utterly and implacably opposed to Sledgehammer because of the fact that for an operation to be mounted that early, the bulk of casualties would be certain to be predominantly British and Canadian, not American.

But Marshall was in a sense right to feel hornswoggled, since the British had given him firm impression of support where in fact none existed. Was he deceived? This is an issue that has exercised American historians in particular ever since—the British deception of 1942! For Churchill now proposed that an American invasion of North Africa (at that time code-named Gymnast) should be the instant second front that Sledgehammer should have been. We shall look at this in more detail later on, but the general's reaction to Churchill's suggestion to Roosevelt is most significant.

As Mark Stoler puts it in his biography of Marshall:

Marshall was incensed. Disagreeing vehemently with such reasoning and convinced the British were guilty of manipulation and a breach of faith, he pushed for a "showdown" by suggesting to Admiral King that they threaten a Pacific-first strategy if London vetoed Sledgehammer and insisted on Gymnast. King concurred and on 10 July the two formally proposed such a shift to Roosevelt.[43]

This was a massive shift by Marshall himself, since he had been one of the key advocates of a Europe-first policy since before Pearl Harbor. Even to think of allying with King was a sign of how truly angry with Churchill he had become.

Therefore, King and Marshall now argued in this strange new alliance:

If the United States were forced to engage "in any other operation than forceful, unswerving full alliance to full Bolero plans" they advised the President, "we should turn to the Pacific and strike decisively against Japan; in other words assume a defensive attitude against Germany...and use all available means in the Pacific.[44]

This was completely revolutionary, and as Stoler rightly continues:

Roosevelt was appalled. "My first impression," he bluntly informed them, "is that is exactly what Germany hoped the United States would do following Pearl Harbor." He rejected their proposal and ordered them to meet with him and prepare to depart for another conference in London, accompanied by Hopkins, during which they would have to agree to Gymnast if the British rejected Sledge-hammer. For emphasis he signed their directive "Commander in Chief" instead of "President."[45]

Roosevelt hoped that ended Marshall's alliance with King over putting the Pacific first.

Is it fair to say that the British had actually been deceptive? I think we should remember what we saw Ismay saying earlier in this chapter: "I think that the British were rather in a way not unfair but not straightforward enough."[46] They were not trying to deceive, but in their terror that the United States *would* put the Pacific first, over Europe and the defeat of Germany, they were nowhere near as candid as they should have been. I think this is fair—the British were not entirely straight with their new US ally, but the charge of *deliberate* deception is probably unfair. Certainly, the very profound US and UK disagreements on strategy were soon to emerge fully in the open and with much animosity between the two countries.

Further, as we shall see, with the British veto over Sledgeham-mer remaining total, this meant not Bolero with Roundup in 1943, but exactly the kind of diversion, to North Africa, that Marshall so feared. As one historian has put it:

> Beyond the personal blow, Churchill's strategy had destroyed Marshall's attempt to create a coherent, unified strategy.[47]

In the last chapter we looked at the views of the historian Tuvia Ben-Moshe. One comment he makes is, I think, telling in all these debates. He writes:

> [Had] the issue been left entirely to the discretion of Churchill and the British Chiefs of Staff, they would not have invaded western Europe before Germany's strength had collapsed or been drastically weakened. Neither eventuality occurred during 1944. It therefore follows that they would not have crossed the Channel in that year.[48]

This seems a harsh judgment, but I fear that it has much to be said for it. Not only that but, as we shall now see, it was to be a costly mistake of gigantic magnitude.

We have looked at some of the issues chronologically, so let us now examine them thematically, so we can see in more depth the damage that Churchill's triumph over Marshall had in fact done. This is not to say that the prime minister could ever have foreseen those consequences back in 1942, something that it is only fair for us to remember. But there were very profound results nonetheless, and to these we now turn.

Second Front Now? Historians Argue for 1943

This is an argument that has gone to and fro among historians now for some years. It was written about from the vitally important British perspective by the late John Grigg in his book *1943*—vital in that the subject of our book, Winston Churchill, was Britain's leader—and from the American standpoint in Walter Scott Dunn Jr.'s book *Second Front Now, 1943*.[49] Significantly this book has a preface by General Wedemeyer, who was in a special position to know that Dunn's case was strong, if not unassailable.

Indeed, as Wedemeyer writes, he was "fully convinced of the operational feasibility as well as the military and geopolitical wisdom of an early, all-out invasion of the continent from Britain."[50] But the Allies allowed themselves to be diverted, and by 1944 "Soviet troops were well on their way to Berlin, and German defenses along the Atlantic coast had been strengthened."

He concludes with the crucial *geopolitical* case: what would have happened *politically and strategically* had D-day been earlier:

> Had the Western Allies faithfully adhered to their plan for assembling appropriate forces in the United Kingdom and for launching the invasion in 1943, I believe they would have succeeded. They, instead of the Soviets, could have seized and occupied much of Central Europe.

The Cold War, I would argue, might still have happened, but with very different borders for the Iron Curtain, millions of Central Europeans living in freedom instead of swapping one tyranny for another, and the world might, just possibly, also have been a safer place.

Dunn summarizes his argument well at the beginning:

The delay of the invasion would have enormous political impact on the post-cold war world...If the invasion had been launched in 1943, when the German army was still deep in Russia, the Allied armies would have penetrated deep into Germany and forced her surrender before the Russians reached the German border in the East. It was nearly four hundred miles from the front line in July 1943 at Kursk to the prewar Polish border and a further five hundred miles to the German 1939 frontier.[51]

Since British historians tend to disagree with the 1943 thesis, I should be careful about what I say now! But one only has to read the wonderful books by one of Britain's most eminent historians, and a leading authority on Central Europe, Norman Davies, to know that Britain betrayed the Polish people horribly—and did so twice, both in 1939, when we did nothing to help them, and then again, as we shall see, in 1944, when the government wished for by the majority of Poles was sacrificed. Stalin was thereby able to impose his will on Poland by brute force, as Norman Davies so movingly portrays in *Rising '44: The Battle for Warsaw*,[52] not least because it was *his* armies that had conquered Poland ("liberated" hardly applies in relation to what the Soviets did, especially in deliberately allowing the Germans to slaughter the genuine, and thus anti-Soviet, Warsaw Polish underground), rather than the Allies.

However, while the betrayal of the Poles by the West in 1944–45 was real, Churchill and those who defended the wartime settlement did have this as their justification: the Soviets were in situ and there was therefore nothing that Britain or the United States could do. Since that is the reality of what *did* happen, as a result of D-day's postponement by a year, Churchill has a fair defense. There really was nothing that the two Western allies could have done.

But what I am saying is that all this is a consequence of the much earlier strategic decision to divert Allied forces in 1942–44 and to throw away the chance of an earlier victory. For as Dunn argues, had D-day been in *1943*:

> The distance from Normandy to the Ruhr was less than four hundred miles. It is possible that Germany could have been defeated before the Russians had completely occupied Poland, providing the West with the opportunity to return the Sikorski government-in-exile. At the least, a Western hold on Germany would have given Churchill and Roosevelt a far stronger hand to play in negotiations in 1944.

To me that is an understatement! The West was four hundred miles from the German border on D-day, and in 1943 the Red Army was still nine hundred miles away, so had D-day been a year earlier, the geographical, let alone military and political, logistics of the situation would have been obvious. Having no Atlantic Wall would have made the D-day landings much easier, and if one considers that had the capture of Arnhem not been blown (as much by bad luck as human error by Montgomery), we could have been in Germany by 1944, then the case that these two authors make for a Western conquest of Germany *by 1943* becomes more overwhelming still. (We also nearly captured Prague as late as 1945—for this see below.)

The fact is that in the key discussions with Stalin up until June 1944, there was no Western Front at all and Stalin and the Red Army were doing all the major fighting. The United States might be the world's greatest power, but in 1943–44 that was, so far as the war in Europe was concerned, still in the future rather than a done deal obvious to all.

Dunn's book spends much time on logistics, a subject that, as we have seen, remained a complete mystery to Churchill, but was, nonetheless, in many ways the key to eventual and certain Allied victory.[53] This is especially true, for example, in the matter of landing craft,[54] an issue often raised by those who argue that there were not enough landing craft *in Europe* by 1943, and thus D-day really did have to wait until 1944 to be effective. Dunn shows that this is simply not the case:

> The landing craft [for Western Europe] were available. Ample supplies of all types of craft were available from early 1943. [By December 1942 Britain and the United States had manufactured, of different types of LST]…three times the number needed for Normandy. The necessary number of craft had been built by early 1943, but many had been sent to the Pacific. Even those available in Europe were sufficient to launch seven divisions in Sicily. These facts reveal that there was not a shortage of landing craft.[55]

In other words, as Dunn argues, the decision when to launch the second front, from 1942 to 1944, "was political not military."[56] Furthermore:

> On the basis of military capacity, according to American military leaders, the second front was possible in 1943, if not in 1942. A German surrender in 1943 would have saved Germany from the heavy bombing of 1944 and 1945 and spared Russia much of the devastation that resulted from the battles of those years.[57]

So in fact everyone would have benefited—especially of course the Jews, millions of whom would have been spared the Holocaust, as I state elsewhere.

Logistics, Dunn demonstrates, were on the side of the Allies *by the end of 1942*, something that Marshall and the Americans fully understood but Churchill and Brooke did not. As a result—ironically, in view of the way in which those wanting delay then (and in argument now) insist—in terms of logistics, "the invasion in 1944 was more difficult than it would have been a year earlier." Not only that, but:

> The British and Americans ignored the value of their lead in 1943 and misjudged the Germans' relative use of time. When the balance was heavily in favor of the Allies, they failed to apply the maximum military use of force at the crucial point with the object of paralysing the German war effort. Instead, they allowed most of their war potential to remain idle, while the Germans rearmed and shifted forces to meet them. By wasting opportunity, the Allies lost the chance for a clean, quick end to the war.[58]

As we have seen, Marshall fully understood the devastating effects this would have on his war plans, which is why he was rightly so opposed to the way in which Churchill inveigled Roosevelt into getting involved in the entirely peripheral struggle in North Africa.

What we are really seeing is the crucial difference, which emerges throughout our book, between the *direct* strategy of the Americans and the *indirect* strategy of the British. While an American author like Dunn is correct to say that during the war, much of the problem was the British planners' anxiety over the "fearsome power of the German army,"[59] I would argue here as elsewhere that it was not so much a question of understandable British terror in the face of the mighty Wehrmacht—although that was not inconsiderably a factor—but that *British policy had always been that way, for centuries,* right back to the time of Churchill's great ancestor Marlborough, and the wars against King Louis XIV of France.

The British, especially Churchill, were not being weak-willed or lily-livered, but traditional, since the United Kingdom, and England beforehand, had never been strong enough *on its own* to prevail over a continental army, whether the French in the eighteenth century or Hitler in the twentieth. Churchill was wrong, I would argue, not out of cowardice—that is never something of which someone like him could ever be accused—but ignorance, in particular, of the mighty effect that a fully mobilized American war machine would have, and indeed did have after 1944 (and in the Pacific, from earlier).

Let us take one example, to which we shall return at the end of the book. One argument for *1943* is that it would have prevented the Iron Curtain from ever happening at all—but, as the following shows, the Allies came close to that in one area *even in 1945*, with a June 1944 D-day instead of the one that should have been in April 1943.

As things turned out, for example, General Patton could easily have liberated Prague in 1945, and thereby enabled the West to be the clear victor in that country's affairs, with what would possibly have been major results come 1948 and the coup in Prague that turned Czechoslovakia from the beacon of democracy it had been 1919–39 into one of the most repressive of all the Soviet bloc regimes (the fleeting Prague Spring of 1968 notwithstanding). Patton was willing to go, and felt he could have done so easily. Churchill strongly sympathized with Patton's aims, but Eisenhower would not be budged: all considerations were to be *military* and not political, and if the Soviets had been designated to capture the Czechoslovakian capital, then it would be the Red Army, not the US Army under Patton, that would do the capturing.[60]

So here Churchill was once again on the side of the angels, but as before, over Poland, he was comparatively far too powerless to do anything to prevent the tragically inevitable fate of Central Europe. Truman would later, as history records, be the man to stand up to the Soviets, and Marshall's aid plan would ensure the economic recovery of the West, and thus, indirectly but firmly, secure Western Europe for freedom and democracy. But when the Czechoslovakian government agreed to join the Marshall Plan, they were summoned to Moscow by Stalin and ordered to renege on their decision. There was to be no Marshall Plan for Czechoslovakia, and instead forty-one years of effective rule from Moscow, as Dubcek and the leaders of the abortive Prague Spring leap for freedom were to find out when Soviet tanks invaded the country in 1968.

It should be said that things could of course have turned out the same in Prague in 1948, and that Czechoslovakia would have still become Communist. But the psychological advantage would no longer have been with the Soviets, nor would there have been Red Army troops in the region, since it is unlikely that a free Czechoslovakian government would have wanted the Americans to leave in favor of Stalin. The Prague coup and the Berlin Airlift were the two pivotal events that helped to alert the United States to the postwar Soviet threat, and thus to create NATO, but since NATO would sooner or later have come into existence anyway, the Czechs would have been able to join it half a century earlier, and with huge psychological results, since the West and NATO would then have had a direct border in the east of the country with the USSR itself.

CHAPTER FIVE

Waiting for Winston

WHILE WAR-CHANGING MAJOR battles raged across the world, from Midway to Stalingrad, Britain was directly involved in neither of these epic struggles. They are of vital importance to Allied victory against both Japan and Germany, but no British sailors or soldiers fought in either. So this chapter will inevitably follow some of the distortion that results in British accounts of the period, Churchill's own fully included, while not forgetting the proper perspective that all this showed was how comparatively unimportant the United Kingdom was in distinction to her ever more powerful Soviet and American allies. This and other issues therefore come up in Churchill's account in his book *The Hinge of Fate*,[1] after his account of the discussions on Allied strategy in London and Washington DC that we have just seen.

We shall look at the big conferences that took place between Churchill and Roosevelt, and their advisers, notably Brooke and Marshall, and see that by the end, Marshall was *finally* able to win through, and have the Normandy landings he had wanted for so long.

Let us first pause to see how Churchill perceived things in July 1942.

By that date, Churchill was still pondering why the German war machine was continuing to do so well.[2] Not only was the Wehrmacht fighting on in Russia, but, as he lamented, when "we feel what a couple of Panzer divisions...can do in North Africa against our greatly superior numbers and resources, we have no excuse for underrating German power in 1943 and 1944." Not only that, but in terms of logistics, the sinking rate in the Atlantic was still considerable, as Churchill fully understood:

> It may be true to say that the issue of the war depends on whether Hitler's U-Boat attacks on Allied tonnage, or the increase and application of Allied Air power, reach their full fruition first.

So Churchill returned to the chimera of victory through air power, or through a mass revolt of brave European civilians—for that is what it would have to be—against their Nazi oppressors. As he put it:

> In the days when we were fighting alone, we answered the question: "How are you going to win the war?" by saying: "We will shatter Germany by bombing." Since then the enormous injuries inflicted on the German Army and man-power by the Russians, and the accession of the man-power and munitions of the United States, have rendered other possibilities open.[3]

How much did all this affect what Churchill wanted to do? I think the sad answer is not by much, as we shall soon see....

He informed Roosevelt on July 8:

No responsible British General, Admiral or Air Marshal is prepared to recommend SLEDGEHAMMER as a practical operation in 1942.... I am sure myself that GYMNAST is by far the best chance for effecting relief to the Russian front in 1942.[4]

To Dill, he was even more explicit a few days later: "GYMNAST affords the sole means by which United States forces can strike at Hitler in 1942."[5]

This therefore meant no second front of the kind that Stalin wanted and needed. As Stalin told Churchill on July 23:

With regard to the...question of creating a second front in Europe, I am afraid it is not being taken with the seriousness it deserves. Taking fully into account the present position on the Soviet-German front I must state in the most emphatic manner that the Soviet Government cannot acquiesce in the postponement of a second front in Europe until 1943. I hope you will not feel offended that I expressed frankly and honestly my own opinion as well as the opinion of my colleagues on the questions raised.[6]

So Churchill now felt that he had to go to the USSR to tell the dictator himself.

His visit was in August 1942. This was, therefore, after the terrible defeats of that year, such as Singapore, but also just as the Soviets were achieving their goal of being able to take the offensive successfully against the Nazis for the first time in the war. Churchill's timing was thus not exactly ideal.

His memoirs are fascinating, but they have been heavily censored!

As Churchill wrote on September 26, 1950, on the final draft of the account of his visit:

> This supersedes & cancels all previous versions of this passage. Previous versions must not on any account be published.[7]

That really says it all—Churchill in 1950 was still a politician and, as Stalin was still alive, the truth could be awkward....

In his party were General Wavell, who, among his many skills, could speak Russian and who had fought against the Communists in 1918; the CIGS, Sir Alan Brooke; and Sir Alec Cadogan of the Foreign Office. Unlike the disastrous British party to Moscow in 1939, therefore, it was the top division of the United Kingdom's political, military, and diplomatic elite. With them was the wealthy man of business so often then found in US administrations, Averell Harriman, later US ambassador to both Moscow and London, and who was also, during the war, to have an affair with Churchill's daughter-in-law, Pamela, whom he was later to marry.[8]

The journey was adventurous, with no proper heating on the plane, and with one of the two planes—containing some of the other officials—having to turn back and arrive separately. For many a bomber crew such deprivations were part of service life, but Churchill was both prime minister and now nearly sixty-eight. It was, as General Douglas MacArthur, not normally an Anglophile, was to comment, very brave of Churchill to risk this in wartime, and deserving of a Victoria Cross.[9]

It was interesting in view of his earlier dislike of the USSR that Churchill was there at all. As he contemplated on his arrival:

> I pondered on my mission to this sullen, sinister Bolshevik State
> I had once tried so hard to strangle at its birth, and which, until

Hitler appeared, I had regarded as the mortal foe of civilized
freedom...Still, I was sure it was my duty to tell them the facts
personally and have it all out face to face with Stalin, rather than
trust to telegrams and intermediaries. At least it showed that one
cared for their fortunes and understood what their struggle meant
to the general war. We had always hated their wicked regime, and,
till the German flail beat upon them, they would have watched us
being swept out of existence and gleefully divided with Hitler our
Empire in the East.[10]

In this Churchill reflects accurately upon the dilemma which
Britain and, since December 1941, the United States faced: that the
Western Allies were, in effect, now allied with a country whose rulers
were as evil as the enemy they all faced. This would become apparent as the discussions between Churchill and Stalin unfolded and
was, one could argue, made worse by the fact that Churchill would
not deliver what Stalin desperately needed, a second front as soon as
possible.

The prime minister and his party soon discovered one of the less
agreeable facets of totalitarian life—their rooms were all bugged.
Churchill was originally going to put this in his memoirs, but, since
Stalin was very much alive as he wrote them, he decided to omit
this fact from the published draft.[11] Sir Alec Cadogan, however, had
no illusions about the dangers inherent in the fact that everything
they said could be overheard and reported to Stalin, something that
Brooke, it seems, had not understood at all. Churchill, however, soon
made fun of the bugs, declaring in mock tones:

The Russians, I have been told, are not human beings at all.
They are lower down the scale of nature than the orang-outang

[*sic*]. Now then, let them take that down and translate it into Russian.[12]

The mind boggles on what the NKVD listeners and transcribers made of that!

Needless to say, Churchill had to spend much time defending the lack of a second front in 1942 to Stalin when the two men finally met in the Kremlin. To Stalin's objections, Churchill replied:

> War was war but not folly, and it would be folly to invite a disaster which would help nobody. I said I feared the news I brought was not good news.[13]

Churchill did say, though, that a second front would be possible in 1943, a view we saw he held sincerely even if his actions did all possible still to militate against the one way in which it could be successful. But there was to be no attack on France in 1942.[14]

Stalin remained resolutely unconvinced by what he felt were Churchill's prevarications.[15] Your author's students each year have to write an essay entitled "When Did the Cold War Begin?," and Churchill's visit to Moscow in August 1942 is as good a starting point as any, since the increasing—and from their viewpoint, militarily understandable—Soviet paranoia over the delay of the second front did nothing to help East-West relations.

(One could, on this analogy, actually take the ultimate origins of the Cold War to the exclusion of the USSR from Munich, and that too would be as good a date as any, especially if, as one can argue, the beginning phases of the Cold War were cumulative rather than dating to one or two specific events.)

So as Churchill then recalled:

There was an oppressive silence. Stalin at length said that if we could not make a landing in France this year [1942] he was not entitled to demand it or to insist upon it, but he was bound to say that he did not agree with my arguments.[16]

Given the vast bloodshed on the Eastern Front, and the desperate struggle for Stalingrad—which, David Reynolds correctly comments, Churchill massively underplays in his memoirs[17]—it is hard not to sympathize with Stalin, not in his capacity as psychopathic dictator but as leader of a nation being slaughtered in their millions by the Nazi invaders.

Churchill's attempts to defend himself to Stalin are highly revealing of his own mentality as to how to win the war.[18] First, he made clear that bombing was in itself a kind of second front, and as this was doing direct damage to the German economy, Stalin conceded that on that Britain was indeed doing *something*. But his other version of a second front was Torch, and here Churchill's analogy to Stalin has become famous as an illustration of his entire strategic approach:

To illustrate my point I had meanwhile drawn a picture of a crocodile, and explained to Stalin with the help of this picture how it was our intention to attack the soft belly of the crocodile as we attacked his hard snout. And Stalin, whose interest was now at a high pitch, said, "May God prosper this undertaking." [After further discussion]...We then gathered around a large globe, and I explained to Stalin the immense advantages of clearing the enemy out of the Mediterranean.[19]

However, things did not go as well for Churchill as he had first supposed: the second day's talks commenced with "a most unpleasant discussion." Stalin, it seems to an outside observer, had not been fooled by Churchill's defense of what, to the Americans as well as the Soviets, was Churchill's penchant for the indirect approach, or, to use his wonderfully memorable analogy, the soft underbelly of the crocodile.

The West, Stalin accused the visitors, was "too much afraid of fighting the Germans,"[20] they had broken their Sledgehammer promises, and the supplies were nowhere near as great as they should have been. In the memo Stalin handed over, it was clear that the Russians had wanted a second front in Europe in 1942, and this promise the West had failed to deliver.

This Churchill vigorously denied, later sending a memo of his own, written with the aid of Cadogan and Brooke, which argued that the only possible second front operation that would work in 1942 was Torch. Any invasion of France would be a "hazardous and futile operation...[which] could only end in disaster."[21]

Churchill summarized his feelings in a telegram he sent to his deputy prime minister, Attlee:

> Perhaps...I took too gloomy a view. I feel I must make full allowance for the really grievous disappointment which they feel here that we can do nothing more to help them in their immense struggle...Everything for us now turns on hastening "Torch" and defeating Rommel.[22]

While the defeat of Rommel was a good thing, and it would come thanks to Churchill's dispositions in Cairo, putting General Alexander in as commander in chief and General Bernard Montgomery, Britain's most famous and controversial commander, in charge of the Eighth Army, nonetheless we should put the whole issue into perspective. Churchill very nearly did not put Stalingrad into his memoirs at all, and in effect did so under pressure from friends and collaborators.[23]

His visit to Stalin in 1942 betrays this same lack of understanding of the difference between the two fronts: in Stalingrad the Red Army lost *half a million* men, at El Alamein the British and Allied forces saw 2350 dead, or just about one-fortieth of the losses suffered by the Soviets. As one of Churchill's biographers records, the entire six volumes nowhere mention the siege of Leningrad in which over *one million* people died—mostly civilians—a death toll higher than that of the *entire* British and American casualty rate *combined*. All this is quite a horrifying lack of perspective from one of the key leaders of the war, and the idea that an operation such as Torch could even be seen as somehow helping to lessen the carnage in Stalingrad and elsewhere is more than telling.

This was, Norman Davies and others now remind us, also the beginning of a major distortion on how we read and understand the war itself. As mentioned earlier, a battle like Kursk was far more important in the defeat of the Axis than countless other battles that were turned into movies or made the subject of myriad books by Western historians.

To be fair, much of this is because of the sheer inaccessibility of Soviet archive material, which took until the advent of Gorbachev to be opened to outsiders (and may now, one gathers, be increasingly closed once again). But a great deal was known during the Second World War itself about, for example, Stalingrad and the comparative death counts; it is very clear, for instance, in reading Churchill's brief references to the Eastern Front, that he was well aware of the scale of the Soviet sacrifice and of the paucity of Western casualties in comparison. It is also why we still tend to think of the Second World War as a "good war," for reasons we have discussed elsewhere.

However, in terms of that big picture, Churchill did get one thing right. At the final dinner the question of Stalin's murderous elimination of the kulaks—the richer peasants—came up in conversation. To the dictator it seemed a simple matter of improving the food supply. Churchill was careful in what he said, but he could not help pondering afterward:

> I record as they come back to me these memories, and the strong impression I sustained at the moment of millions of men and women being blotted out or displaced for ever... With the World War going on all around us it seemed vain to moralise aloud.[24]

Indeed—for more kulaks were butchered on Stalin's orders on account of being the wrong social class as were Jews by Hitler for being the wrong race, a perspective that was all too lacking at the time, since, for reasons of wartime propaganda, Stalin was portrayed benignly as "Uncle Joe," and indeed often referred to as such by both Churchill and Roosevelt themselves. In fact, between "Uncle Joe" and "Uncle Adolf" there was little moral difference, something that the needs of war disguised, and that was also hushed up and even denied in the USSR itself until Khrushchev, the Communist Party boss of Stalingrad, was to let the cat out of the bag in the 1950s, and in practice right up until the 1980s when Gorbachev decided that honesty was after all the best policy.

Much of the rest of Churchill's *Hinge of Fate* was therefore taken up with what to Britain were key victories, especially at El Alamein, but which, in terms of the wider war, were in essence sideshows, vital though El Alamein was to the much-battered British morale.

In terms of the actual war, therefore, while the critical battles in Europe were being fought in Russia and their Asian equivalents by the Americans and Japanese in the Pacific, one of the key meetings of the war was that held by the Western Allies in Casablanca early in 1943, after El Alamein but before final victory had been won in North Africa.

But here we ought to look briefly at what happened in relation to Torch, as it was all related to the talks held in the city made famous by the movie of that name.

Although historians maintain that it would have helped if the American troops had landed nearer to the British—as we shall see—one can call the Torch landings a success. But as one writer has rightly put it, this "should have been followed by a quick return to the crucial campaign—the invasion of France...Instead, one diversion led to another, and the conquest of Sicily was the next logical step."[25]

However, this was a crucial step *not* taken, and all this despite the fact that General Marshall was, quite correctly one would argue, against all major diversions to the Mediterranean or, for that matter, anywhere that would stop the truly important battle in northwestern Europe from taking place.

As Walter Dunn puts it, the American campaign in North Africa was a success:

> The attack proved our logistical capability—compared to a short trip across the [English] channel of perhaps fifty miles, the ships were loaded in Scotland and England more than fifteen hundred miles away and in the United States three thousand miles away from the North African coast...The Americans fought well, except for the setback at Kasserine [which we will look at later]...In succeeding invasions, new divisions with no battle experience were used for the initial landings, proving that combat experience was not essential.[26]

In fact, as we now know, most of the *American* and many of the British and Canadian troops landing on the beaches of Normandy on D-day were all novices who had not been under fire before. The more experienced troops were often those fighting in Italy, which, as we also now know in retrospect, proved a much tougher battleground than northwestern Europe.

Dunn sagely concludes on the issue of Torch:

> In summary, although military reasons were given for the rejection of the invasion of France in 1943 and the substitution of the November 1942 invasion of North Africa, the true reasons were political—the need for a quick, easy victory.

What delayed the subsequent campaign is where the Americans landed—too far away from Tunisia and in a place that could be taken by Rommel's forces.

By the end of 1942 the Allies had not swept the Axis forces from the North African shore. But Montgomery, with a combination of firm but cautious generalship and overwhelming supplies, was able to beat the Germans at El Alamein; and while Germany was still able to mount offensives on the militarily far more important Eastern Front, the fact that the USSR was able to hold Stalingrad made a huge difference, both in terms of the battle and surely psychologically as well.

However, Churchill still believed that a direct assault upon the Third Reich was out of the question. Instead his preferred place to invade was Sicily, which was Italian and not German, and hundreds of miles from the borders of the Reich.

But although he was not unsympathetic to the Soviets' fury that it was still the Red Army bearing the disproportionate load of fighting the Wehrmacht, Churchill still prevaricated against the idea of a direct assault *in 1943*. Claims about the weather and landing craft and all sorts of other delaying tactics were used by him in the House of Commons and elsewhere to stem the clamor—some of it led by his old friend Lord Beaverbrook, the press baron—that the second front should be launched, and *now*.

He then received a major shock—it became apparent that the rate of delivery of Bolero was being heavily reduced by the Americans, who were, understandably, getting fed up with British prevarication, and were therefore beginning to send supplies to the Pacific that had originally been earmarked for the invasion of France. Not only that but the "production of landing craft was being reduced to build more warships."

He told Roosevelt that it would be "most grievous" that the postponed Roundup should mean a diminution of supplies and that "this matter requires most profound consideration." He even now professed to be "deeply impressed" by Marshall's attitude, which was not at all the truth.[27]

(Thankfully it seems that Churchill was scared for nothing, and it seems that it was all a misunderstanding. But the reason was unquestionably Churchill's insistence on keeping the war going elsewhere and thereby delaying the decision in France.)[28]

This possible reallocation was naturally great news for the US Navy, and for those in its senior posts for whom the war in the Pacific had always been far more important. This is a key issue, since one of the major reasons why Churchill had prevaricated over the 1943 date for Roundup was the lack of landing craft.

This now became a circular argument, since the United States reduced the amount available for use in Europe *because of Churchill's delaying tactics* and thus, ironically, were validating his excuse! As we shall see later, the landing craft argument against an early D-day is thus wholly spurious, since there were always enough landing craft *if the political decision had been made to earmark them for Europe.*[29] In fact, if John Grigg's guess is right, if one looks at the amount of them used in the Mediterranean, there were in reality plenty enough if Italy had been stood down as a major theater of operation and the craft used to land Allied soldiers on Anzio and elsewhere had been sent instead to Britain for the invasion of France *in 1943.*

Needless to say, this did not help with Stalin, who by November 1942 was becoming all the more suspicious as Red Army casualties mounted at a far higher rate than that of Britain and the United States.

As Churchill's people in Moscow told the prime minister in December:

> It is impossible to say exactly what form these suspicions may take. It might be anything from a relatively innocuous belief that something has gone wrong with our plans, that as usual we were hopeless bunglers...to a far more dangerous belief that because the threats to Stalingrad and the Caucasus seemed less, we now felt that we need no longer make the same effort, and had even better not make that effort to soon, for fear that the USSR might emerge too strong at the end of the war...No suspicion is too fantastic to be entertained.[30]

While Stalin's paranoia—which sentenced millions to death during his purges—was usually indeed "too fantastic to be entertained," it is entirely understandable that he was angry at the continued lack of a second front.

In October 1942, Churchill was still dangling all sorts of alternatives to a simple and straightforward invasion of France.

He wrote on the twenty-fourth of that month to his Chiefs of Staff in his capacity as minister of defense. Churchill felt vindicated that Marshall's Sledgehammer plan had been unrealistic—and in a way that backs up Tuvia Ben-Moshe's notion, expressed in his book on Churchill, that the prime minister felt that British and therefore by extension American troops were not up to an invasion of France in 1942:

> Personally I was sure that the newly raised United States formations, as well as our own somewhat more matured forces, could not establish themselves on the French coast, still less advance far inland, in the teeth of well-organised German opposition.[31]

In June 1944 they did just that, of course.…

Not only that, but Churchill then proceeded to use this as an argument against the Soviet desire for a second front:

> The Russians, meanwhile, completely ignorant of amphibious warfare and wilfully closing their eyes to the German strength on the French northern coast, continued to clamour for "a second front in Europe." On this we have protected ourselves by written declarations from all reproach of breach of faith.[32]

The idea that the Soviets did not know about German strength was, of course, insulting—and as we have seen, German defenses on the Normandy coast were *stronger in 1944 than in 1943*. The Soviets also knew about river crossings, so what Churchill wrote was simply mistaken.

Just before Churchill and Roosevelt were to meet in Morocco, at Casablanca, Churchill summarized his own thoughts in a Minister of Defense memorandum to the Chiefs of Staff.[33]

First:

A prime object of British and United States strategy in 1943 should be to bring the maximum force into contact with the enemy both on the ground and in the air…Our action in the various theatres now under discussion should have continuous regard to this object.[34]

This was vital to Churchill's argument—and was to be the key determining factor in winning over a very willing Roosevelt to ignore Marshall and go with the prime minister. Politicians want *instant*, not long-term, action—Churchill could guarantee it.

Second:

By the great operation of "Torch" we have placed ourselves in a position to threaten or attack the enemy both from the West and from the South. We ought to take advantage of this.[35]

Churchill was promising war in North Africa, not a buildup in Britain for a future date. Once again, the real action would be delayed.

Play It Again, Winston: Casablanca 1943

Let us now look at the Casablanca conference,[36] and, first of all, at the person who lost out most, George Marshall.

We have seen that although General Marshall was completely right on the key issue of the war—how to end it as swiftly as possible—he was, nonetheless, by no means always right. It would, in any case, be ridiculous to point out the defects of one great genius of the Second World War, Winston Churchill, and then create a new infallible figure in the form of General George Catlett Marshall.

Writers and military pundits across the board seem to agree that the Americans landed in the wrong place in North Africa in 1942, with the result that it took until well into 1943 to beat Rommel out of the region and win the southern shore of the Mediterranean for the Allies. In this Marshall is therefore not without blame.

The other thing to recall is that it was firmly his view that Torch ruled out Roundup in 1943. Logistically and otherwise there is much to be said for this argument, and it was certainly one in which he believed strongly.

The result, however, was to wreck chances of an earlier D-day and postpone it well into 1944, and, as we shall soon see, it was not until the Allied meetings in Canada much later in the year that the Americans were able to tie Britain down to an invasion in 1944 at all, and even then Churchill was still able to lose time in his successful postponement from May to June, a month delay which could well have been the factor that elongated the war well into 1945.

And, righteous and understandable as Marshall's wrath at the decision in 1943 to continue the war in the Mediterranean and invade Sicily once North Africa was concerned, it does not really justify the de facto decision by the American military and naval leadership in effect to give brief priority to the Pacific over the war against Germany.

For what I want to say here is that while Marshall was right to say that Torch derailed Roundup and victory in 1943, it *might* have been possible to put the train back onto the tracks, and make a political decision to go for Roundup anyway. This would have still left *some* troops in North Africa, or allowed for a far more limited version of Husky (the successful invasion of Sicily), but would have placed the overwhelming number of British and especially American troops who did serve in Italy on the beaches of Normandy instead.

Remember too one of the themes of this book: but for the debacle in Greece in *1941* and Churchill's decision to throw away what would have been an easy victory over the Axis *that year*, no American would ever have needed to have landed in North Africa in *1942*. There would have been no need for Torch, and if the Americans had needed immediate battle practice, as both Roosevelt and Marshall agreed that they should have, something like the invasion of Sicily could have been attempted a year earlier, in 1942, instead of 1943 when it actually took place. And, for that matter, had Britain won in 1941, there is no reason why an invasion of Italy could not have followed straight away, so that by the time the American forces under Eisenhower landed in reality in 1942, Britain might already have captured Sicily, and the war in the Mediterranean might have been *very* different altogether, and immeasurably to the advantage of the Western Allies.

Nothing is inevitable therefore. If Marshall was wrong to say that pursuing Torch *entirely* ruled out an early invasion, maybe the place where the mistaken decisions of April–June 1942, to go to North Africa at all, were consolidated in irreversible form was at the Casablanca conference of 1943. For once the invasion of Italy (via Sicily) got truly under way then a full-scale landing in Normandy *the same year* removed itself from the realm of possibility, to the great loss of all.

The conference in Casablanca nearly did not take place at all. Roosevelt initially wanted only a meeting of experts, and Stalin, who was always paranoid about leaving Soviet territory, refused to come abroad at all. Roosevelt was always aware of the need to demonstrate to the Soviet leader that there was no Western conspiracy against the USSR, and so was sensitive to the appearance to Stalin of a meeting between the Western leaders only. (This was probably why the president felt it would be politically unwise for the meeting to have taken place in England.)

It would in any case have been difficult for both Roosevelt and Churchill had Stalin been there, for, unsurprisingly, Stalin's main goal was to ask what had happened to the second front the president had promised in 1942, and the prime minister for early 1943, a date that was now only a few weeks away.

(Churchill was to be quite hurt by this later in the war, but by that time Britain's comparative insignificance in relation to her two more powerful allies was fully established.)

However, despite all this, the Churchill-Roosevelt meeting, with their staffs (but, significantly, no secretary of state or foreign secretary allowed), was fixed for Casablanca at the beginning of 1943.[37] The code name, which is not often used in accounts of the meeting, was Symbol.

As Churchill records, the British Chiefs of Staff were still not in agreement with the American way of waging war, a "serious divergence" that was nonetheless "one of emphasis rather than principle" and the main task of the gathering would be to sort all this out. Churchill's understanding was that they wanted both Torch pursued and Bolero continued, while Marshall and the Americans wanted Roundup sooner than later and operations in North Africa "standing fast" rather than being given further priority. The British Chiefs of Staff did not rule out a Roundup in August or September 1943, but they did add the important caveat that this should only proceed "if the conditions are such that there is a good prospect for success."[38] This was, of course, the archetypal "get out of jail" card, since it became clear to Marshall and others that if British policy was followed, then conditions for 1943 would never be right.

(Not only that, one could add, but August or September would take the start of the invasion rather near to winter than was wise. There would be more adverse weather conditions from January onwards.)

After a terrible journey, in which he either boiled or froze in a converted bomber, Churchill arrived in Casablanca, with the president arriving on January 14, and General Eisenhower the following day. Also present were the Chiefs of Staff from both countries and this is where the keen debates then began. In the words of John Grigg, this was the "first great event of the momentous, though also disastrous, year 1943."[39]

As General Marshall was to rue and as Maurice Matloff, the American official historian, was to write later:

> The British brought to the conference a full staff and carefully prepared plans and positions. The Americans came with a small staff with preparations incomplete.[40]

In particular, Admiral King not only wanted to give the Pacific war greater priority, but he disliked the British and was, alas, to consume many of the landing craft for the war against Japan that could easily have been used in Europe had the *political* will existed so to deploy them—it is a very important part of the arguments of both John Grigg in *1943* and Walter Dunn in *Second Front Now* that where to place these various landing craft was ultimately a decision made by the political leaders, Churchill and Roosevelt, not their military leaders, such as Brooke, Marshall, and King. In this instance, the fact that Marshall, who saw the issues clearly, did not get his way is one of the main reasons why so many such craft remained in the Pacific rather than being transferred to Europe.

As Sir Basil Liddell Hart put it drolly in his *History of the Second*

World War, the idea that the British and US top brass constituted, as officially described, the "Combined Chiefs of Staff" was a misnomer, since when it came to what to do and where next to do it, they were anything but combined in their views.[41]

However, despite being the people who made the ultimate decisions, neither Roosevelt nor Churchill attended the actual staff conferences themselves. If one reads Churchill's account one gets the impression that the main and significant differences were actually not between the British and Americans but between the senior commanders and their respective planning staffs, some favoring Sardinia as the best place to invade next and others plumping for Sicily, with Churchill on the winning side. But this is an entirely inaccurate picture, since the divergences of view, while sometimes between ranks,[42] were often of a more fundamental nature. For example, Marshall was determined to hold on to his key plan for 1943 to save both Bolero and Roundup for *that* year, and the American sources make this abundantly clear but Churchill ignores it altogether.

(He does mention his conversation with General Eaker, the commander of the US Air Forces in Britain, and how Eaker was successful in persuading him to accept the American policy of daylight bombing, a controversy at which we shall look elsewhere.)[43]

As the official historian, Sir Michael Howard, puts it in his essay "The Mediterranean and British Strategy," written while he was writing the official volumes in the *Grand Strategy* series, British strategy on arrival at Casablanca "was as yet undecided."[44]

> The British were only concerned, when they met the Americans at Casablanca...to persuade them neither to write off the European theatre nor to suspend operations there until 1944; but to continue with operations in an area where they could operate effectively and

immediately, to bring help to the Soviet Union, weaken the Axis and pave the way for eventual cross-Channel attack.

Indeed, Sir Basil Liddell Hart was to comment:

Allied planning continued at a leisurely gait.... The question of how it [their final decision, to invade Sicily] should be exploited was left open... Nor was there an emphatic sense of urgency in the planning of the Sicilian stroke.[45]

Howard notes that Marshall "accepted these arguments with the greatest reluctance." But can one agree with what Sir Michael then goes on to add: "He could offer no alternative"? It is surely right to say that Marshall correctly gauged that the British had no dark, hidden imperial agenda lurking unspoken beneath the surface—something that Wedemeyer thought at the time,[46] or indeed some American historians since then.[47]

(In fact some American service planners thought much the same: they were particularly worried about the British desire to keep India—something, as we all know, that was very dear to Churchill's heart—and this therefore gave the Mediterranean, which was, via the Suez Canal, Britain's shortest route there, an especial strategic significance. This would, the joint planners worried, make the United States end up serving the British Empire, which was emphatically not why the Americans were at war.[48] Admiral King, the main proponent of switching priority to the war in the Pacific, was also firmly of this school, and both Eisenhower and Marshall, who did not share his Anglophobia, were both worried at the extent of prejudice against Britain held by many in the United States. Needless to say, Churchill's and Brooke's desire to give the Mediterranean favor over a direct assault on France did not help.)

In fact, so keen was Wedemeyer to ensure Marshall's ability to put the American case to the UK Chiefs of Staff that he told his puzzled superior that the US plans should not fall into "hostile hands"[49]—by which he meant not the Axis but Churchill and the British! Unfortunately for Marshall, the plans were in fact leaked, so that when the US delegation arrived at Casablanca, the United Kingdom delegation was already fully aware of the US proposals. Wedemeyer thought they were leaked by Field Marshal Sir John Dill, a man whom Marshall completely trusted. While the Dill/Marshall relationship actually improved after this, the American Chief of Staff was careful that such a leak did not take place again.

The staff talks began on January 14, which Brooke described as a "very long and laborious day,"[50] since after he had begun to outline British views General Marshall came in and explained why the Americans disagreed.

Brooke was right to say that to try to allocate priorities by percentage was a strange thing to do—Admiral King wanted 30 percent for the Pacific and agreed to 70 percent for Europe. King, according to Brooke's diaries, became increasingly drunk as the day progressed, which was hardly conducive to good interallied relations, and managed to argue ferociously with Churchill before the day was up.

By the fifteenth the Combined Chiefs were down to serious business, or as Brooke put it, another "hard day." Marshall remained as eager as ever to make sure that Germany was hit directly. As he put it:

[The] British are extremely fearful of any direct action against the continent until a decided crack in German efficiency and morale has become apparent...while the British wish to build a strong force in the United Kingdom for possible operations against Germany in case a weakness develops, it must be understood that any operation in the Mediterranean will definitely retard Bolero...the two critical factors in the decision as to whether the operation is to be in the north [i.e., France] or the south [i.e., the Mediterranean] were (1) the safety of the lines of communication and (2) the fact that there will be an excess of veteran soldiers available in North Africa to mount an operation.[51]

Marshall was as adamant as ever about keeping the Western Europe option, Brooke against him in going for the Mediterranean.[52] As Brooke laconically noted in his secret diary, there was "no doubt that we are too closely related to the Americans to make co-operation between us anything but easy."

However, were there no alternatives? I think it fair to say that Marshall, having perhaps overcommitted American troops to Torch in terms of numbers,[53] now despaired at what was to be the inevitable corollary of invading Sicily—the decision to launch a full-scale invasion of the Italian peninsula itself.[54] This is also exactly what happened.

But what if Marshall had insisted on Roundup in 1943? April, the original target date, might have now become a bit soon, and rather too many landing craft had now ended up in the Pacific, thanks to his and others' despair in 1942. These craft could, though, have been brought back, and, as we shall see, the numbers of landing craft which were soon to be used *in 1943* in both Sicily and then in the invasion of Italy itself might have been enough in and of themselves for a successful Normandy landing the same year.

In fact Sir Alan Brooke outlined what could and should have been done in 1943—and his sadly strong disagreement with such a policy, to the assembled Combined Chiefs of Staff. If only he had followed this instead of the Mediterranean policy he preferred, and which prevailed at Casablanca, things would have been very different.

> The first was to close down in the Mediterranean as soon as the North African coast had been cleared and the sea route through the Mediterranean had been opened, and to devote every effort to building up in the United Kingdom for an invasion of the north of France at the earliest possible moment. The British Chiefs of Staff had examined the possibilities and calculated that twenty-one to twenty-three divisions could be made available for this purpose by September 15.... The other broad possibility was to maintain activity in the Mediterranean while building up the maximum air offensive against Germany.... The Mediterranean offered many choices.... One of the great advantages of adopting the Mediterranean policy was that a larger force of heavy bombers could be built up in the United Kingdom for the attack on Germany than if they were concentrated for an invasion of France.[55]

Needless to say, Marshall disagreed completely. He pointed out to the British that it was important that:

> [We] now reorient ourselves and decide what the "main plot" is to be. Every diversion or side issue from the main plot acts as a "suction pump." [While invading Sicily had its merits...] before deciding to undertake such an operation, he thought it necessary to determine just what part it would play in the overall strategic plan.[56]

An argument against needless Allied diffusion could not have been put better.

But all this was alas lost on Brooke, who treated his American allies with the disdain usually used by teachers trying to explain simple mathematics to numerically illiterate and intellectually dim pupils. He wrote in his diary that getting Marshall away from the direct approach was a "slow and tiring process which requires a lot of patience" and, as he reflected some years later, Marshall, to him, "did not possess...[the qualities] of a strategist."[57] Marshall was not alas at all helped by Admiral King, who remained fixated on the Pacific, and thus did not come to the aid of his colleagues at Casablanca in the same way that all the British Chiefs (Brooke, Pound, Dill, and Portal) were careful to do for each other.

The British were alarmed at Admiral King pressing for so much of the Allied resources to go to the Pacific, and the meetings on the seventeenth and eighteenth were taken up on this very issue.[58] Would Europe as a priority survive a major transfer of resources to the war against Japan? Since Brooke and his colleagues had done so much to delay what Marshall regarded as the best way by far to beat Germany, it is not surprising that the American Chief of Staff began to wonder whether in fact it was worth keeping to that priority after all. Until now the war in the Pacific was essentially a defensive one—now Marshall decided that taking the offensive against the Japanese was necessary, with the extra resources that that would entail. Neglecting the Pacific war would be a mistake that the United States would not now commit.

Now Sir John Dill, the wise former Chief of the Imperial Staff and the main British military man in Washington DC, intervened, and his friendship with Marshall was put to good use. A compromise was reached: Europe would remain the main theater of war, the U-boat menace in the Atlantic would gain major priority, the invasion of Sicily (Husky) would go ahead, and Bolero would remain, just in case there was a sudden German collapse.[59]

To all this Roosevelt and Churchill thus gave their blessing, and for all intents and purposes it looked as if any liberation of the Continent in 1943 was now off the cards, and for good. The Americans were to spend much of the rest of that year persuading the British to agree to having D-day at all, and by now, in *1944*, with all the dire consequences that this book has made so clear.

Now, I think it fair to argue, as will soon emerge, that the decision to push the liberation of northwestern Europe into 1944 was as much *political* as it was military. Priorities could have been changed, and if the Allies had made the decision to stand fast in the Mediterranean and devote all their resources to Normandy, then there were probably also enough American soldiers in the United States ready to cross the Atlantic (if they were not in Britain already) to make a serious invasion of France possible. One look at British military histories shows us that *most British troops* were either in the United Kingdom or in a position to be returned there rapidly, ready for cross-Channel action.

As Sir Michael Howard puts it:

Once more Marshall agreed with profound reluctance. Behind the British attachment to Mediterranean operations the Americans were beginning to see, not devious political calculations, but an unwillingness to commit themselves to large scale operations on the Continent.... They were determined to risk neither a slaughter nor a debacle, and it sometimes seemed to them that the Americans were light-heartedly heading for both.

Professor Howard, the accepted doyen of British strategic studies, accurately reflects the view on his side of the Atlantic, and most United Kingdom historians would probably agree. We saw earlier how Churchill's Chief of Staff General Ismay recalled the 60,000 dead on the *first day* of the Somme, and as Howard reminds us, the British Chiefs had as "young officers...been through" that battle and that of Passchendaele.

But, to repeat a refrain of this book, this once again shows the utter British failure to appreciate the sheer scale of the American offer, and the fact that an Anglo-US invasion would, by its overwhelming size, be of an utterly higher and more successful order of magnitude than the kind to which the British were used.

This is crucial because I think it fair to say that historians on the United Kingdom side of the pond tend to take the fears of the former officers of World War I very seriously, and then forget that by 1943 the whole nature of warfare had drastically changed. Had things been no different from 1916, then the most understandable horrors of the Somme would and should have been enough to end all further discussion. But by the time we get to Casablanca, the nature of battle had already changed—tanks, bombers, artillery, and many similar parts of the paraphernalia of war had changed immeasurably and entirely to the benefit of the Allied armies contemplating the invasion and liberation of northwestern Europe. This the Americans, such as Marshall, understood, but the British, from Churchill to Brooke, did not.

Furthermore, one can argue that it was in fact Sir Alan Brooke, rather than Churchill, who was the main proponent at Casablanca for a Mediterranean-based strategy.[60] This is important, because it was not that Brooke (or indeed the British) was too scared to take on the Germans per se, rather that they lacked confidence in the ability to take them *head on* in northwestern Europe itself until they felt that conditions were right. In fact one could say, as John Grigg does, that "Churchill...did not favour any specific strategy."[61] Rather he was all over the shop, wanting to attack, as we saw, in the Mediterranean, in Norway, *and in northwestern Europe.* But in practice, there were now so many obstacles to what Marshall knew to be the main need— Roundup *in 1943*—that all the agreements made at Casablanca in effect made that overriding priority all but impossible, in the light of the decisions made.

As Grigg puts it (his italics) concerning the decision to put the clearing of North Africa and capturing Sicily first: *"This action was tantamount to postponing cross-Channel action until 1944."*[62]

(Although this book concentrates principally on Europe, the Pacific was of enormous importance, especially to the US Navy, and the use of American troops there and the idea of launching a campaign in the British sector against the Japanese in Burma also ate up huge amounts of resources that could easily have been employed in Europe.)

The other major decision made at Casablanca was also one of the most controversial of the war, enunciated by what Marshall called one of Roosevelt's cigarette holder gestures: *unconditional surrender.*

This has been described by some of the participants at the conference, such as Albert Wedemeyer, as a massive mistake.[63] It is perhaps also fair to say that neither Italy nor Japan surrendered unconditionally, so that the Allies were actually inconsistent on this matter. But is this fair? And did Churchill truly know about it ahead of time, or was he right to tell his colleagues that this was something of a surprise sprung upon him unawares by Roosevelt?

Either way, it has been blamed for prolonging the war, most notably around the time of the plot to kill Hitler in 1944: had the conspirators been able to negotiate a deal with the Allies, it has been alleged, then they could have surrendered *in the West* to the British and Americans.

But surely this forgets many things, not the least of which was the way in which Germany surrendered to the Allies in 1918 on the basis of Woodrow Wilson's Fourteen Points, and then, after the Treaty of Versailles turned out to be far more harsh than they expected, led to the fatal legend of the "stab in the back," which stated that the army was undefeated in 1918 and the war could have continued, with German victory still possible. This myth was especially supported and fostered by the Nazis, who were able to use it greatly to their advantage on their route to power in 1933 and after.

By 1945, however, no one could dispute that Germany was well and truly beaten, if not all but annihilated militarily. No false "stab in the back" legend could arise from the rubble and ashes of Berlin and countless other cities in the remains of the Third Reich. Germany was *defeated* and everyone knew it. Not only that but except for in the dreams of a minuscule minority of fanatics, there has been no desire for a Fourth Reich: the era of German menace (roughly 1870–1945) has departed from the earth, with no desire ever to see it rise again.

Japan, however, as many Chinese will argue, has never had to face its past, such as the Japanese apologizing formally for the Rape of Nanking and countless other atrocities in the same way in which Germany has felt it necessary to atone to Israel and global Jewry for the Holocaust. Similarly a Mussolini (his granddaughter, Alessandra) is a player in contemporary Italian politics, and fascist parties have held seats in Italian coalitions in recent years. Is the fact that both Italy and Japan had *conditional* surrenders a factor in this? One can wonder....

Not only that but in January 1943 there was, as we have just seen, still no proper second front in northwestern Europe, whatever claims Churchill could make for war in the Mediterranean. One can argue, as biographers of Roosevelt do,[64] that at least unconditional surrender told Stalin that his Western Allies would join him in fighting to the death, and that they were taking the total elimination of Nazism from Europe as seriously as he did. Who in their right minds—except of course for Stalin in 1939 (and *possibly* even in 1941)—would have wanted a conditional surrender that allowed the Third Reich to exist for so much as another day? We may not have known the full horror of the death camps by the time of Casablanca, but it was obvious by then that one was not dealing with a normal regime in any understandable sense of the word.

What is surely wrong is that, as with so many of Roosevelt's other wartime decisions, it was made without proper consultation either with his own senior military or with Churchill (although here it is correct to say that Roosevelt's announcement was not a *total* surprise to the prime minister, as it had been discussed even if inadequately during the conference and thus before the press briefing).

For it made all the difference to the *way* in which the war would now be fought.[65] The traditional way of winning—Churchill's favored strategy of the indirect approach, and the idea so beloved of the Royal Air Force that the war could be won simply by a policy of attrition—was now in effect rejected by Roosevelt by his signal to Stalin and to the world in general that now it was to be won by *total war*. This was conflict to the bitter end, with no nice peace talks and bargains along the way. You either surrender totally or get defeated totally—there is now no other option.

And this surely meant winning Marshall's way in the end: with an attack where it needed to be, in northwestern Europe. Only by such means, rather than by assaulting the soft underbelly, could a total war to the bitter end be fought and won.

This therefore makes Marshall's and Wedemeyer's despair at Casablanca somewhat ironic, for I think it is true to say[66] that while they had lost the *immediate* battle—abandoning the invasion of Sicily (or Husky)—they had won the *long-term* strategy that, however much

Churchill might want to postpone the long-awaited frontal assault on northwestern Europe, the direct defeat of the Third Reich could not now come about by any other means.

So perhaps one can be less pessimistic for Marshall than Marshall was himself.

However, and this is a significant *but*, Casablanca did postpone an early end to the war. Thus whatever Marshall's foreboding and misgivings were, one can argue[67] that actually Marshall in effect threw in the towel too early, because the decision for Husky was not in any sense inevitable given that American troops were already in North Africa. We have seen that Marshall felt Torch and Roundup in 1943 were incompatible, and that this might have led him to send more troops than were strictly necessary to that front in late 1942.

But might it not have been possible to say something quite different at Casablanca? Could perhaps not much more than a token force have been kept in North Africa, to remove the remaining Axis presence, and to guard it against any attempt by the Germans to reenter the area? Then could not the American troops that ended up in Sicily and, following the anti-Mussolini coup, in Italy itself, have been sent back to Britain and ready for the landings in Normandy that *could still have taken place in 1943?*

This would have needed a political decision by Roosevelt, since Marshall could not himself have overruled the powerful navy lobby that still preferred to fight the war in the Pacific against Japan and which had commandeered so many of the vital landing craft that would otherwise have been available for Europe.

(As we have seen, and as seems apparent throughout Dunn's book,[68] there were always enough landing craft for wherever they were needed—the decision to send so many to the Pacific and thus

deny them to Europe was always a *political choice* not a military neces-
sity, and those craft used in landing both on Sicily and on mainland
Italy could *all* have been used in northwestern Europe had the decision so been made.)

It is also true to say that a decision as late as January 1943 to launch
D-day only three months later would have been a very tall order. The
right time to make such a decision was always between April and
July *1942*, the correct choice that was so badly thrown by Roosevelt's
option for Torch.

But one can say that it was still not *entirely* too late to have opted
at Casablanca for an *invasion* of France in 1943, even if the optimum
date of April that year was now, because of the delays, probably out
of reach. Even June, or more likely September would still have been
feasible, and this is still therefore something that would have dramatically shortened the war to the advantage of the Western Allies.

At Casablanca, Marshall was still doing his best to get the Allies
to get on with the job of attacking the main enemy, Germany. But
Churchill was as adamant as ever at what Wedemeyer was right to
call a peripheral strategy. Admiral King was not helping either side,
since he was as much in favor of giving the Pacific priority as ever.

Churchill's view prevailed over Marshall's, and the last chances
for a D-day in 1943 were now fast ebbing away. As Churchill told his
war cabinet colleagues:

I am satisfied that the President is strongly in favour of the Mediterranean being given prime place... Although nothing definite has
been settled between us pending the result of staff conversations, I
feel sure that we are in solid agreement on the essentials... Personally I am very satisfied with the way this has gone.[69]

The other issue at the conference was the noncooperation of General de Gaulle, the Free French leader. Churchill was understandably despondent at de Gaulle's resolute distaste with General Giraud, the unfortunate American choice for leader of France.[70] "The man must be mad," Churchill groaned to Eden, and it is hard to know with whom to sympathize the most: the aggrieved de Gaulle, who felt slighted by American power, or Churchill, who had done everything possible for de Gaulle but who, by early 1943, was now in no position of political bargaining strength to overturn a firm US decision.

(Roosevelt was kinder, when he met de Gaulle, than Churchill had been to the recalcitrant general[71] but the damage had been done. Eden was rightly wary of Churchill's rough treatment of de Gaulle, as Churchill acknowledged, but to the prime minister, there were "dangers to Anglo-American unity"[72] in Eden's "championship of de Gaulle," and, so far as Churchill was concerned, that was therefore that!)

While this might seem a spat with no consequence—de Gaulle prevailed in the end and was to go on first to liberate Paris and then to be president of France from 1958 to 1969—it was a disagreement with dire consequences for Britain, since de Gaulle, a man of notoriously thin skin, was not someone ever to forget a slight. In 1963 and then again in 1967 he was to veto Britain's entry to the European Economic Community (now the European Union) with dire short-term economic consequences for Britain, and with a legacy of British anti-EU sentiment that still haunts the country in the twenty-first century, nearly seventy years after de Gaulle's rough handling in North Africa in 1943. Never can such an issue of protocol have had such unfortunate long-term results.

Churchill had put the relationship with the United States above everything else, including the one with France. Defending de Gaulle would be, as he told Eden, in danger of "marring my relations with the President," Roosevelt.

Since this book is about the war, not what happened years afterward in British/European politics, the long-term effects are therefore, strictly speaking, not part of the remit. But it is important briefly to state one thing.

The revisionist view of Churchill is one that I have stated as being mistaken, albeit, in the case of serious writers such as John Charmley[73] and Correlli Barnett, "wrong but wromantic" [*sic*], to adapt the post-1918 British joke.[74] America was always going to emerge as the number one world power, as I have argued elsewhere.

But when it comes to British foreign policy after the war, it is surely worth a paragraph to say that John Charmley has a good point in arguing that the romantic pro-American streak in Churchill did Britain much harm in the *1950s*—Churchill was as we know prime minister again from 1951 to 1955—since he completely failed to see that Britain had to develop far closer links with its immediate European neighbors, rather than pursue a will o' the wisp attempt to make the wartime relationship with the United States the *prime* feature of British policy. Britain was to be humiliated at Suez in 1956, the year after Churchill's final retirement, by Eisenhower, of all people, whose performance at the Casablanca conference Churchill could not praise highly enough. Also in North Africa was the British minister to Allied Headquarters, Harold Macmillan, and it is no coincidence first that Macmillan realized post-Suez that Britain now needed to join in more closely with Europe, and second, that his attempt to do so was vetoed in 1963 by de Gaulle. Such were the long-term effects of a few days in 1943 in the Moroccan sun.

To return to the conference, Churchill felt things had gone well— Husky, his project for invading Italy via Sicily, had prevailed over Brimstone, the alternative plan, which would have involved the invasion of Sardinia instead.[75] The good news, too, was that the defeat of

Germany was still the priority over Japan—and here one can add, Marshall had thus won over King as well as Churchill. But while Churchill noted that "we have secured the priority of the Mediterranean over ROUNDUP"—the invasion of Europe in 1943—"without prejudice to the maximum development of BOLERO"—the buildup of US forces in Britain for the eventual invasion of northwestern Europe[76]—nonetheless one can look at Churchill's triumph as a disaster.

For now the chance finally to go for Hitler directly had gone. Bolero, the sending of US troops to Britain, would continue. But now the *main* thrust was inevitably Husky, the invasion of Sicily, and thence of the Italian mainland, an operation that was to prove to be one of the slowest of the entire war.

Needless to say, and with good cause, Stalin was, as Churchill told Eden and the war cabinet, "disappointed and furious"[77] at the postponement of the second front in France. The overwhelming burden of fighting the Third Reich would remain the responsibility of the Red Army, with, as we now know, all the dire political consequences that were to follow, not to mention the large-scale atrocities that the Soviet troops were to carry out against millions of German civilians by way of revenge against those inflicted on Russian civilians by the Wehrmacht and the SS.

Of course, the American military did not give up, and now, when they all met again with the British in DC in May 1943, things were to be a whole lot better.

The Trident conference, as the meeting was code-named, was to see Marshall finally able to get a commitment to Britain fighting a second front in Europe and in 1944.[78] Sending American troops to Italy would be all right, but seven divisions would have to be sent from the Mediterranean theater to fight in northwestern Europe, the real invasion to defeat Germany for which Marshall had been plan-

ning and hoping for so long. Not only that, but, unlike earlier conferences, when the politician in Roosevelt caused the president to side
with the prime minister over his own Chief of Army Staff, Roosevelt
finally backed Marshall and refused to side with Churchill. The goose
was now cooked and the American view had, sadly too late for a 1943
D-day, ultimately prevailed.

Churchill had wanted to fly, but his recent serious bout of pneumonia (disguised in his memoirs as anxiety about flying at altitude)[79]
meant that he had to go the slow way, by boat.

Brooke and a whole host of British luminaries, including Churchill's
scientific adviser Lord Cherwell, came with him, as did Field Marshal Wavell to talk about the Asian issues. Brooke was worried about
what might happen:

> I don't feel very hopeful as to results. Casablanca has taught me too
> much. Agreement after agreement may be secured on paper but if
> their hearts are not in it they soon drift away again.[80]

As for Churchill, Brooke was to moan toward the end of the
conference:

> And Winston??? Thinks one thing at one moment and another
> at another moment. At times the war may be won by bombing
> and all must be sacrificed to it. At others it becomes essential for
> us to bleed ourselves dry on the Continent because Russia is doing
> the same. At others our main effort must be in the Mediterranean,
> directed against Italy or Balkans alternatively, with sporadic desires
> to invade Norway and 'roll up the map in the opposite direction to
> Hitler!' But more often than all he wants to carry out ALL opera-
> tions simultaneously irrespective of shortages of shipping![81]

As Field Marshal Alanbrooke, he was to comment later in the 1950s:

> Winston's attitude at the White House Conference was tragic. He had originally agreed to the paper we were discussing and with Roosevelt had congratulated us on it. How at the eleventh hour he wished to repudiate half of it...in later conferences he always feared that we should 'frame up' (he actually accused me in those terms one day) with the American Chiefs of Staff against him![82]

There is an irony in what Brooke goes on to comment, since in 1942, as we saw, Roosevelt had, for political reasons of his own, ostensibly sided with Churchill against Marshall. But that is not how Churchill perceived things by 1943:

> He knew the Americans could carry the President with them, and he feared being opposed by a combined Anglo-American block of Chiefs of Staff plus President. As a matter of fact on those occasions I was far from 'framing up' with Marshall and on the contrary was more liable to be at loggerheads with him over Pacific and cross Channel strategy. Under such circumstance it may be imagined how complicated matters became!

This was indeed true! As Marshall and Brooke chatted at the time (as recalled by Brooke years later):

> I was walking with Marshall and Dill to one of our meetings [and] Marshall said to me, 'I find it very hard even now not to look on your North Africa strategy with a jaundiced eye.' I replied, 'What strategy would you have preferred?' To which he replied, 'Cross

Channel operations for the liberation of France and advance on Germany, we should finish the war quicker.'[83]

While Brooke disagreed, it is to dissent from Marshall's wisdom, with all the millions of Jewish and Russian civilian lives that would have been saved had Marshall prevailed.

Brooke was not the only Chief of Staff to be worried—so too, after the debacle in Casablanca, when early victory was thrown away, was Marshall. He was determined that diversion from what he knew to be the only swift path to victory would not be deflected again this time.

He made it very clear in a memorandum he drafted before the conference that Churchill's ideas were "not in keeping with my ideas of what our strategy should be. The decisive effort must be made from the United Kingdom sooner or later."[84]

Marshall had realized one important political lesson: politicians needed constant activity.[85] He realized that American troops would therefore be required to be in action in Europe *somewhere* and that operations could therefore legitimately be used to follow up the successful invasion of Sicily.

So when he saw the president before Churchill's party arrived, he made clear that he opposed an invasion of Italy, and that the other Joint Chiefs agreed. In fact, while the British were crossing the Atlantic, the Joint Chiefs told Roosevelt that from now on, the *main* Allied objective had to be "to pin down the British to a cross-Channel invasion at the earliest practicable date and to make full preparations for such an operation by the spring of 1944."[86]

Both the Chiefs, the secretary of war, Henry Stimson, and several leading members of the Congress, such as Senator Vandenberg, were all deeply concerned that as in 1942 the wily Churchill was going to be able to persuade Roosevelt to abandon a policy that met with US interests for one that used brave American soldiers for essentially British ends! As we saw, the actual reasons for the president's decisions in 1942—Torch over Sledgehammer—were probably political and his own, rather than the result of Churchill staying in the White House and inveigling a naïve Roosevelt, but the feeling was strongly there all the same.

This therefore was the opposite of what Churchill feared! Far from controlling their president, and scheming together with the British Chiefs of Staff, the US Joint Chiefs were doing all possible to persuade the president to agree with them and not with Churchill and were thus completely opposed to the policy of slowing up victory of their British equivalents.

As noted by Robert Sherwood in his edition of *The White House Papers of Harry Hopkins*:

> Roosevelt needed no urging from Churchill (and if he did need it, he did not get it) to concentrate his primary attention on the major operations on the continent of Europe. Now, at last, he was firm on his insistence on the massive invasion of Northern France, which was given its ultimate code name, OVERLORD, and detailed plans for which were ordered to be drawn in London immediately.[87]

It was what to do about Italy that the president and prime minister had many a discussion, as well as about matters to do with the war in Asia.[88]

To Churchill, invading Italy was bound to help Stalin and the Eastern Front, but as for Normandy, there were bound to be problems in landing, though he did concede to his American hosts that as soon as a reasonable plan could be made, the British government would naturally support it. Such a plan had of course been given him by Marshall in April 1942, over a year before, but this Churchill had obviously chosen to forget.

Roosevelt made his position plain:

> The President ended by saying that in order to relieve Russia we must engage the Germans. For this reason he questioned the occupation of Italy, which would release German troops to fight elsewhere. He thought that the best way of forcing Germany to fight would be to launch an operation across the channel.[89]

But Churchill determined to stick to his old ways:

> I now replied that as we were agreed that the cross-Channel operation could not take place until 1944, it seemed imperative to use our great armies to attack Italy.

As Forrest Pogue relates: "For once the President took the lead in arguing the case of his military advisers."[90] What a shame, one can add, that he had not done so before.

In one sense Churchill was to win the battle but lose the war when it came to the final decision. Italy was invaded, and Allied troops were still struggling there in 1945 as Germany surrendered. But the key decision, the issue that worried Marshall, was won: D-day in France could now not be kicked into the long grass and postponed indefinitely. It was going to take place in 1944 whether Churchill wanted it to or not.

He and Brooke did not give up easily. The British CIGS continued to push for his Mediterranean strategy, and even believed that he had been successful in making his case.[91] But with Marshall successful in getting US and British troops withdrawn from the Mediterranean, and future US troops landing in divisional strengths now coming to the United Kingdom for D-day rather than to the Mediterranean for further adventures, Marshall had finally won the argument.[92]

Defeat on a now immovable date for D-day, and all it implied for British strategy, did not go down too well with Churchill. As John Charmley is right to say:

> Churchill's concentration on [what his secretary John Colville called] victory rather than ideology also exacted a price... The Washington conference... was to reveal the vanity of Churchill's hopes that the friendship which he had forged with Roosevelt, and which he sought with Stalin, could supply the place of real power to influence events... the American answer at and after the conference... not only belied Churchill's fond hopes, but also provided a more realistic answer to the question of who would wield the power.[93]

One could say something like, "Welcome to the new world of 1940s geopolitical realities." For how, one asks, could it have been otherwise? Britain may, in the twenty-first century, be one of the G8 nations, at the top international table. But did that make the United Kingdom, even with its empire, the equal in weight of the United States and the now powerful USSR? It is easy to feel sorry for Churchill, for whom imperial glories were a present reality in his mind. But even in 1943 his views were surely fantastic, and the treatment he was increasingly receiving from both Roosevelt and Stalin was only reflecting the realities of the harsh new world.

Writers both pro- and anti-Churchill have pointed out his remarkable short-term prejudices, of concentrating on victory rather than on what the world would be like after the war was over.[94] By 1944, as we shall see, he was to realize the folly of this, but in 1943 the world after the defeat of the Axis and how it should best be managed was still far from his mind.

We see this in memoranda he wrote at the time, one-half omitted from *The Hinge of Fate*, perhaps, as David Reynolds has speculated, because by the time he wrote the book, the Cold War was already and indisputably under way.

Since as early as October 1942 his foreign secretary, Anthony Eden, had been trying to persuade him to take the postwar planning issues seriously. For Churchill, winning the war came first and he ended the memorandum to Eden using a phrase he had earlier used in *The World Crisis*, his book on the First World War and its aftermath:

> I hope these speculative studies will be entrusted mainly to those on whose hands time hangs heavy, and that we shall not overlook Mrs Glass's Cookery Book recipe for Jugged Hare—"First catch your hare."

Churchill was not entirely without thought of how things might look whenever victory took place. He was, for example, rightly worried that it "would be a measureless disaster if Russian barbarism overlaid the culture and independence of the ancient States of Europe" (a letter to Eden he *did* put in the book),[95] but both then and in Washington in 1943, he was rather vague on what kind of world body would exist to police the globe after the Allies had won.

Much of it centered around his vision of his mainly written but as yet unpublished book *The History of the English Speaking Peoples*. This is what in the twenty-first century is sometimes called the Anglosphere, and it remains an alternative for those in Britain wanting to have a closer link with distant Australia and the United States rather than with nations speaking foreign languages just over the English Channel. It is also the beginning of that great chimera, the "Special Relationship," which in reality is a way of Britain enabling itself to look more important internationally by appearing alongside the United States than the United Kingdom's actual resources allow. As we shall see, though, it was already an illusion in Churchill's time as prime minister during the war, with Roosevelt wanting to show to Stalin that Britain and the United States were not ganging up on their Communist ally.

In addition, it is probably fair to say that Churchill is what we would now, in international relations jargon, call a *realist*, a thought we shall revisit when we examine his time with Stalin later on, carving up the different parts of Central and Eastern Europe into zones of influence. Old-fashioned notions such as the balance of power were very important to Churchill. In 1943 it was impossible to presume that US troops would hang around for all that long in Europe after Allied victory—they are still there, well over sixty years after VE Day—and thus more theoretical notions of issues such as the future United Nations were of less importance to him than they were to someone more *idealist* in foreign policy such as Roosevelt, a Democrat. As one historian has commented of the president: "Churchill was a man of the past, Roosevelt saw himself and Stalin as men of the future."

Stalin was also angry, and again with good cause, that there was still no major second front that would help the Red Army knock the Third Reich out of the war. (In fact, as Harry Hopkins noticed, they were actually now worse.)[96] Remember this was May 1943—under the original victory plan that Marshall had put together, the Western Allies were, by this stage, supposed to have been in northwestern Europe for a whole month, whereas in reality they were still over a year off invading France, and had not as yet even landed troops on the European mainland against Italy.

As always, Churchill did not give up and soon both he and Marshall found themselves across the Atlantic and in Algiers, better to discuss the course of the war.[97]

Whatever else it may have achieved, taking Marshall with him to see Eisenhower in situ in North Africa certainly helped Churchill's attitude toward the most important soldier of the Second World War. As the prime minister later recalled:

> Hitherto I had thought of Marshall as a rugged soldier and a magnificent organiser and builder of armies—the American Carnot.[98] But now I saw that he was a statesman with a penetrating and commanding view of the whole scene.[99]

It took some while to get to Algiers, this time by plane. Churchill was to describe his time with Marshall thus: "I have no more pleasant memories of the war than the eight days in Algiers and Tunis."[100]

Crucially, this was the very last time that Britain was to have more troops in the field than the United States had. Until D-day altered the picture and gave the Americans overwhelming military predominance, this was the last imperial hurrah.

As Churchill put it:

> The circumstances of our meeting were favourable to the British. We had three times as many troops, and almost as many aeroplanes available for actual operations as the Americans.[101]

But despite this, as Churchill also noted, the British had agreed to be commanded by an American!

All this, as Marshall's biographer Forrest Pogue tells us, was part of the buttering-up process to see if more could be done to get troops to Italy, not France—Churchill's title in his memoirs is, significantly, "Italy the Goal," even though they include talks of other things, such as patching up relations between the two feuding French generals, Giraud and de Gaulle. Pogue notes:

> The Prime Minister may have been diverted from his Mediterranean obsessions during the trip, but once he landed in Algiers he lost no time in getting back to them.[102]

Eisenhower and Marshall, though, were determined not to be sidetracked or bamboozled, especially with Montgomery arriving on June 3 to put his weight on Churchill's side.

For all intents and purposes, especially as the Italian government was now poised to implode, with Mussolini being deposed in a coup by the king and Marshal Badaglio, it might seem that Churchill prevailed in Algiers—he was, ostensibly, able to persuade the Americans that Italy should now be invaded after all.[103] Although the seven divisions were to leave the Mediterranean to go to Britain, there would still be a large army, under Eisenhower's command, with which to invade Italy.[104] But this was an illusion, certainly so far as Marshall was concerned, as the Chief of Staff was to return to Washington determined that the agreement at Trident was still fully in place.[105] Soon the Americans would have far more troops in place than the British, and things would never be the same again.

Churchill was still not *inwardly* convinced, however, as Secretary of War Stimson was now to find out.

In July 1943, Stimson was going on to visit Eisenhower in North Africa, but he naturally came through London, and wrote up his experiences for Roosevelt, which the president then used as background briefing for the conference (code-named Quadrant) in Quebec the following month.[106]

As he told Roosevelt, "Although I have known the PM for many years and had talked freely with him, I have never had such a series of important and confidential discussions as this time," so much so, in fact, that Stimson changed his itinerary to spend more time with Churchill than he had planned.

(Here we should add that, thankfully only briefly, the invasion of northwestern Europe was called Roundhammer—what appears to be a mix of "Roundup" and "Sledgehammer." Fortunately for the confusion this would cause, it was soon known by the code name familiar to all of us: Overlord.)

Stimson did his level best to try to persuade Churchill of the correctness of the American plan.

> I asserted that it was my considered opinion that if we so allowed
> ourselves to become so entangled with matters of the Balkans,
> Greece and the Middle East that we could not fulfil our purposes
> of ROUNDHAMMER in 1944, that situation would be a serious
> blow to the prestige of the President's war policy, and therefore to
> the interests of the United States.[107]

This angle was clearly new to Churchill, whose main reply seems to have been towards "favoring a march on Rome...and the possibility of knocking Italy out of the war."[108]

Stimson then spent much of his time visiting US forces and D-day planners in Britain. He had dinner during this time with Churchill and the US ambassador, John Gilbert Winant, and the prime minister seemed up to his old tricks, determined to believe that everyone was supporting his Italian designs, something that Marshall, on hearing about this from Stimson, was quick to correct.

The significant meeting was on July 22. Stimson once again—one can detect the inward groan as he wrote his memorandum to the president—made the case for giving the invasion of France the overwhelming priority.

Churchill, however, would have none of this, and what he now told Stimson is, I think, one of the most revealing conversations he had during the war that is on record for us to ponder years later:

> He [Churchill] at once broke out into a new attack on ROUND-HAMMER. The check [i.e., military setback] received by the British at Catania, Sicily, during the past few days had evidently alarmed him. He referred to it and praised the superlative fighting ability of the Germans. He said that if he had fifty thousand men ashore on the French channel coast, he would not have an easy moment because he would feel that the Germans could rush up sufficient forces to drive them back into the sea. He repeated the assertions he had made to me as to the disastrous effect of having the Channel full of corpses of defeated allies.[109]

One would now love to have been a fly on the wall, as Stimson recounts that the two men now went "hammer and tongs" against each other!

> I [Stimpson] told him that we could never win any battle by talking about corpses. On this he said that, while he admitted that if he was C-in-C he would not set up the ROUNDHAMMER operation yet, having made his pledge he would go through with it loyally.

This, one suspects, was Churchill's inner attitude right up until D-day itself and probably for months afterward as well—for all his outward profession of fealty to what was supposed to be a joint plan, it is evident that the prime minister's heart was indeed not in it, as Stimson correctly surmised for the president. After the war, and especially in his memoirs, Churchill was to deny this,[110] but I think one can make an excellent case for saying that this was special pleading long after the event was over and the American policy had been proved to be triumphantly correct.

As Stimson sagely summed it up for the president (and for Marshall):

> When I parted with him I felt that, if pressed by us, he would sincerely go ahead with the ROUNDHAMMER commitment but that he was looking so constantly and vigorously for an easy way of ending the war without a trans-Channel assault that, if we expected to be ready for a ROUNDHAMMER which would be early enough in 1944 to avoid the dangers of bad weather, we must be constantly on the lookout against Mediterranean diversions.[111]

Stimson then went on to see Eisenhower. But he had become aware of Churchill's delaying tactics, and so warned the president that in effect British plans in Italy were "not put forward as an aid to ROUNDHAMMER but as a substitute to supplant it." Eisenhower did agree that there was one possible advantage of having Allied troops in the mainland of Italy, namely, that this would enable Allied bombers to be able to target sites in Germany from the south as well as from Britain.[112] But it remained clear to Stimson that while this was true: "A slow progressive infiltration of the Italian boot from top to bottom, time consuming and costly, would be sure to make ROUNDHAMMER impossible."[113]

On his return, Stimson advised Roosevelt:

The main thing therefore to keep constantly in mind is that the Italian effort must be strictly confined to the objective of securing bases for an air attack [on Germany] and there must be no further diversions of forces or materiel which will interfere with the coincident mounting of the ROUNDHAMMER project.[114]

Roosevelt was now duly prepared.

CHAPTER SIX

Churchill Finally Has to Give In

THE MEETING BETWEEN the British and the Americans in the French-Canadian city of Quebec in August 1943—code-named Quadrant—was the first time that Marshall was able to get his own president to try to nail Churchill to the floor and agree to a firm May 1, 1944, date for D-day, Overlord. While there is a case for saying that it was not until Teheran, at which Stalin was also present, that Churchill finally had to capitulate, the meeting at Quebec was beyond doubt a move in the right and war-winning direction.

Churchill arrived in Canada on August 11 and he and his daughter Mary (now Lady Soames) went briefly to see Roosevelt for a few days' break at Hyde Park, over the border in New York State.

The serious business began back in Quebec, at the Citadel, on August 19, and the various Chiefs of Staff had already begun their work, on the fourteenth.[1]

This time, so unlike at Casablanca, the Americans had got their act together long in advance, especially since Churchill and Brooke were trying to use the collapse of the Fascist regime in Italy to delay the dispatch of the seven divisions needed for Overlord from Italy to Britain ready for D-day. As Mark Stoler puts it in his biography of Marshall, unlike earlier in the year, this "time, however, the army chief emerged triumphant."[2]

Marshall also had backing in high places:

> Stimson further warned Roosevelt that the indirect British approach, which he labelled "pinprick warfare", not only would not work but would violate pledges given to the Soviet Union and would create serious problems with Stalin in the postwar world. If left in British hands, the cross-channel invasion would never take place, for the "shadows" of the World War I trenches as well as Dunkirk "still hang too heavily over the imagination" of Churchill and other British leaders. The time had come... [Stimson] insisted, for Roosevelt to assume responsibility for and leadership of the 1944 cross-channel attack by pressing for Marshall to be given command of the operation.[3]

As we shall see, Roosevelt's need to have Marshall at his side in DC prevented the last part from coming to pass. But this time, Roosevelt was indeed convinced by his own Chief of Staff, and was to back him to the hilt at the discussions that now took place. It was, one could add, a case of better late than never....

We can see this victory in the account Churchill himself gives of Quadrant, in his publishing highlights of the Combined Chiefs of Staff memorandum that he was given the opening day, CCS 303/3.[4]

It begins:

OPERATION OVERLORD

(a) This operation will be the primary United States-British ground and air effort against the Axis in Europe. (Target date, May 1, 1944)

This was good news in itself. The third paragraph began:

As between Operation "Overlord" and operations in the Mediterranean, where there is a shortage of resources available resources will be distributed and employed with the main object of ensuring the success of "Overlord."[5]

Needless to say, this did not go down well with Churchill.... As he put it with understatement in his own account of the meeting, these "paragraphs produced some discussion."[6] He insisted he favored Overlord in 1944 although he "had not been in favour of 'Sledgehammer' in 1942 or 'Roundup' in 1943." He was now also happy for an American commander for Overlord, even though he had originally favored Brooke for the command earlier that year. But in one sense, although Churchill probably persuaded himself that he now truly did believe in a May 1944 D-day, there was still plenty of resistance left in him.

Much of this was in an area at which we are not looking closely in this book, the war against Japan. As Churchill recorded, much of the dispute was the extent to which Britain could be involved in the Pacific once Germany had been defeated.[7] Here Churchill was to get a minor victory, in that a South East Asia Command was set up, in effect to liberate areas that had once been British, such as Burma, and Vice-Admiral Mountbatten, a minor British royal to whose father

Churchill felt a sense of obligation back from 1914,[8] was duly made Supreme Commander.

This is all the impression we get from Churchill's account. But, as David Reynolds has demonstrated so clearly in *In Command of History*, Churchill's account is in fact completely disingenuous, since it deliberately omits all the prime minister's caveats about D-day.[9] He'd told the British Chiefs of Staff in July, the month before, that he was worried about the "extraordinary fighting efficiency of the German army," and therefore felt that after Husky, the Allied invasion of Sicily:

> I have no doubt myself that the right strategy for 1944 is:
>
> (a) Maximum post-"Husky" certainly to the Po, with an option to attack westwards in the south of France or northwards towards Vienna, and meanwhile to procure the expulsion of the enemy from the Balkans and Greece
>
> (b) "Jupiter" [the invasion of Norway] prepared under the cover of "Overlord"[10]

Reynolds points out Churchill's policy at this time:

> His reticence is not surprising for the 19 July minute calls into question Churchill's claim of consistent support for Overlord... A similar sleight of hand may be found in Churchill's account of the Quebec conference... he skates over the "lengthy discussions" in the Combined Chiefs of Staff, where the suspicious Americans tried to elicit a firm British commitment to give Overlord "overriding priority" over all the other preparations in the European theatre.... In other words, like previous conferences, Quebec pro-

duced formulae that each side could use to advance its strategic preferences. In what the Americans hoped would be a straight-jacket, the British still discerned plenty of wiggle room.[11]

This is surely correct, and, as we will see later on, Churchill did not give up his ideas of Balkan invasions. That is why, although I quoted earlier American optimism that they had got their way, nevertheless I think it fair to say that it was not until Teheran, when Stalin came down so very firmly indeed on the American side, that the United States can finally be said to have prevailed. All this also makes the helpful general point that we see once more Churchill was making a legend about himself that did not always dovetail with the actual facts at the time. As we saw in the last chapter, he saw US Secretary of War Stimson at this time, and it is clear from Stimson's notes that Churchill's thinking about D-day was still more than fuzzy.

As for Jupiter—the attack on Norway—we have seen the rightness of Paul Kennedy's comment that while this was a pure piece of nonsense on Churchill's behalf, which his own Chiefs of Staff opposed both resolutely and successfully, the *threat* of it worked brilliantly, tying down tens of thousands of German troops needlessly up in Norway for an invasion that never came, and without the loss of any Allied lives in the process.[12] Sometimes, one could add, the flaws in Churchill's genius worked positively in ways he could never have expected. . . .

Now it was time for all three of the Allied leaders to meet, and for the first time. The logistics of this were not easy to arrange, but eventually all finally came together.

Teheran (now Tehran), the Iranian capital, was the place that proved mutually acceptable to both Stalin and Roosevelt as a venue for an Allied meeting (in the latter's case only after much persuading), as well as to Churchill.[13] The conference, usually known by its place name, was code-named Eureka. By this time, the prime minister was well aware of the comparative insignificance of his own position:

> There was emerging a strong current of opinion in American Government circles which seemed to wish to win Russian confidence even at the expense of co-ordinating the Anglo-American war effort.[14]

This Churchill was naturally keen to avoid, yet even now, in his telegram to Roosevelt on October 23 he was trying to argue for divisions remaining in Italy and for a month's postponement of Overlord.[15] As Warren Kimball notes in his commentary on the telegram:

> American military leaders constantly advised the President against delaying OVERLORD in order to build up Allied strength in an area that would fall within the British sphere of post-war influence. Churchill's tactic seemed to be to get Roosevelt committed on a Mediterranean strategy before meeting with Stalin, leaving such a tripartite meeting to deal with post-war politics rather than military decisions.[16]

Thankfully, one could add, in this Churchill failed.

This was also one of the reasons why Roosevelt refused to have a preliminary meeting with Churchill, in which the two Western leaders could stitch things up between them before then going on to meet with Stalin and present the Soviet ruler with a fait accompli. Roosevelt, it has long been felt, wanted to get close to Stalin, and felt that this would send the wrong signals, and Churchill, to be fair to the prime minister, probably did not so much want to snub the USSR as to keep up the exclusive relationship with the United States that was at the heart of his policy.[17]

(One by-product that Roosevelt did not expect is that, paradoxically, the president's ostentatious snubbing of Churchill to get close to the Soviets did not go down well with Stalin himself, who saw the action for what it was. As he was to comment, he preferred "a downright enemy to a pretended friend" and that while Roosevelt would take nothing less than a ruble out of your pocket, Churchill would take just a kopeck.)[18]

Alas for Churchill, "so far as...[his] interests were concerned, Tehran had been little short of disastrous,"[19] since, as Richard Holmes has noted, "FDR convinced himself that Winston was now the fly in the soup of fellowship with the Soviet tyrant."[20]

As Churchill was later to put it himself, to his old friend Lady Violet Bonham-Carter (the daughter of his old Liberal colleague, Prime Minister Herbert Asquith):

I realised at Teheran for the first time what a small nation we are. There I sat with the great Russian bear on one side of me, with paws outstretched, and on the other side the great American buffalo, and between us sat the poor little English donkey who was the only one, the only one of the three, who knew the right way home.[21]

This is quintessentially self-confident Churchill at his best! (Or worst?) It does seem amazing that it had taken him so long to realize the way in which international grand strategy had changed. But now the terrible understanding of how comparatively insignificant in the new world order the British Empire and its prime minister had become had finally struck him.

Understandably, historians of the Teheran conference have concentrated upon Churchill's divergence of view with Roosevelt, and how the president was to humiliate his old ally to gain curry with Stalin. No one has put this better than General Sir Ian Jacob, one of Churchill's key military aides during the war, who correctly assigns this feeling to the American reaction earlier in the war about how Britain squashed what the United States wanted to do. As he writes in *Action This Day*:

> It was...somewhat galling to the Americans that, except in the Pacific, where the United States Navy ruled the roost and would allow no interference with its plans, they were necessarily constrained to fall in with British plans, as their force had not developed and we were already in action.[22]

The point Jacob makes is a fair one and it is, as we saw with the decision to veto Sledgehammer, an understandable one, as that operation was, in effect, an American one that would principally have used British and Canadian lives to put it into operation. But, as Jacob correctly observes, things changed as the war progressed:

> This situation ruled up to the Casablanca conference...and it gradually changed in the following year. The change was obvious at...Teheran...and it presented Churchill with problems that even he could not solve.[23]

Not only that, but:

> When the first conference was to take place at Teheran between the three leaders instead of two, it soon became clear that the President

had determined to break free from entanglement with Churchill
and the British, and to meet Stalin without any prior consultation
or agreement on a common line beforehand. Churchill was gravely
perturbed by this development.[24]

This is an understatement! But we do not sense it from Churchill's
memoirs, which accentuate the positive in dealings with the United
States;[25] since he was still a practicing politician when they came out,
that is easy to comprehend.

It was, though, a major dilemma, and one that his critics feel was
the direct result of his decision in 1940 to throw all his eggs into the
American basket.[26] One does, though, need to ask the same question we posed when we looked at Britain alone: *short of defeat, what
other option did he have?* Defeat by Nazi Germany, being reduced to a
puppet state of the Third Reich, was beyond the bounds of all decent
options, and Churchill rightly rejected that choice.

But traditionally Britain had always needed a powerful allied
army to fight its battles on the Continent. France was now out of the
war, and to depend entirely on Stalin would have made the bad situation in 1943–45 far worse, as the Red Army could have conquered
Europe as far west as the English Channel. Britain would have
escaped being a Nazi satellite only to become one of the USSR. So it
was *only the American army that could do the job.*

Since, proportionately, the United States was bound to become
massively more powerful than the United Kingdom and its empire
combined—a point we shall explore elsewhere—American predominance was bound to make its mark sooner or later. Now at Teheran,
Churchill was finding those chickens of 1940 coming home to roost.
But I do not think we can in any sense blame Churchill for this, as he
had made the correct decision to defend the United Kingdom from

conquest, and in doing so made the right moral, military, and political choice.

So did Churchill thereby make the United Kingdom a satellite state of the United States of America, which is precisely the accusation his detractors make against him?[27]

Well, perhaps yes and no. So far as the nations of Western Europe were concerned, they were soon to swap one dire threat for another, namely that of the Cold War, and the ever-present danger created by the Soviet Union and its post-1945 Iron Curtain empire. No European country could face the USSR on its own, and it was only thanks to Marshall Plan aid that the countries so battered by war were able to recover economically at all. Obviously, this restricted the ability of such countries to have interests contrary to those of the US, but, given such an existential threat, who would really have wanted to do such a thing? American hegemony was inevitable, and all that was happening at Teheran and after was that this was now becoming clear.

Not only that, but was Britain—or any other NATO country post-1949, for that matter—really no different from Czechoslovakia or Poland? Having direct experience of how dissidents were treated in such countries during the Cold War, your author would very strongly beg to differ from those who would argue any such thing.

So Britain's glory days were over, however painful that must have been for someone of Churchill's age and imperial nostalgia. Not only that, but, as General Sir Ian Jacob continues, on the prime minister's hurt at Roosevelt's actions:

It went clean against his concept of the English-speaking peoples as a combined force for good in the future world. It seemed to give Stalin, who was answerable to no one, and whose troops were not fighting alongside the British and Americans, a great opportunity of driving a wedge between the Western Allies and to plant ideas which would ease the Russian path to the domination of Europe. That the President should deal with Churchill and Stalin as if they were people of equal standing in American eyes shocked Churchill profoundly, and seemed to nullify all the patient work he had done during the previous three years.[28]

Sadly, though, such feelings of hurt, while indeed profound, were alas imperial fantasy on Churchill's part. We saw earlier, in looking at 1942, that in some instances, there were battles in which the Red Army lost in a single campaign as many troops as the United States and UK combined during the entire war. For this reason alone, the Soviet Union was of far greater strategic importance than Britain, whose contribution was far smaller, but, and thankfully one might add, whose sacrifice was considerably smaller as well. This was, as we saw elsewhere, simply geopolitical reality, however unpalatable that might be.

Not only that, but we are in danger here, I think, of *anachronism*. We know that Truman was eventually to see things very differently, and to create the NATO structure in which we have lived since 1949, one that during the Cold War entailed a large US armed presence in Western Europe to protect that area against Soviet attack.

But it is also apparent that Roosevelt, thinking both in electoral terms as a US politician, and in strategic terms of the Pacific, was contemplating taking American troops either off to defeat Japan—no one in 1943 seems to have envisaged the impact the atomic bomb would have in shortening that war—or home to their families and friends in the United States. To both ends some kind of understanding with Stalin was important, looked at from the perspective not of London but of Washington DC. British politicians think in terms of British interests, and US politicians of American interests, and that Roosevelt would put British interests ahead of what he perceived to be those of the United States is thus unthinkable, however needlessly hurtful he was to Churchill in the process.

Without wishing to get too involved in early-twenty-first-century political issues, it is also worth saying that this has actually *diminished* British power vis-à-vis the United States, since not merely is the UK nowhere near as powerful as it was, say, before 1914 and two world wars, but, if Britain can always be taken for granted entirely as a loyal ally by the United States, then its concerns can be safely ignored— no British prime minister is ever going to upset the applecart, in a way that a French president or German chancellor might be inclined to do.

So yes, Churchill is not guiltless in failing to understand the long-term implications of his brave and morally correct decisions in 1940, but he is by no means alone, since most of his successors in 10 Downing Street have, if guilt is indeed the right word, been equally complicit.

Nor, in the context of Churchill's legitimate concerns on Roosevelt's policies, is it correct to say that the Americans were ignorant of what might happen as the result of the rise of Soviet power following an Allied victory over the Third Reich. This was something that many in the armed services were fully aware of as a serious danger, including General Marshall himself.

As one of his key aides, General Handy, said at the time:

Victory in this war will be meaningless unless we also win the peace. We must be strong enough at the peace table to cause our demands to be respected. With this in mind, we should only give such equipment to our Allies [especially the USSR] that they can put to better and quicker use than we can.[29]

A State Department official was to make an equally important point:

If Germany collapses before the Democracies have been able to make an important military contribution on the continent of Europe, the peoples of Europe will with reason believe that the war was won by the Russians alone.[30]

(In fact in the Iron Curtain states this was the myth the Soviets fostered assiduously as the reason for their continued military presence in the so-called liberated countries, with therefore more harmful effects than the UK and US film versions of events had, even though many of these films ignored the contribution made by other countries.)[31]

Both Sumner Welles, Roosevelt's own point man at the State Department, and Ambassador William Bullitt also made sure that the president was aware of the long-term Soviet threat. This was a point reinforced by no less than Hopkins himself, who was worried that "either Germany would go Communist or an out and out anarchic state would set in." Hopkins then went on to make what one can argue is the key statement:

It will, obviously, be a much simpler matter if the British and American armies are heavily in France or Germany at the time of the collapse [of German forces to the Soviets] but we should work out a plan in case Germany collapses before we get to France.[32]

Thankfully things did not get *that* bad! However, as we shall see, there was to be a major difference between meeting the Red Army on the Elbe (which is what did happen) and on the Vistula (which is what *could* have happened if Marshall had been successful in 1942).

This was also a nightmare for other leading Americans, including General Hap Arnold, the Chief of Staff of the US Army Air Corps (now the USAF). As he told Eden, who was visiting DC, "if we do not watch our step we could still be discussing ways and means for operating BOLERO while the Russians were marching into Berlin."[33]

Above all Marshall was very aware indeed of the hideous possibilities open to Stalin were the second front to be delayed again. As Marshall made abundantly clear to Roosevelt, it was:

> highly important for us to have at least a strong Army Corps in England because if events did suddenly culminate in an abrupt weakness of German resistance it was very important that there should be a sizeable American representation on the ground whenever a landing on the continent of Europe was made.[34]

Even more crucially perhaps, in Marshall's discussion with Roosevelt:

> I also gave him my personal opinion that if we were involved at the last in Western Europe and the Russian Army was approaching German soil, there would be a most unfortunate diplomatic situation immediately involved with the possibility of a chaotic situation quickly following.

(Let us note that phrase "at the last"—we can see Marshall's frustration at all the messing around in the Mediterranean and the delays for D-day are clearly showing through!)

All this is very important when we go on to look at the Yalta conference of early 1945, the last time that Stalin, Roosevelt, and Churchill were ever to meet. Much ink has been spilled over American foolishness at that gathering, but it is clear from all these accounts that many US officials knew full well what the Soviet Union was really like. To me, though, the issue is equally now a *military* one. Given the very different positions of both the Red Army and that of the Western Allies—at the time of Teheran there was not a single US soldier in France, and at the time of Yalta the Soviets were closing in far faster than the Western armies—how could it have been different even though we knew that the USSR was as unpleasant as it was?

This anxiety at the possible collapse of Germany under Soviet invasion was the origin of a plan called Rankin, which American historian Mark Stoler has well described:

> RANKIN was a political plan designed to keep alive the 1943 promise to Stalin, force a continuation of BOLERO for the 1944 assault, hamper British Mediterranean plans, and place American forces in Europe in the event Germany weakened or collapsed before the 1944 target date.[35]

As we know, this did not happen, so Rankin proved unnecessary. But it certainly made Roosevelt realize that an invasion of northwestern Europe was needed, as he now understood, "at the earliest possible date."[36]

Roosevelt's concerns about where Stalin stood influenced his policy at Teheran.

Much of the actual discussion at Teheran was on Asian issues, with the Americans (especially Roosevelt) keen to help China in any way possible. But on Mediterranean vs. Overlord, it is hard to disagree with those historians who say that in effect what Roosevelt and Churchill were doing was looking to Stalin to solve the impasse between the British and Americans. Fortunately Stalin chose to support Overlord but it could have been a close thing, and revealing differences between the two democracies was not a wise move in the face of someone as wily as the Soviet dictator.

One thing that Roosevelt did was to insist on seeing Stalin alone, and here we should agree with Richard Holmes that he behaved in a way that was not exactly honorable to his British ally.[37] He raised with Stalin the question of India. Having both rubbished the French, the conversation continued:

> The President...felt it would be better not to discuss the question of India with Mr. Churchill, since the latter had no solution of that question, and merely proposed to defer the entire question until the end of the war.[38]

Stalin agreed that "this was a sore spot with the British" and then Roosevelt continued:

> The President said that at some future date, he would like to talk with Marshal Stalin on the question of India; that he felt that the best solution would be reform from the bottom, somewhat on the Soviet line.

This is somewhat of a dreadful interference in the internal affairs of an ally, and to reform India on *Soviet* lines is an extraordinary statement! What if Churchill had raised with Stalin the racist makeup of the segregated American forces in Britain—which was in fact an issue that caused not a few British people grave and legitimate concern. This is not to defend Churchill on India—far from it! His policy on India was appalling and wholly reactionary, as we have seen. So what we are really seeing is Roosevelt trying to ingratiate himself with Stalin at Churchill's expense, which, as Richard Holmes is right to say, was equally bad behavior.

The first plenary session was on November 28, 1943, and took place at the Soviet Embassy, with Roosevelt in the chair.[39]

After a general survey, including details of the Pacific conflict, Roosevelt honed in on Europe, which he regarded as "the most important theater of the war."[40]

> He said he wished to emphasize that for over one year and a half in the last two or three conferences which he had had with the Prime Minister all military plans had revolved around the question of relieving German pressure on the Soviet front; that because of the large difficulties of sea transport it had not been possible until Quebec [in August 1943] to set a date for the cross-channel operations.... the plan adopted...involved an immense expedition and had been set at that time for May 1, 1944.

(He chivalrously did not say that in April 1942 his own people had set a date for April 1, 1943, or he may well have forgotten....)

Roosevelt then went into the issue of whether or not Allied action in the Mediterranean would help on the Eastern Front, and that "he and the Prime Minister had desired to ascertain the views of Marshal Stalin on this point"—in other words, the two democracies were making the Soviet dictator their arbiter! Thankfully Roosevelt also let slip his own clear view, namely "that in his opinion the large cross-channel operation should not be delayed by secondary considerations," which is exactly what Marshall and the others knew Churchill's Mediterranean interests to be.

Stalin reminded his Western allies of the realities of the war—there were no fewer than 210 German divisions on the Eastern Front, along with 50 of the Reich's allies: 260 divisions in all. The dictator then cut to the chase. Italy was not a suitable place for operations, and the barrier of the Alps was insuperable (a strategic factor with which the American military were later to agree when we look at the issue of the so-called Ljubljana Gap in 1944).

> He [Stalin] added that in the opinion of the Soviet military leaders, Hitler was endeavouring to retain as many Allied Divisions as possible in Italy where no decision could be reached, and that the best method in the Soviet opinion was getting at the heart of Germany with an attack through northern or northwestern France and even through southern France...northern France was still the best.

Marshall had been trying to persuade Churchill of this for over eighteen months; now here was Stalin saying the same thing.

Churchill now, rather disingenuously, tried to say that he did of course support Overlord, as it was now called, but that it had been impossible to carry out in 1943. Nevertheless 35 divisions would be available for Overlord in 1944 in the initial assault.

(One vital thing we should note as Westerners: Stalin had just stated that there were *330* Red Army divisions fighting the Germans. Churchill was talking of *35* Western divisions in Normandy, in other words, between nine and ten times *fewer* divisions than Stalin was employing on the Eastern Front.)

However, Churchill went on, "the summer of 1944 was a long

way off." So since Rome ought to be captured by January 1944, "it would be six months before OVERLORD would begin." So there was a good chance of "at least mauling 10 to 15 German divisions" in Italy. He also now launched into his perennial fantasy—which was never fulfilled—of Turkey entering the war on the Allied side.

None of this convinced Stalin, who agreed with the American military view that such dispersals were useless:

> Marshal Stalin replied that in his opinion he questioned the wisdom of dispersing allied forces…[for] the various operations such as Turkey, the Adriatic and Southern France since there would be no direct connection between these scattered forces. He said he thought it would be better to take OVERLORD as the basis for all 1944 operations.[41]

Once more, this is exactly what the American military had been saying since early 1942!

He did, however, agree with what the Americans were calling Anvil, an operation in the south of France to take away German troops from Normandy (the operation was later to be called Dragoon). But he favored doing this two months *before* D-day, whereas, because of steadfast British opposition to the idea, the actual invasion in that region did not in fact take place until several months *after* D-day, by which time one can legitimately ask if it had ceased to be helpful.

All this was good news for Roosevelt and bad news for Churchill. While the prime minister wanted to "develop arguments to demonstrate why it was necessary for the allied forces to capture Rome," the president's immediate response was to state that "he personally felt that nothing should be done to delay the carrying out of OVERLORD."

While Churchill persisted, it was plain that thanks to Stalin, Roosevelt had won the day.

Similar themes emerged in the meeting that the Combined Chiefs of Staff had the following day, November 29.[42]

Brooke did his best to make sure that the British options remained alive, pointing out to a skeptical US and Soviet delegation that Allied troops in Italy were keeping German forces contained.

Marshall, however, brought them back to realities, and in doing so reminded the Soviets of the sheer scale of the American effort— only the United States was fighting *major* wars in both the Atlantic and the Pacific theaters. (This was not, one should add, to ignore the British activities in Asia, simply that they were not on the same scale as the Americans'—and the Soviets were not fighting the Japanese at all, something that the Americans were very keen to change.) He then went on to make the crucial point: "he wished to repeat and emphasize that there was no lack of troops or of supplies." One could also interject here that in so saying, he was pointing out the folly of the British argument as well: that there *was* a limited amount of supplies and that this therefore curtailed possible Allied action.

He then added that a key reason "for favouring Overlord from the start is that it is the shortest overseas transport route"—the Mediterranean was farther and this, Marshall was right to say, was a major issue.

Marshal Voroshiloff came in strongly on the side of the Americans as they had hoped that he would. Was Brooke in favor of Overlord? he asked.

General Marshall intervened—all was on target and it remained "now only to bring the troops up to the supplies."

Brooke's reply was of a different nature altogether. He supported Overlord, he said, but the British "stipulated that the operation must be mounted at a time when it would have the best chance of success." The fortifications on the French coast were of a "serious character," for instance, and this meant that invasion would be possible by 1944. (As we have seen, Rommel in fact greatly increased the German fortifications in France in 1944—they were far stronger by D-day than they were at the time Brooke was speaking in Teheran.) But the British bottom line remained:

> The British wished, during the preparation for OVERLORD, to keep fighting the Germans in the Mediterranean to the maximum degree possible.[43]

This is where the issue of landing craft comes in. The British maintained that one could not have full troop strengths in the Mediterranean without them, and this limited the amount for D-day, whereas Marshall was able to show that such craft could simply be transferred to Britain for France—and that of course meant far fewer troops in Italy than the British wanted. It was not a question therefore of landing craft but of where best to fight the Germans, and that was thus a *political* as well as military decision, as becomes clear reading the transcripts of the Teheran discussions.

Voroshiloff now came in on the part of the United States and against Britain, saying that:

> OVERLORD is the most important operation and that all other auxiliary operations such as Rome, Rhodes [one of Churchill's many alternative bright ideas] and what not, must be planned to assist OVERLORD and certainly not to hinder it. He pointed out that it was possible now to plan additional operations that may hurt OVERLORD and emphasised that this must not be so. These

operations must be planned so as to *secure* [*sic*] OVERLORD, which is the most important operation, and not to hurt it.[44]

Brooke continued to do the best he could for the British point of view, but he was outgunned. While he saw problems, Marshall "emphasized that no catastrophe was expected, but that everyone was planning for success." D-day was to prove this right—the only near-disaster was on Omaha, and, as we have seen, this was because the Allied delay had given the Germans a whole extra year to reinforce the Normandy beaches.

Stalin was determined to press home his advantage in nailing down both Britain and the United States to a very firm date for an actual Overlord.[45] He did so by bringing up the awkward question of who would actually command the Western forces invading France, a decision that Roosevelt had to admit was not yet taken.

(Here one can feel sorry for both Brooke, who had thought from Churchill that he would be the commander in chief, and Marshall, who had nursed similar expectations of the Supreme Command. The decision was not made in Teheran but later, and as we all know Roosevelt felt safer with Marshall by his side in Washington DC, and Eisenhower got the job commanding D-day.)

What is truly extraordinary is the opening statement of the session:

The President said since there was no agenda for the conferences he thought it would be a good idea to have a report from the military staffs who had met...[that] morning.

What a way in which to start so important a meeting....

Once again the discussions got bogged down in Churchill's favorite chimera, Turkish entry into the war. Stalin swatted this away, and insisted on knowing who the commander would be for D-day and:

> In order that Russian help might be given from the east to the execution of OVERLORD, a date should be set and the operation should not be postponed.

Here one should remember the Russians had been told as early as the start of 1942 that there would be a second front *that year*—i.e., 1942—by Roosevelt, and nothing had as yet happened. One cannot blame Stalin for seeming a bit desperate. One can add too that if one is looking for the origins of East/West suspicion, and thence the Cold War, we can see their distant origins in the meetings in Teheran.

One sees this further in the different account of the meeting given by the Combined Chiefs of Staff. The following conversation is more than revealing:

Roosevelt had allowed himself and Stalin to talk about intrigues in the Balkans. Stalin was almost certainly worried about Western troops entering an area he wanted under Soviet control postwar. But I think Stalin also had some legitimate *military* concerns, not least because of the ongoing carnage and high casualty rate on the Eastern Front. So Roosevelt finally agreed:

> The President said that we should therefore work out plans to con-tain...[the twenty-five German divisions in France]. This should be done on a scale as not to divert means from doing OVERLORD at the agreed time.
>
> Marshal Stalin observed, regarding the President's statement, "You are right, you are right."
>
> The President said we again come back to the problem of the

timing for OVERLORD. It was believed that it would be good for OVERLORD to take place about 1 May, or certainly not later than 15 May or 20 May if possible.[46]

Remember the *actual* date of D-day: June 6, or over a week later. (Brooke was to see the delay as a major British triumph[47] and as he put it after the November 28 discussions, the Allies "were reaching a point where Stalin's shrewdness, assisted by American short-sightedness, might lead us anywhere."[48])

The reason for all this delay now becomes clear from the minutes:

The Prime Minister said he could not agree to that.

Marshal Stalin said he observed at yesterday's conference that nothing will come out of these proposed diversions. In his opinion OVERLORD should be done in May. He added that there would be suitable weather in May.

The Prime Minister said he did not believe that the attitudes of those present on this matter were very far apart. He said that he (the Prime Minister) was going to do everything possible to begin OVERLORD at the earliest possible moment. However, he did not think that the many great possibilities of the Mediterranean should be ruthlessly cast aside as valueless merely on the question of a month's delay in OVERLORD.

Marshal Stalin said that all the Mediterranean operations are diversions...He accepted the importance of these other operations but definitely considered that they are diversions.

Stalin was of course right, although proponents of a Mediterranean strategy would no doubt still think otherwise. Discussion continued, with Churchill fighting his corner, until Roosevelt pitched in:

The President said he found that his staff places emphasis on OVERLORD. While on the other hand the Prime Minister and his staff also emphasize OVERLORD, nevertheless the United States does not feel that OVERLORD should be put off.[49]

Stalin was also clearly feeling antagonistic, including to Brooke. Since time was passing, and Roosevelt was not entirely well, the president announced that it was clearly time to eat! And Churchill, feeling the need to be mollifying, stated:

> The Prime Minister replied that if the conditions specified...[at the earlier talks in Moscow] regarding OVERLORD should exist, he firmly believed that it would be England's duty to hurl every ounce of strength she had across the Channel at the Germans.

The dinner, from Churchill's point of view, was truly horrible, as Charles Bohlen's minutes make clear.[50]

> The most notable feature of the dinner was the attitude of Marshal Stalin towards the Prime Minister. Marshal Stalin lost no opportunity to get in a dig at Mr. Churchill. Almost every remark that he addressed to the Prime Minister contained some sharp edge, although the Marshal's manner was entirely friendly. He apparently desired to put and keep the Prime Minister on the defensive.

Bohlen also gives what he thinks was the reason, in which the American diplomat is almost certainly correct, presuming, though, that one can discern the mind of a totalitarian monster like Stalin:

Marshal Stalin was obviously teasing the Prime Minister for the latter's attitude at the afternoon session…he was also making known in a friendly fashion his displeasure at the British attitude on the question of OVERLORD.

A 1920s British historical satire calls a seventeenth-century group of Puritans "right but repulsive."[51] Can one say the same of Stalin on this issue? He was right that Overlord should begin soon—indeed, as we have argued it was nearly eight months later than Marshall had planned for it already—but he was not the ideal person to be ragging a democratic prime minister.

Now things got even worse, with Roosevelt joining in on Stalin's appalling behavior. Stalin now suggested that 50,000 to 100,000 "of the German Commanding Staff must be physically liquidated."

Here Bohlen omits what Churchill recalls as his (the prime minister's) shocked reply, so, although Churchill's memoirs are not always one hundred percent reliable, I will use them for what followed:[52]

On this I thought it right to say, "The British Parliament and public will never tolerate mass executions. Even if in war passion they allowed them to begin they would turn violently against those responsible after the first butchery had taken place. The Soviets must be under no delusion on this point."

Stalin then insisted that at least 50,000 "must be shot." Churchill was furious.

"I would rather," I said, "be taken out into the garden here and now and be shot myself than sully my own and my country's honour by such infamy."

Roosevelt now tastelessly decided to defuse the situation by suggesting that "only forty-nine thousand" be shot, and his son, Elliot Roosevelt, present at the dinner, supported his father's bad joke. This was all too much for Churchill:

> At this intrusion I got up and left the table, walking off into the next room, which was in semi-darkness.

He was then prevailed upon to return, and in his memoirs firmly lets everyone off the hook, pretending that "the rest of the evening passed pleasantly."

His physician, now Lord Moran, noted in his diary Churchill's horror at what was unfolding. This, not what Churchill wrote in *Closing the Ring*, is what the prime minister actually felt:

> Stupendous issues are unfolding before our eyes, and we are only specks of dust, that have settled in the night on the map of the world. Do you think...my strength will last out the war? I fancy sometimes I am nearly spent.[53]

As Moran himself then went on to observe about his patient, about whose "Black Dog" depression he was very aware:

> Until he came here, the PM could not bring himself to believe that, face to face with Stalin, the democracies would take different courses. Now he sees he cannot rely on the President's support. What matters more, he realises the Russians see this too. It would be useless to try to take a firm line with Stalin. He will be able to do as he pleases. Will he become another menace to the free world, another Hitler? The PM is appalled by his own impotence.

It is not surprising that Churchill's new bout of depression was to last for some while to come, with the prime minister soon succumbing to an even worse pneumonia in North Africa.[54]

I think too we must agree with Richard Holmes's judicious summing up of the situation from Churchill's point of view:

> On his sixty-ninth birthday, during the Teheran conference… Winston saw all too well that the indispensable role Britain under his leadership had played in the Grand Alliance was coming to an end.[55]

In terms of politics, and the comparative strengths of the different nations, your author would say that Churchill was now bowing to the inevitable. But Holmes is surely right to continue:

> If any tangible American advantage had followed FDR's humiliation of Winston during the conference, history would judge him to have made a hard but correct decision. But it is still profoundly chastening that a man who considered his nation to be in the vanguard of human civilisation sought the friendship of a despot whom he knew to be responsible, among other monstrous crimes, for the murder of some twenty thousand Polish officers and men at Katyn and elsewhere, and made jokes with him about doing the same to the Germans.

It is not therefore remotely surprising that Churchill was so upset, as Holmes concludes:

> Winston had just learned that the man in whom he had deposited his hopes for a decent post-war world was an appeaser, and had

seen FDR make mock of him while sharing a genocidal joke with a mass murderer.

You would not know this from reading Churchill's memoirs, which also include the moving tale of Stalin being given a ceremonial Sword of Stalingrad on behalf of the British people.[56]

Part of the problem is the myth of the glowing US-UK "Special Relationship" by which Churchill set such store, and which is a leitmotif of his *History of the Second World War*. As we have seen, it ought to be incontestable that only the United States could have come successfully to Britain's rescue in 1940–41 and it was the realization of this, unlike the blinkered approach of a Chamberlain, that makes Churchill so stand out in this period as the leader who saved his country by seeing the truth.

Now however he was being shut out—the poor donkey between the bear and the buffalo!

Richard Holmes has summed this up better than anyone:

Winston and the British Chiefs of Staff found it hard to adjust to the gloomy fact that their views had become increasingly suspect in the eyes of an ally [the United States] who was able to monitor their good faith, while those of the ultra-secretive Soviet dictator were no less automatically accepted at face value. This was something far deeper than the issues of ego that sometimes disfigure some senior officers' memoirs. Winston's own history of the war created a myth of Anglo-American unity of purpose that successfully diverted the attention of posterity from the dispiriting reality he was obliged to wrestle with in 1944–5. Those who lived through it with him generally follow his lead, but passages here and there testify to an abiding sense of betrayal.[57]

So in a sense one can say that at Teheran Churchill was hoist with his own petard—he had been obliged, because of his dreadful strategic inheritance in 1940, to put all his eggs in the American basket, and the United States had indeed prevented Britain from being invaded and now put the United Kingdom firmly on the winning side. But America had its own agenda and Roosevelt, being a democratically elected politician, like Churchill himself, had his. We can be thankful that Marshall, who, as we saw earlier, was very aware of the nature of the Soviet threat long-term, was in charge of US foreign policy after the war, and that Truman was quickly to see things in a more realistic light than an idealist such as Roosevelt failed to do.

However, although we can thus legitimately feel sorry for Churchill, is it that simple?

One can, I would argue, say that, while that is all true, we must not forget our own different perspective on all these issues, namely that it was very much Churchill's own fault that the Western Allies were in such a terrible position vis-à-vis Stalin at all. Think how utterly and radically different the position would have been *if D-day had already taken place seven months earlier* as Marshall had first proposed back in early 1942. The balance of power between Stalin on the one hand and the West on the other would have been different by a vast magnitude, entirely to the benefit of the West.

So Stalin's victory at Teheran, which is essentially what it was, would never have happened *in the way that it did*, if, indeed, it would have happened at all, which under our alternative scenario is therefore very unlikely. Given the rapid advance upon Central Europe in the real world, in 1944, and the fact that with the Atlantic Wall being nowhere near as strong in 1943 as it was to be in 1944, it is more than likely that the Western Allies would have advanced into Germany itself far quicker in 1943 under our alternative scenario than they did in real life a year later, since France would have been easier to invade, and the German armies would have been far further apart. (We shall come back to this later on, as it is a point that bears repetition.)

Not only that, but the US resentment, to which Jacob referred, would have never taken place. This might, and probably would, have led to British resentments! But the United Kingdom was the dependent power, and the United States the senior partner, and so, in terms of importance, this would have mattered far less than the feelings Churchill provoked among many members of the US high command.

Roosevelt would still have wanted to come to terms with the USSR, since the need to defeat Japan, and to take as many US soldiers home as possible, would still have been there. But with the West in a far stronger military bargaining position, many of Churchill's very legitimate fears about Soviet intentions, which were now (finally, one might add) beginning to grow, would have been groundless. For let us remember the key thing about the actual Teheran conference: *when it took place, there was not a single British or American soldier in northwestern Europe*, and Stalin's sense of paranoia about this was very profound, with good cause, given the scale of the carnage on the Eastern Front.

One can therefore feel legitimately sorry for Churchill—but not *that* sorry, since so many of his wounds were self-inflicted going back to 1942, and the decision to reject the American way of winning the war more quickly. Not only that, but one could also add that in putting the UK well above its actual rank in world affairs—in the top five for certain, but nowhere near as high as number two to the mighty United States of America—Churchill was beginning a process among British politicians that has continued ever since, as one

British foreign secretary put it during the 1990s, of hitting above its weight.[58]

The point about how different Europe would have been on an earlier D-day comes home especially strongly when we think of the conversations that both Roosevelt and Stalin, and Churchill and Stalin (usually apart, alas, not together) had on the future of Europe, and on the fate of poor Poland in particular. Here we must remember the central point made so significantly by historians such as Norman Davies[59] on Poland during the war and on the fate of Central and Eastern Europe in general to which I have referred elsewhere. Stalin wanted Poland, hitherto a free country, under his control, and would soon wreak the most savage horrors on those Poles brave and independence-loving enough not to want to be under Soviet rule; in the uprising in Warsaw he would deliberately allow thousands of Polish freedom fighters to die at the hands of the SS.

Churchill, in writing *Closing the Ring*, clearly exudes a sense of guilt about what happened to Poland after 1944–45, with the Soviet occupation of that country, and the tens of thousands murdered by the NKVD, and the crushing of Polish independence into what then seemed like permanent occupation.[60] It was obvious what Stalin wanted to do and equally plain that there was absolutely nothing that the two Western Allies could do to help Poland in its fate.

Just one example, a statement of Stalin's on December 1. The Polish government in exile knew full well that the murders of the thousands of Polish officers whose bodies were found in the forest at Katyn had been committed by *Soviet* troops, something that the USSR, under Gorbachev, finally admitted decades later after many years of lies and cover-up. Stalin had broken off all relations with the London Poles, and had bludgeoned his Western allies into secrecy on the issue. This is how the discussion went:

Marshal Stalin replied that Russia, probably more than any other country was interested in having friendly relations with Poland, since the security of Soviet frontiers was involved.... He added that they broke relations with Poland [in exile] not because of a whim but because the Poles had joined in slanderous propaganda with the Nazis.[61]

This was entirely untrue—the London Poles knew full well it was NKVD troops, *not* the Nazis, who had massacred all the victims of Katyn. But no one contradicted Stalin, even though they knew the truth.

Stalin continued:

The Russians would welcome relations with a Polish Government that led its people in the common struggle but it was not sure that the Polish Government in exile could be such a government. However, he added, if the government in exile would go along with the partisans and sever all connections with German agents in Poland, then the Russians would be prepared to negotiate with them.

In fact the collusion with the Germans was to be the Red Army in 1944, since the Soviets did nothing to prevent the SS from slaughtering thousands of innocent Poles during the Warsaw uprising. However, Stalin did not see things that way, and the West was to be shameful in colluding with him to put pressure on the London Poles to conform. Not only that, but the Allies were, eventually, forced to recognize legally all the Soviet seizure of Polish territory in 1940, which, as British Foreign Secretary Eden briefly and bravely mentioned at Teheran, was the Ribbentrop-Molotov Line, or Polish-Soviet border.

(To which Stalin replied, "call it what you will, we still consider it just and right.")[62]

Churchill, as he reminded Stalin, was very aware that Britain had gone to war in 1939 to defend Poland.[63] Now he was beginning to see that in one sense that had been in vain, as the Soviets were moving in to take over where the Nazis had left off. As a no-doubt guilty-feeling Churchill put it at the end of his Teheran chapter in *Closing the Ring*:

> I do not feel any break in the continuity of my thoughts in this immense sphere. But vast and disastrous changes have fallen upon us in the realm of fact. The Polish frontiers exist only in name [this changed in the 1970s, as part of Germany's *Ostpolitik*, but after Churchill's death in 1965] and Poland lies quivering in the Russian-Communist grip... About this tragedy it can only be said IT CANNOT LAST [Churchill's capitals].[64]

We shall revisit the Polish issue when we consider the final decisions made at the Yalta conference. Much ink has been spilled over the fateful meeting in the Crimea in early 1945. I think, though, that the key thing to remember is that by the time of Yalta, the pass had *already* been sold—Poland was, for all intents and purposes, sunk in Teheran, and Yalta only sealed a deed already done.

But let us take this as a practical instance of what *might* have happened *if* D-day had met Marshall's schedule instead of Churchill's delayed one of fourteen months later. Well over a million *Western* Allied troops would be in France, and, since the Atlantic Wall would have been weaker, they might well have been on the borders of Germany itself by December 1943. Meanwhile, Stalin's troops were still many miles from Poland, let alone Germany itself. There would have been no cause for Stalin's moral outrage at British prevarication, since the United Kingdom would be fully engaged in fighting on the mainland.

Roosevelt might have seen less of a need to do a deal with Stalin, and, significantly from the US point of view, with victory nearer, there would have been far less of a panic to ensure that the USSR joined in the war against Japan, since, to be fair to Roosevelt, that was an issue very much on his mind as it was on that of the American Chiefs of Staff. In addition *American* suspicion of and sheer frustration with Churchill, and of Britain generally, so evident to anyone reading the American accounts of Teheran, would not have had cause either, or certainly not with the profound good reasons that Churchill's delaying tactics at Teheran provoked.

This does not mean that all would have been well for Poland, a country whose most unfortunate fate it was to be in between an eastward-expanding Germany on the one hand and a westward-going Russia and then USSR on the other. (If Churchill thought he had problems being wedged between the Soviet Union and the United States, that pales into minor insignificance compared to Poland's dire geographical position.) But the West would certainly not have been in anything near as weak a military and moral state as was the case at the actual Teheran conference in 1943. Churchill's prevarications over D-day would cost the Poles and the other peoples of Central Europe very dear come 1945.

CHAPTER SEVEN

Churchill and America at War

WE WON THE *war in 1944!*
    Well, so goes the rhyme I heard so often as a schoolboy, back in the 1950s, just over ten years in my case after the titanic battles of World War II were finally over.

So far as the Western Front in Europe was concerned, there was a great deal of truth in the saying. For while the battles raged until the German surrender of May 1945, there is a real sense in which, on the *western* side of the struggle, the fate of the Third Reich and the eventual demise of the Nazis were effectively determined on the Normandy beaches eleven months earlier, in June 1944.

This view has also been perpetuated in the movies, in films such as *The Longest Day* and, more recently and with huge success, *Saving Private Ryan*, along with the equally acclaimed television series *Band of Brothers*.

In and of themselves, all of these are great movies and make for wonderful entertainment. But in reality they distort the picture of what World War II was like, and do so very badly indeed. This is not just the traditional British gripe that states, with some degree of fairness, that the Western Front was an Allied effort, and that British soldiers also fought in Normandy and in the liberation of Europe—a fault that a film such as *A Bridge Too Far* avoids, by showing the bravery of American, Polish, and British forces fighting side by side.

Rather it is the fact that the Hollywood version perpetuates, rather than creates by itself, a total myth: *the Allies beat the Germans in the West and therefore won the war.*

This is, in reality, a complete distortion. The truth, however uncomfortable, is as follows:

a. The Americans won the war against Japan in the Pacific, with the British effort in Burma effectively a sideshow.

b. The Russians won the war against the Germans in Europe, with the American and British effort, while not entirely a sideshow, playing a much smaller role in defeating the Third Reich, but probably ensuring that *Western* Europe stayed outside the Soviet bloc.

This is not a new point—the notoriously irascible and later right-wing hardliner US General Albert Wedemeyer made it as early as the 1950s in his wartime memoir *Wedemeyer Reports!*, a book now mainly remembered as one of the many that claimed the Truman administration "lost" China to the Communists, since much of Wedemeyer's time was spent in the Pacific theater of war. This theory also became famous with the bestseller by Chester Wilmot, at which we shall be looking further as this chapter unfolds.

So while we naturally feel for Churchill, the fact that his role becomes ever more insignificant is not a personal reflection on him, but more the reality of what was now happening: *however truly heroic the British war effort was, Britain was now the junior partner in a much bigger war.*

Let us now look at how things developed after D-day, but bearing all this in mind as we do so.

D-day brought the troops to Europe at last—fourteen months later than Marshall would have wished them to be there, and, as we have seen, over a year too late to save the lives of well over a million Jews who, had the war ended earlier, would otherwise have survived the Holocaust. But better late than never, and whatever nightmares Churchill and Brooke might have had about another Somme on the beaches of Normandy, no battles on the *Western* Front in the Second World War were to approach the carnage either of the same area in the First World War, or of the *Eastern* Front in the Second.

So in one sense our argument is over—there now was a second front and British and American soldiers (not to mention Canadians) were fighting bravely in northwestern Europe for the liberation of those countries conquered in 1940 and for the defeat of the Third Reich itself.

However, life was not that simple!

First, Churchill and Roosevelt *still* disagreed on strategy, and strongly so. Nor had the prime minister given up on his wish for a Mediterranean strategy, and in particular for what Marshall and the others regarded, with good cause, as suction pumps taking vitally needed Allied troops away from the main battlefield in France.

Not only that, but Churchill was now slowly waking up to something that should have been glaringly obvious to someone as distrustful as he had always been to Bolshevism, namely that the USSR, although an ally against Hitler, was going to become rather too powerful as a result of the war, and perhaps a major threat to the free world that Churchill wished to see come into being once the Allies had won.

But, as we shall see, the prime minister would now be hoist with his own petard, since the fourteen-month delay in launching D-day was to cost not only the lives of millions, but also the freedom of millions more, as it was now to be the Red Army that stormed into Central and Eastern Europe, and not the British and Americans. One of the great tragedies of Churchill is that he now understood what victory would entail, and that it was too late to do anything to prevent it.

So let us look first at the Soviet issue in particular, and then at one of the ways in which Churchill sought to stem the advance of the Russian juggernaut, by means of a *Western* invasion of Central Europe through an area known as the Ljubljana Gap.

But before we do so, we need to remember one key thing: *we know the Cold War came into being and lasted until 1989 but that is with the benefit of hindsight. Up until the time we are considering, the main thought of the Western leaders was that of beating Hitler, and not what Stalin would be up to once victory had been achieved.*

Much has been written on how Western leaders were to get all this wrong, most notably, as just mentioned, in Chester Wilmot's book *The Struggle for Europe* and many histories written during the Cold War (up until 1989) as well.[1] But while it is possible to blame Churchill and Roosevelt for what now unfolded, one does have to remember, in their favor, that they were fighting a massive war, on a scale hitherto never seen. We can, as will become clear, say that they were wrong, but in a good cause.

We can start, in the light both of the subsequent Cold War, and also of what the Allies decided at the time, by looking briefly at the views of one of the most famous of all Cold War warriors, the American diplomat George Kennan.

George Kennan, who lived until 2005, was the man who, as an American official in both prewar and postwar USSR, invented the idea of *containment,* of keeping the Soviet Union in its borders, or, once the Cold War had begun, within the confines of the existing Soviet bloc. His famous "Mr. X" article in *Foreign Affairs,* called "The Sources of Soviet Conduct," in 1947, was the first publication outlining American Cold War policy and a way of thinking that continued right down until the collapse of the Soviet Union in 1991.

Kennan was not someone who agreed with the major thrust of US policy during the war years themselves—though, as we shall see, this was a somewhat simplistic understanding of the American view, since there were many people in the administration who were well aware of the potential Soviet threat to the democratic West long before Truman became president and changed the more sympathetic course Roosevelt had charted.

Kennan felt that Roosevelt and Marshall were too influenced by the entirely military aspects of strategy, at the expense of the political ramifications. There is a good case for this, as Marshall's chronicler Forrest Pogue admitted in an interview with Kennan as part of his research.[2]

With this, Kennan agreed: General Marshall "was a man of such integrity that when he was called upon to deliver the major military effort he wasn't patient with anything that seemed to be a diversion from that effort, anything that we condict [*sic*]. And many of these decisions did...it was quite unnecessary to promise the Russians anything to get them into the Far Eastern War [i.e., the war against Japan]."

Furthermore:

And in general it was very strongly my view that after the Warsaw uprising in September 1944 we should have had a basic clarification with these people. And we should have asked them in effect, what are you up to here in Eastern Europe, because if you are going to behave just the way that Hitler does, we don't know if it is worth our while to support you in this war effort for another half of the remainder of this war or not.... [However...] I am sure that this would have been unacceptable at home, because people would have thought... those hundreds or so many divisions are absolutely necessary to us. But I felt that at the same time we had already liberated Paris, we were on the borders of Germany, the Russians had made their intentions very clear in the Warsaw uprising, and it would have been very difficult for them to negotiate any sort of dependable peace with the Germans. In fact the Germans would have been glad to surrender to us alone.

Needless to say, even after the Cold War has now been over for nearly two decades, such views remain controversial.

But the sheer horror of the Warsaw uprising, a Soviet-permitted atrocity that should rank as one of the worst of the war, should have alerted the West to the full nature of their Russian ally. Authors such as Norman Davies, in his book *Rising '44: The Battle for Warsaw,* have described for us the terrible extent of the Nazi massacre of Poles, including Poland's young elite, while the West's supposed ally, the USSR, looked on and did nothing. Most of the future leadership of a free (and thus non-Communist) Poland lost their lives in the carnage, and that, one can surmise, was Stalin's intention all along.

Indeed as Davies puts it in his wider-scope history *Europe at War,* the uprising actually lasted from August 1 to October 3, 1944, and was the biggest national resistance movement uprising against the

Nazis of the whole war. It was, Davies writes, "confusion...followed by treachery and tragedy," with over 200,000 *civilians* losing their lives, let alone armed combatants.[3] Churchill asked for permission to fly in aid to the Poles via bases in Italy—Stalin refused.[4] Churchill was right to find the whole affair profoundly distressing and he was clearly well-informed from sources within the Warsaw uprising itself, which he quoted at length to Roosevelt.

At least one can say in mitigation that Churchill tried, but by this time it was physically impossible to get anywhere near to the region from Western-occupied territory.

Indeed one can also agree with George Kennan, who felt that an entirely different Allied policy should have been made after the genocide in Warsaw. To him, it was a "real mistake...giving Lend Lease to the Russians to justify their requirements...by [mid to late 1944] they had liberated their own territory, they had no kick coming to us now about the Second Front. Paris was already in Allied hands, we were at the German borders ourselves, and they spilled their own hand very clearly in Poland, and...this was a time when we could have cracked down."

As Averell Harriman, Roosevelt's envoy to Russia (and later US ambassador to the United Kingdom), admitted to Pogue, "Stalin was utterly ruthless to Poland,"[5] which one might add is an understatement in the light of the carnage wreaked upon the Poles by their supposed Soviet liberators.

And it was now, of all times, that Churchill went to Moscow to see Stalin, to carve up Central and Eastern Europe into zones of occupation! Forrest Pogue has commented that Churchill "destroyed his moral position" on matters to do with this region by his talks with Stalin on the issue, in October 1944, and it is hard to disagree, especially since the prime minister was later on going to complain bitterly that we were giving Poland away to Stalin, just after he himself had signed away half the Balkans to the USSR!

Much has been written on this issue, and it is certainly one of the most controversial actions Churchill took during the war, and one, interestingly, that he did not hide in writing his memoirs. It is usually described as the "percentages agreement."

It is outlined in volume six of his memoirs, and, as writers have commented,[6] Churchill does not beat about the bush.

As he puts it:

The arrangements which I had made with the President in the summer to divide out our responsibilities for looking after particular countries affected by the movements of the armies had tided us over the three months for which our agreement ran. But as the autumn drew on everything in Eastern Europe became more intense. I felt the need of another personal meeting with Stalin, whom I had not seen since Teheran, and with whom, in spite of the Warsaw tragedy, I felt new links since the successful opening of "Overlord." The Russian armies were now pressing heavily on the Balkans scene, and Rumania [*sic*] and Bulgaria were in their power. As the victory of the Grand Alliance became only a matter of time it was natural that Russian ambition should grow. Communism raised its head behind the thundering Russian battlefront. Russia was the Deliverer, and Communism the gospel she brought.[7]

I have started here, some while before Churchill arrived in Moscow, and have done so deliberately—books and articles examining the notorious Churchill-Stalin discussion on carving up Central and Eastern Europe usually commence when Churchill is already in the

Soviet capital, since that is a more dramatic place to start. But we do need to know something first—what was actually in Churchill's mind before he set out. We can then look at whether he was being disingenuous in his memoirs, because it is clear from the evidence that he did not have anything like the American sanction for his actions that the preceding quotation would suggest. Far from it—this was Churchill on a gallivant of his own making. Then we can see, with the help of David Reynolds's account of Churchill's history, exactly how truthful he was being with us.

Churchill did not go without Roosevelt's knowledge. He had already, back in August, told the president of his profound concern for Greece—first that Greece would not go Communist, which was a very real possibility, and second, being a romantic, that Greece would retain its monarchy (though on the latter issue he downplayed that with Roosevelt).[8] Ten thousand British troops could be sent to Athens as soon as the time was ripe. This, it seems, was something to which Roosevelt consented, albeit strongly against the wishes of his State Department, even giving Churchill permission to use American transport planes.[9]

So when Churchill decided on some personal diplomacy with Stalin, he made sure to cover himself in writing to Roosevelt, which he did on September 29.[10] Stalin had refused, not surprisingly, to come to a conference in the West, so the prime minister therefore decided he would go to Moscow. As he told the president:

> Our two great objects would be, first, to clinch his [i.e., Stalin's] coming in against Japan and, secondly, to try to effect a friendly settlement with Poland. There are other points too about Greece and Yugoslavia which we would also discuss. We should keep you informed of every point.

However, as is clear from this, "other points" about Greece and Yugoslavia do not give any indication of what Churchill was actually going to do—a straightforward old-fashioned balance-of-power carve-up of parts of Europe with Stalin. As Kimball comments, Roosevelt "chose to remain aloof" from the Moscow visit. He did, however, allow Harriman to be there as an observer.[11]

So we now come to the infamous fifteenth chapter of *Triumph and Tragedy*, which Churchill entitled "October in Moscow."

The first meeting was on October 9, in the Kremlin, with Churchill, Eden, Harriman, and Stalin, plus the interpreters.

As Churchill puts it:

The moment was apt for business, so I said, "Let us settle about our affairs in the Balkans. Your armies are in Rumania and Bulgaria. We have interests, missions, and agents there. Don't let us get at cross-purposes in small ways. So far as Britain and Russia are concerned, how would it do for you to have predominance in Rumania, for us to have ninety per cent of the say in Greece, and go fifty-fifty about Yugoslavia? While this was being translated I wrote out on a sheet of paper:

Rumania	
Russia	90%
The others	10%
Greece	
Great Britain (in accord with USA)	90%
Russia	10%
Yugoslavia	50%–50%
Hungary	50%–50%

Bulgaria

    Russia   75%

    The others   25%

I pushed this across to Stalin, who had by then heard the translation. There was a slight pause. Then he took his blue pencil and made a large tick upon it, and passed it back to us. It was settled in no more time than it takes to set down.[12]

The actual final drawing-up is in the archives of Churchill's private secretary, John Martin, and can be seen as one of the illustrations in Reynolds's book *In Command of History*.[13]

Not surprisingly, since what they did was entirely disgraceful, the participants, even clearly Stalin himself, wondered whether they should keep it. As Churchill recalls:

After this there was a long silence. The pencilled paper lay in the centre of the table. At length, I said, "Might it not be thought rather cynical if it seemed that we had disposed of these three issues, so fateful to millions of people, in such an offhand manner? Let us burn the paper." "No, you keep it," said Stalin.

This is an understatement! At the time of writing, the last head of state of World War II is still alive—King Michael of Romania, a cousin of the royal families of Britain, Greece, and Yugoslavia. He is now finally allowed back into his own country, and he is also, as we see elsewhere, the king who enabled the Soviets to seize his kingdom from the Nazis and local Iron Guard fascists almost without a conflict, a good deed for which he was expelled from his own country, to spend over fifty years as an exile in Switzerland. Yet here was Churchill, condemning Romanians—and Bulgarians—to decades of Soviet rule and oppression, and in the former case, to the psychopathic dictatorship of the Ceausescu family until 1989.

As David Reynolds puts it, Greece is what mattered to Churchill: "conceding Romania to Stalin was a paper sacrifice."[14] Churchill had told Eden that there was nothing in any case that the West could do for the poor Romanians, and with that one must agree—Stalin was by now much too far east for the West to be able to get even near the region, let alone try to gain some kind of predominance there.

This particular part of *Triumph and Tragedy*, which Reynolds correctly describes as one of the most dramatic in all of the six volumes, was composed in late 1950, when Churchill was still leader of the opposition party, but, since the general election earlier that year, now with an excellent chance of becoming prime minister soon (which he did indeed achieve the very next year). It is now clear that Churchill did not discuss the notorious "percentage agreement" even with his foreign secretary, Anthony Eden, let alone with Roosevelt, and as one biographer has written, Churchill "never used it again," although he would later refer to it as his "naughty document." The war cabinet, fully including the foreign secretary, and the Americans—furious at not being consulted—were all appalled at what Churchill and Stalin had done.

So why did he do it? Over this issue much ink has been spilled.

Churchill gives a self-defense in *Triumph and Tragedy*, including a memorandum to Roosevelt that he decided not to send formally to Stalin, and indeed to "let well alone" upon the matter.[15]

He wanted Britain and Russia to have a common Balkan policy to present to the United States. Furthermore:

These percentages which I have put down are no more than a method by which in our thoughts we can see how near we are together, and then decide upon the necessary steps to bring us into full agreement. As I said, they would be considered crude, and even callous, if they were exposed...all over the world. Therefore they could not be the basis of any public document, certainly not at the present time. They might however be a good guide for the conduct of our affairs. If we manage these affairs well we shall perhaps prevent several civil wars and much bloodshed and strife in the countries concerned...At this point, Mr. Stalin, I want to impress upon you the great desire there is in the heart of Britain for a long, stable friendship and co-operation between our two countries, and that with the United States, we shall be able to keep the world engine upon the rails.

As he told his cabinet colleagues, what he was doing was "not intended to be more than a guide, and of course in no way commits the United States," which was an understatement, "nor does it attempt to set up a rigid system of spheres of interest."

However, despite Churchill's caveats to his colleagues, several of whom, like Attlee, Morrison, and Bevin, were anti-Communist leaders of the Labour Party, this is, evidently, old-fashioned, 1815 Congress of Vienna, great-power diplomacy all over again, 129 years since the diplomats in Vienna sorted out the map of Europe after the Napoleonic Wars. Churchill was, though, nothing if not old-fashioned, so this in itself should not surprise us.

I would agree with the biographer who says that what "Churchill really wanted on 9 October was a free hand in Greece," or, as the same author puts it, "trading Romania for Greece."[16] This makes a lot of sense. Churchill was seriously worried about a Communist take-over in Greece, and with good cause—the country was plunged into civil war and there is little doubt that but for the presence of British troops the Communists might well have been successful. The only other thing next to British force that prevented their victory was Stalin's decision not to intervene on their behalf, and also to restrain Tito, the new ruler of neighboring Yugoslavia, and a Communist, from doing so himself.

One historian points out that Churchill does not mention much about either Yugoslavia or Italy.[17] Yugoslavia was, I would argue, by way of being a success. In 1948, Tito effectively took his country out of the Soviet bloc, and although it was to remain a Communist country, with the tragic results of which we are all aware when it broke in violent pieces after Tito's death, it was thereafter always a genuinely nonaligned country. As one Yugoslav put it to me in the 1980s, Yugoslavia was a cage, like the Iron Curtain countries nearby, "but it is a *big* cage."[18] Stalin did not invade in 1948 to crush Tito's rebellion, very unlike the actions of his successors with Hungary in 1956 and Czechoslovakia in 1968. So one could say that Stalin respected the fifty-fifty split—Yugoslavia was a Communist state (Stalin's 50 percent), but unaligned and friendly to the West (Churchill's 50 percent). And as David Reynolds points out, Churchill went into 1945 having to trust Stalin "because the alternatives seemed much worse."[19]

Needless to say, the Americans were not at all pleased at Churchill's freelance actions, something that does not emerge in his own war memoirs. In fact later Soviet historians even disagreed that such a deal ever took place—albeit waiting until 1958 to do so.[20] Nor, historians now feel, does Churchill's account in his memoirs tally with what actually happened in Moscow those evenings in October 1944. Things other than the Balkans were discussed, for instance, notably the thorny issue of the Montreux Convention of 1936, which forbade the Soviet Union to send warships through the Bosporus and the Dardanelles without prior Turkish permission.[21] Furthermore, Churchill may not, according to the official records, have been quite as insistent as his memoirs suggest—and as he told his colleagues—that the deal with Stalin was intended to be entirely temporary and not permanently set in stone. Not only that, but it is clear that, unlike the impression given in *Triumph and Tragedy*, Italy was spoken of, and Stalin was well aware of the large Communist Party in that country.

It is also clear that the poor Hungarians lost out badly. Churchill in his account shows that he intended Hungary to be a fifty-fifty equal-shares country—and within a day of that agreement, Molotov, the Soviet foreign minister, was able to insist to Eden that Hungary be 75 percent in favor of the USSR, the same as Bulgaria.[22] (Eden was, it seems, able to stop him from demanding a similar percentage in Yugoslavia—just as well for Tito four years later.)

In any case, one can add two things.

Firstly, it is surely true to say that before Churchill and Eden even arrived in Moscow, "the British bargaining position in the Balkans had crumbled."[23] This was of course simple military reality—the Soviets were invading the region, their armies were successful, and, as Molotov reminded Eden, it was Soviet blood being spilled in the Balkans not British. Within days, in fact, Bulgaria signed an armistice with the victorious and conquering Red Army, on October 28, and any attempt by the British to gain 25 percent of control of that nation now vanished into the mist.

This goes on to the second point: what on earth is 25 percent of control of a country anyway? As one American wag put it in relation to all this, can someone be only 25 percent pregnant?[24] Fifty-fifty makes sense as Tito discovered—and one could argue much the same applied in reverse with Finland, which was a Western democratic country after 1945, but obliged to be both neutral and to have a policy that did not clash in any way with that of its Soviet neighbor. But 75/25 or 90/10: surely such percentages do not make sense when applied to national governments in the real world.

Historians debate over the *meaning* of all this[25]—I think I would also want to discuss the results, especially in the light of the thesis of this book that the only reason why Soviet troops now occupied much (and soon most) of Central and Eastern Europe by October 1944 was the fateful decision, in which Churchill was instrumental, of delaying the second front by a year. (Needless to say, the academic discussions of the percentages agreement ignore that as a factor.)

So is it right to say that the agreement "merely formalized an already existing situation, except that the original percentages, in so far as they had meaning, understated actual Soviet predominance"?[26]

If this was the case, surely, I would argue, the Americans were right to ask what on earth Churchill actually thought he was doing in formalizing the Soviet conquests with Stalin, except, as David Reynolds is right to argue, Churchill was trying to save Greece, or, perhaps, to be nice to Stalin because of what was then regarded as the urgent need to get the USSR on our side for the invasion of Japan.

(In this book I concentrate on my area of expertise, which is European/Middle Eastern rather than East Asian history. We have to remember, as we will see elsewhere, that the leaders of the Grand Alliance made decisions on *what they knew at that time*. A visit to the Truman Presidential Library in Independence, Missouri, will reveal how very complex was the decision to drop the atomic bombs on Japan, and it is also fair to say that many of the top military and naval commanders were highly dubious, *before* Hiroshima and Nagasaki, what actual effect the two bombs would have. Most planned for a full-scale invasion of Japan in which the casualties, including American, would have been gigantic, and so seen from the perspective of 1944, wanting Stalin to help with the invasion made a great deal of sense. The results, one could argue, were tragic—not only for the Japanese, although they were at least spared Soviet occupation, but also for the wretched Central and Eastern European countries handed to Stalin in order to get his support for an invasion thousands of miles away in Asia.)[27]

As Averell Harriman, who was there with Churchill's permission, put it: "I don't understand now, and I do not believe I understood at the time...just what Churchill thought he was accomplishing by these percentages."[28] Nor, it seems, did Charles Bohlen, who was head of the State Department's Eastern Europe Department.

It is just as well that Churchill did not consult Cordell Hull, the secretary of state himself, since Hull, writing his memoirs four years later, made it clear that he was "flatly opposed to any division of Europe into spheres of influence," which, one could argue, was exactly what Churchill was doing despite his protestations to the contrary that we saw earlier, and which he had also told Roosevelt he had no intention of doing back in May, when the issue had first arisen:

> There have recently been disquieting signs of a possible divergence of policy between us and the Russians in regard to the Balkan countries and in particular towards Greece...We therefore suggested to the Soviet Ambassador...that the Soviet Government would take the lead in Roumanian affairs, while we would take the lead in Greek affairs.[29]

But as we have seen, the actual discussions in October covered far more than just Greece and Romania; they included Turkey and the straits, and events within Italy.

Furthermore, as well as Hull, Admiral Leahy, Roosevelt's personal Chief of Staff, was also adamantly opposed to Congress of Vienna–style carve-ups into old-fashioned spheres of influence,[30] and it was only Churchill using the specter of Greece going Communist to the president in June[31] that enabled Roosevelt to back off. By this time Roosevelt was also contemplating reelection for what, in the light of subsequent change to the US Constitution, was to be a unique fourth presidential term.

Consequently, Churchill was able to get away with it—for the time being. As Roosevelt told Harriman, his "active interest in the Balkans is that such steps as are practical should be taken to ensure against the Balkans getting us into a future international war."[32] The great nineteenth-century German leader Prince Otto von Bismarck once proclaimed that a territory was not worth the bones of a Pomeranian Grenadier, and, in effect, one could argue, Roosevelt was saying that Central and Eastern Europe were not worth the lives of an American Marine.

And as George Kennan wrote to Charles Bohlen in early 1945, to take us full circle, the United States itself was doing nothing to prevent things from happening. He told his State Department colleague:

> Although it was evident that the realities of the after-war were being shaped while the war was in progress we have consistently refused to make clear what our interests and our wishes were, in eastern and central Europe. We have refused to name any limit for Russian expansion and Russian responsibilities...we have refused to face political issues and forced others to face them without us.[33]

So while Roosevelt dithered, Churchill at least did something, even if one is obliged to regard it as distinctly morally reprehensible. We will see the result of Roosevelt's well-meaning dithering in the next chapter, not least his decision to let Stalin know that the United

States might only keep American forces in Europe for two years at most, something that in the long run might well have done as much damage to the poor Central and Eastern Europeans as Churchill's infamous percentage deal.

To conclude our theme here, therefore, we need to ask:

a. Could it have been otherwise?
b. Did good come out of bad?

The answer of this whole book to (a) is naturally "yes": the only reason why we had to give so much to Stalin was that, as Churchill fully understood, the Red Army was in control of all these areas, and, as John Grigg once put it, to Stalin possession was nine-tenths of the law.[34] Had D-day been a year earlier it goes without saying—or should do so, I would attest—that John Grigg is entirely right to say that the Western Allies and the Red Army would have met on the Vistula and not on the Elbe.

But, reprehensible though I would want to say that Churchill's percentages agreement surely was, one could make a case in (b) for saying that good came out of bad.

First, as countless historians have argued, Stalin kept his word over both Greece and Yugoslavia, which is surely a very Good Thing, as a spoof British history book once put it in another context.[35] Yugoslavia remained neutral, which was probably just as well during the Cold War, as this denied the Soviet bloc a warm-water port on the Adriatic. Greece may have had its ups and downs, especially the period of quasi-fascist military rule under "the Colonels" in 1967–74, but it has never been under Communist tyranny and is a pluralist democracy in both the EU and NATO.

Not only that, but for example, Stalin was also not able to get his way over opening the Bosporus and Dardanelles to Soviet warships, which would have allowed the Russian fleet egress from the Black Sea into the Mediterranean. Stalin tried hard for this in 1936 and in 1939–41 and failed both times. He failed again with Churchill in 1944 and all attempts thereafter.

Finally Italy, which we now know he discussed with Churchill even though the latter omitted this from *Triumph and Tragedy*, also never went Communist. Whatever one thinks of the sadly unstable nature of postwar Italian politics, with a dizzying propensity to change government, and despite for a long time having one of the biggest and most intellectually influential Communist parties in Europe, Italy did stay free of Soviet clutches. If Italy *had* gone Communist, as might have been the case, the effects throughout Europe would have been potentially devastating, especially during the Cold War.

And thinking of the Cold War, one of the major problems in discussing all this is the fact that we now know[36] that there was a Cold War at all, for at least forty years, depending on when one begins and ends that historic time period. In 1944 Churchill was entirely ignorant of future events, and for this we cannot blame him—how many *genuinely* predicted the fall of the Berlin Wall in 1989 and did so *before* that epochal event took place? Hindsight is wonderful, but Churchill was not superhuman, and nor for that matter are the rest of us.

Should he have made such an agreement with Stalin? I would say not. Did it actually matter in the long run, given the overwhelming success of the Red Army in the field? I would say not, since Stalin failed to get his way on many things, something we forget because he *did* win on so many others.

Let us now look at the way in which Churchill tried to use his love of Mediterranean strategy as a way of getting to Central Europe first, ahead of the Red Army, and why the Americans opposed such a move not on *political* grounds, but on the purely *military*.

The Ljubljana Gap, to use the current name of the capital of Slovenia, or Laibach, to use its old Hapsburg nomenclature, is a way through the mountains and into the plains of Central Europe. In the war, whether or not to advance Allied troops, from Italy, through the Gap and into what was then the Third Reich itself (now Austria, and beyond that country to Hungary), became one of the biggest controversies of the war.[37]

The reason is simple—and the retrospective historical debate on whether or not this was the best thing to do has been waged by writers from Chester Wilmot, whose famous book *The Struggle for Europe* we have encountered before, and onwards.

In essence, the Wilmot view (a thesis also held, one can argue, by Churchill himself) is that if the Allied forces, under Field Marshal Alexander and General Mark Clark, had been able to keep all the divisions they had in Italy in mid 1944, they could have blasted through the German Gothic Line in northern Italy, passed through the infamous Ljubljana Gap, and then gone on to Vienna and perhaps even Budapest.[38]

(The military operation, had it actually taken place, was provisionally called Armpit! It is hard to presume that so strange a name would actually have survived had the attack on Istria and the eastern Adriatic gone ahead. Anvil, the campaign to support Overlord from southern France, became Dragoon once it became operational, and one hopes for those who would have taken part in it that the final name of the Ljubljana Gap invasion would similarly have altered. Field Marshal Alexander later on came up with another putative campaign in the area, code-named Gelignite, and this too was stillborn. I will use the more euphonious term Ljubljana Gap, or simply Gap, in this chapter.)

The advantage to the Allied cause was supposed to be twofold. First, it would have meant the actual territory of the Third Reich itself being attacked in 1944 from three directions—from the Soviets in the east, the Western Allies in the west, and, had the Gap been breached, by the *Western* Allies in the south.

Here I have italicized the word *Western* deliberately. For the essential argument about the so-called Ljubljana Gap strategy is that it was essentially a *political* issue rather than a purely *military* one; and where Wilmot and his successors have been so accusatory is that in the American high command's purely military/strategic/tactical decision to insist on sending key Allied divisions in Italy to support Overlord by way of a parallel invasion of France, through the south (Anvil), while also having denuded Alexander and Clark of many of their soldiers, preventing an Allied push through the Ljubljana Gap into central Italy, the Americans, in effect, allowed Stalin, not the West, to seize physical, and thence subsequent political, control of Central Europe.[39]

As one historian has noted, "there is no consensus on whether Anvil was 'the biggest strategic blunder of the war'.... the unanswered question remains: could British policy generally have done any better to prevent one brutal hegemon from replacing another. Churchill lamented in 1944 that 'Stalin will get what he wants'. Was there no alternative?"[40]

So the issue at hand is simple: was Churchill right to argue for what was basically a politico-military campaign, one with both political and military objectives, or were the American leaders, in this case both the civilian political leadership along with the military professional command, right to say that the *key* thing was to defeat Germany and then work things out afterward?

This is how the argument is normally presented. But in this

book, we have taken things a step further, by suggesting that *even if Churchill rather than Roosevelt/Marshall/Eisenhower was right in 1944,* Churchill's actions in postponing Overlord by that crucial year in fact meant that he had so circumscribed the Western Allies that Marshall, Eisenhower, and Roosevelt were right to argue for action that supported the troops in Normandy rather than engage in adventures in the Balkans and eastern Adriatic.

In other words, Churchill, while unquestionably right in the political case that he was making—don't let Stalin walk all over Eastern and Central Europe—had, in delaying the second front from April 1943 to June 1944, made his strategic goals *militarily* impossible. This is why, for example, American historian Thomas M. Barker is convincing when he says that had the Allies opted for the Ljubljana Gap strategy over and against Anvil (or Dragoon, as it became after August 1944), it "would have prolonged the war by several months."[41] And here the historian is supported by no less an authority than Eisenhower's right-hand man, General Beddell Smith, who told Marshall's biographer Forrest Pogue that had the invasion of the Gap taken place, it "would certainly have prolonged the war a year longer."[42]

In fact, if Barker's guess is correct, it might even have had an adverse effect on the Battle of the Bulge, since the troops that ended up in Dragoon were used to take the pressure off the main Western invasion force, and had they been attempting to breach the Gap, they would not have been in France when they were needed. Far from stopping the Russian juggernaut conquering all in Central Europe, a decision to opt for the Gap over Anvil/Dragoon might, Barker surmises, have ended up with Soviet troops on the River Rhine, a fate too horrific to contemplate as a better alternative to what actually happened.[43]

We must also make the point that while Churchill was, by 1944, surely morally and politically correct to think about the geostrategic map of Europe postvictory, he had, in reality, left it far too late—one could say that he was hoist with his own petard, since in the earlier stages of the war his thoughts had been concentrated solely on survival and what happened thereafter was a matter of complete irrelevance. While the very integrity of Britain was at stake, in 1940 and 1941, this is wholly understandable.

But the fact that it was clearly not an issue to Churchill even after America joined in the war after Pearl Harbor shows that this "victory at all costs" mentality had now, alas, continued unchanged, as John Charmley is right to argue in his article (which we saw when we examined the vexed issue of Churchill and de Gaulle). The time when Churchill could have made all the difference was now gone—with the United States overwhelmingly the military power on the Western Front (let alone in the war against Japan in the Pacific), no US president was going to be told what to do by a British prime minister, and especially, as Roosevelt was more than aware, in a presidential election year.

So how did the issue unfold?

If one considers the issue from the United States viewpoint, a different picture emerges. This was more than apparent to Eisenhower, who was clearly beginning to tear out whatever little hair he had left as he was obliged to listen to Churchill's pleas for a major dispersion of forces *after* Overlord had begun—something which, as we have seen, goes against every grain of American strategy and military doctrine on how to win a war: hit your *main* enemy and hit him where it is going to hurt most, which to Eisenhower, Marshall, and, one might add, anyone with clear strategic sense, meant in northwestern Europe, where the Allies had *already* landed.

As an exasperated Eisenhower wrote to Marshall on June 23, 1944 (and one could hardly put it better): "OVERLORD is the decisive campaign of 1944. A stalemate in the OVERLORD area would be recognized by the world as a defeat, and the result on Russia might be far reaching."[44]

Anvil, Eisenhower argued, was the direct route to northern France, where, from the viewpoint of the Western Allies, the key battles were to be fought.

Furthermore, as Eisenhower stated cogently to his superior in Washington:

Our forces in Italy do not directly threaten any area vital to the enemy who, therefore, has the initiative in deciding whether or not to withdraw out of Italy…An advance on Ljubljana and Trieste would probably contain a considerable amount of German strength, but there would be no guarantee that it would divert any appreciable number of German divisions from France. Neither would it give us an additional port which could be used in the deployment of divisions from the US [a key argument in favor of Anvil, according to Marshall], and this we believe to be one of the most important considerations. It is believed that it would have very little positive effect until 1945…France is the decisive theater. This decision was taken long ago by the Combined Chiefs of Staff. In my view the resources of Great Britain and the US will not permit us to maintain two major theaters in the European war, each with decisive missions.[45]

The next day, Marshall replied to his harassed colleague:

The proposal made by General Wilson for commitment of forces in northeastern Italy and the Balkans is unacceptable…Concentration of maximum forces in the decisive theater of France is the essential requirement.[46]

This should have been enough! But Churchill continued to ply his case, and at a time when Eisenhower was doing his best, despite the prime minister's diversions, on actually winning the war in Normandy. A deeply frustrated Eisenhower therefore wrote back to Marshall:

> It is my belief that the Prime Minister and his Chiefs of Staff are honestly convinced that greater results in support of OVERLORD would be achieved by a drive toward Trieste rather than to mount ANVIL.[47]

(As we shall see, this was not in fact the case—Brooke was simply being loyal to his political master, Churchill, since he supported the prime minister's overall Mediterranean policy but not Balkan intervention.)

Eisenhower continued:

> They are aware, of course, of the definitive purpose of the United States Chiefs of Staff to mount ANVIL, and I have been even more emphatic in my support of this operation than have your telegrams on the subject. I have further the impression that although the British Chiefs of Staff may make one more effort to convince you of the value of the Trieste move [which was a necessary precursor to Armpit], they will not permit any impasse to arise, and will, consequently, agree to ANVIL...All the above is tinged with conjecture but does represent the impressions gained by me and by General Smith in separate conversations with the Prime Minister.[48]

Now Roosevelt made the decisive intervention—he was not going to have the main thrust of the Allied war against Germany diverted by Balkans sideshows, especially not, as is clear from his message to Churchill, in a presidential election year.

As he now wrote to the prime minister:

> At Teheran we agreed upon a plan. That plan has done well up till now. Nothing has occurred to require a change. History would never forgive us if precious lives and time are lost as the result of indecision and debate. My dear friend, I beg you to let us continue my plan.
>
> Finally, in addition to the military, there are political conditions here which must be considered. I would never survive even a minor set-back in Normandy if it were known that substantial troops were diverted to the Balkans.[49]

So that, as they say, was that.... As Eisenhower wrote to Marshall on July 1st:

> I have been informally advised that the Prime Minister will probably telegraph the President today agreeing to ANVIL. This information has not been verified and is extremely confidential... What we need is speed in order to get a port through which the maximum number of American divisions can come to France.[50]

Eisenhower could now get on with the job of defeating Hitler's armies in northwestern Europe.

However, in historical terms, the argument had only just begun, as the many who have read Churchill's *History of the Second World War* and Wilmot's *The Struggle for Europe* and the comparatively few who have perused the Clark and Alexander memoirs will know.

The purely military argument against Armpit and Gelignite was surely overwhelming, and this becomes especially clear if one examines the Marshall archives at the Virginia Military Institute's George C. Marshall Foundation.

Pogue's interview with Brooke (by then Field Marshal Viscount Alanbrooke) is interesting.[51] Brooke, like Churchill, was a keen supporter of the indirect approach, the Mediterranean strategy. But he did not see the Balkan idea in the same light at all. When Pogue asked him if he held "with this so-called Balkan strategy...to push to the east as a means of forestalling the Russians," Brooke's reply was simple: "No, very definitely not. Winston was toying with it. Of course, Alex [Alexander], being his front and having to go down and do what he could there..."

As for what one presumes is the Wilmot thesis point about Anvil/Dragoon preventing moves to stop the Soviet onslaught, Brooke told Pogue:

> No, it was not, and I never presented that argument to Marshall at all. I never supported Winston or Alex in that maneuver, because it didn't seem sensible. But what I did support was the retention of forces to carry on in Italy and maintain pressure in holding German forces and not withdrawing them from there, giving them the opportunity of withdrawing their forces to meet us in Normandy.... There is no doubt that Winston had a Balkan liking...and he used to make matters rather difficult for me with Marshall with statements he would make, which Marshall would often think were inspired by me and they were not...at all...And I couldn't go to him [Marshall] and say I don't agree with a word my Prime Minister is saying.

So not even Churchill's principal military adviser during the war went as far as supporting his political master in what the Americans regarded as dubious adventures in the Balkans.

Nor, it now emerges, did the other very senior British commander in the field, General (later Field Marshal) Sir Henry Wilson.

Wilson originally agreed with the plan—only to change his mind. This has been interpreted, slightly unfairly perhaps, as Wilson wanting to have his own way over Alexander.[52] But whatever the case, by the time he was interviewed by Forrest Pogue, his views on the technical, logistical, and military folly of an invasion through the Gap were very clear.[53]

"Marshall," Wilson began, "in his masterly way, argued the US case." He continued:

> I must say, after he had finished, he convinced me that the US case vs. our case wouldn't stand up...It really was a question of once Marshall told me that—I knew that strategically that was the only way. We had to clear our sails and get those ports [i.e., the ports in southern France, at which Anvil/Dragoon was aimed] going. Alexander was visibly disappointed because he said that it was knocking the stuffing out of his offensive. None of us liked the offensive against Italy really, against those mountains.

Here one of course needs to ask: in view of the slowness of the Allied approach *after* Dragoon and the seven divisions had left Italy for France, how much of a difference would they have made had they stayed, as Alexander (and, one can add, Churchill as well) would have preferred? They *might* have made all the difference, but then, as Wilson infers here, it could have been an equally hard slog in terrible terrain, geographical obstacles that were, as all the American planners knew, nothing compared to what needed to be overcome should the eastern Adriatic be invaded.

Wilson continued:

> [T]here was no doubt that the US had Balkan phobia and they
> always looked on it as more political than military ... The only fel-
> low in America I knew who was keen on blowing up the Balkans
> was Wild Bill Donovan [the founder of the OSS]...a weakness
> really in our going over the Adriatic was a logistic one, and what it
> comes to is if we had a pushover we would do jolly well, but if we
> got stuck in heavy battle, the question of the supply and mainte-
> nance would have become very difficult...[especially] if you went
> beyond the Ljubljana gap.[54]

I think Wilson is right—conquering the northern part of Italy
and trying to land Allied forces in some of the most inhospitable parts
of Europe was never really going to be a starter. The *military* logic
against it was surely correct.

However, if we think again of our own thesis, the main thing is
that all this postwar argument utterly misses the point—a theme to
which we will return in the next chapter. *If D-day had been in 1943
there would have been no need to attack or try to liberate Central Europe
through terrain as unsuitable as the Ljubljana Gap.* For as we shall see,
Patton very nearly made it, in reality, to Prague in 1945 and similarly the *Western* Allies were over a hundred miles *within the Soviet-
allocated zone* of Germany by VE Day, and this with D-day being in
June 1944. Had it been in April 1943, as it should have been under
Marshall's plan, who knows how many hundred miles *farther east* the
British and American armies would have been? Not only that, but in
1955 the Soviets freely withdrew from Austria, so capturing Vienna
ahead of them would have made no difference to what actually took
place.

Churchill's Ljubljana Gap strategy would almost certainly have been doomed to failure and cost thousands of lives needlessly. But it was his decision in 1942 to postpone or reject an early D-day that made the *true* difference. By the time he was arguing for what the Americans felt were Balkan adventures, the fate of Central and Eastern Europe had long since been decided.

How Things *Might* Have Been
Very Different

U NTIL NOW WE have looked, from primary and secondary sources, at what happened under Churchill's leadership in the Second World War, and how the decisions he made cause one to call him by the subtitle of this book: a *flawed genius*.

It should be clear that in calling Churchill the greatest Briton of the twentieth century—and, many believe, of all time—we are stating an obvious truth. There can surely be no question that he saved Britain in 1940 from the most horrific of fates, and that had the United Kingdom surrendered to the Third Reich in 1940, not only would that country have been conquered but Nazi Germany would have been able to consolidate its power over continental Europe and might possibly have been able even to defy the normal laws of military history and actually conquer Russia itself. It would have been virtually impossible for the United States to do what actually happened in 1941–45, and use Britain for all intents and purposes as an aircraft base from which to launch the liberation at least of the western and southern parts of Europe.

One could say that in that sense Churchill's main and greatest achievement was (a) to realize that without the United States there was no hope and (b) in that light to keep fighting in 1940–41 until the folly of Germany and Japan propelled the United States into actual war.

But it is also a theme of this book, and others quoted earlier, that had the United States been allowed its way in early 1942, and launched D-day on the original target date of April 1, *1943*, the war would have been shorter and ended very differently indeed from the way it did in real life, in Europe, in May 1945.

Counterfactuals, as what I am going to attempt here, are always difficult to prove. But since Churchill himself contributed to such history, I think there is good precedent, and, in any case, historians as eminent as Niall Fergusson of Oxford and Harvard (via Cambridge and New York) have, one could argue, made it respectable.[1]

The books edited by Robert Cowley on alternative endings have contributors as deeply scholarly as David McCullough and Sir John Keegan. All of them are careful not to take their imaginary scenarios *too* far from what happened, and I think that this is surely wise. So what follows is in the spirit too of John Grigg's famous *1943: The Victory That Never Was* and retired curator and Soviet history specialist Walter Scott Dunn Jr. in *Second Front Now, 1943*.

Could the Grand Alliance have won in 1943? Grigg and Dunn certainly think so and it is certainly a real possibility, given the fact that in 1944 the Western Allies had to conquer a far better defended France, and a reequipped Wehrmacht, yet, despite all that, came very close to making the key breakthrough that would have ended the war that same year.

However, Ronald Lewin[2] and Paul Kennedy[3] have a strong point to make that the best Allied warplane, the Mustang, was not fully operational until some while into 1943. Here the discussion and hypothetical scenarios become interesting! Can one say that if, in 1942, for example, the decision had been made to go for 1943, the technological changes that did take place would have been speeded up? John Grigg is persuasive in saying that Churchill dreamed up another one of his strokes of technical genius—the Mulberry harbors—as early as 1917, and so it is *possible* that technical innovations such as the Mustang and other similar inventions might have come onstream earlier in a way that would have made 1943 not only possible but have given the Allies the air cover for the invasion that proved to be so critical in 1944.

It could be, therefore, that an early D-day might not have brought victory in the year of its launch, but, like the actual date, have provided victory within the year: it was eleven months from June 1944 to May 1945, and Allied victory might therefore have been realistically possible by some date in 1944.

Let us say then that the war ended early in 1944.

To begin with, over a *million* Jews who perished in the Holocaust in 1944–45 would have survived, and possibly higher than that, since precise statistics are hard to come by, and it is in fact possible that more than the normally accepted figure of six million Jews actually perished in the death camps or by being murdered directly in Russia and elsewhere. Far more Jews would thus have been rescued had the war finished a year earlier, and since the evacuations from nations such as Hungary, which still have not inconsiderable Jewish populations today, took place in 1944.

Afterward, as a result, there might still be large numbers of Jewish people in Central Europe today, since one must remember the principle of *population replacement*: if, for example, one million Jews survived, and they had gone on to produce the descendants who never in fact came into being, then there would be a good six to eight million *more* Jews alive today. These might be living in Israel, or perhaps in the United States, but quite possibly, as might have been the case with Hungary, they would never have left and would be living in Europe now, to the immeasurable benefit of their home countries. Since Churchill was strongly pro-Semitic, this outcome of his delay is especially tragic.

We should also remember that several times as many non-Jewish Soviet citizens were similarly butchered, with perhaps over two million prisoners of war being among them. Millions of *Soviet* citizens died during the war—perhaps upwards of twenty million or more, or well over three times the number of Jews who perished in the camps and elsewhere. Norman Davies is correct to point out that here one should use the word *Soviet* rather than *Russian*, since a look at the map of where the Nazis reached at their peak in 1942 does contain some Russian territory, but virtually all the territory of Belarus and the Ukraine. So I think it is safe to say that millions of Poles, Ukrainians, and Belarusians would have survived, and, once more, would have left millions of descendants who were, thanks to the prolongation of the war, never actually born.

This raises a moral question, which historians, for professional reasons, usually try to avoid.[4]

It is quite possible, for example, that if the Allies had taken longer to gain effective air cover over Western Europe—say several weeks or months *after* the new D-day of April 1943—Allied casualties might have been higher, albeit if the detailed statistics in Dunn's book are anything to go by, not nearly as great as defenders of 1944 would have us believe. But be that as it may, let us suppose that Western casualties *were* slightly higher after a 1943 D-day. Would the sacrifice have been worth it if millions of Jewish and Slav *civilians* had thus been spared, let alone the hundreds of thousands of German civilians who perished in the Allied bombing raids of 1944–45, or who were slaughtered by the Red Army in the invasion of the Reich from the east? Any death is of course horrible, whether military or civilian, but one of the greatest horrors of the Second World War was the fact that such a uniquely high proportion of the fifty-five million–plus who died during it were noncombatants, not soldiers fighting in the field.

It could be that this is a question for theologians and philosophers to answer rather than a military/historical biography of Winston Churchill. But it is surely worth pondering, since the high civilian death toll of World War II has alas created a precedent of similar carnage in wars that have happened since.[5]

This in fact brings us on to the origins of the Cold War, the issue that so vexed Chester Wilmot in the last section of *The Struggle for Europe* and his famous thesis that we threw away victory in 1944–45, in effect letting Stalin win the war.

Unlike Wilmot, we can now write in the happy knowledge that the Cold War is over, even though some attempt to make the awkwardness of the Kremlin some kind of resurrection of the older struggle.

But there is no question that the peoples of Central and Eastern Europe paid a huge cost, from, I would argue, 1944 to 1989, a forty-five-year span, for the way in which the Second World War ended.

Here an earlier invasion would have made an incalculable difference. One can also argue (as John Grigg does) that Wilmot is actually wrong, since he presumes the case for 1944, and thus fails to grasp the difference 1943 would have made in rescuing the peoples of Central and Eastern Europe from Communism.

The enormous changes would have been seen most in Poland and

Czechoslovakia, the latter being a beacon of democracy in a region of monarchical and quasi-military dictatorships.

As we saw from the narrative, the fact that the Allies waited until 1944 to invade the Continent meant that to rescue the Poles was a complete nonstarter, and thus the country on whose behalf the British went to war in 1939 was beyond hope so far as the West was concerned. The British (and, as we discovered, the Americans as well) were far from happy, but by 1945 there was nothing they could do.

With a 1943 invasion, meeting on the Vistula rather than the Elbe might have been a distinct possibility. With Poland this would have had a profound effect. The slaughter of the brave Polish patriots in July 1944, watched by a Red Army who probably hated them as much as the Nazis, would either never have happened at all (which is more likely), since the Allies would have liberated Warsaw with active Polish resistance help, or, at the very least, Stalin would have been unable to prevent the Allies from getting aid to the uprising, as he succeeded in doing with such devastating results in the real 1944. The cream of non-Communist Poland would thus have survived; the tens of thousands of Polish exiles who stayed in the West would have come home[6] and a solidly non-Communist government would have taken control, whatever Stalin might have preferred.

There would have been the problem of a Soviet occupation zone of Germany, and access to it, but this would have been solved in a markedly different way, since there would have been a much stronger and more independent Poland, perhaps with a Polish zone of occupation in Germany, an option their sacrifices during the war would surely have merited.

Likewise, the Czechs and Slovaks would have been liberated by the West, not by the Red Army.

(We saw earlier that Patton came within a whisker of being able to free Prague in 1945 in the real outcome—it was only earlier agreements that prevented him from doing so, and, needless to say, these actual deals would never have taken place in our scenario.)

The last paragraph being the real case in 1945, there is no question but that the West would have entered Czechoslovakia long before the Red Army with a 1943 D-day. In fact such an outcome—and its near reality—shows that the Marshall case was correct, since the Western armies would have begun their journey in Normandy, not, as Wilmot, Winston Churchill, Field Marshal Alexander, and General Mark Clark would all have preferred, through the highly inaccessible Ljubljana Gap. Adventures in the harsh terrain of the Balkans were not needed to have liberated the peoples of Central Europe before the Red Army.

The political outline of Central Europe would therefore have been considerably altered. For example too, the Western Allies would have reached Austria long before the Soviets, and while this ultimately did not matter—the Red Army left Vienna of its own free accord in 1955—Austria could and might have been like Japan, a former enemy area occupied not by four powers but by the West, with perhaps even Czechoslovakian and Yugoslavian occupation zones to take the place of the one actually taken by the USSR in 1945–55.

How different would Yugoslavia have been? Here the answer is not *directly* related to the 1943 issue, since although the reason why that nation went Communist had everything to do with Churchill, specifically it had to do with his decision to back Tito's Partisans rather than Mihailovic's Chetniks. An earlier invasion might have made no difference, but since Tito might have been further away from the Soviet bloc than was actually the case in 1945, he might possibly have broken away slightly earlier than he did.

In Hungary, a quasi-fascist dictatorship between the wars, it is hard to see what might have happened differently. Horthy was not much of an anti-Semite (though far from perfect) and the Jews of Budapest would not have needed the brave Swede Raoul Wallenberg to save them, since Allied troops would have done that instead. Hungary was also a country over which Churchill wanted fifty percent control, and with an Allied occupation instead of a Soviet, Hungary could well have been kept for the West, and been spared not just 1956 but forty-five years of alien rule.

How about the Cold War itself?

I think there is little doubt that Stalin was, with excellent cause, horrified by Munich and the appalling Western betrayal of Czechoslovakia to Hitler. We have also seen that the events of 1938 probably caused him to switch sides in the internal debate within the USSR, though, as complete dictator, anything he commanded would happen. But if he were open to both sides—and some historians, as we have discovered, think he did not *finally* decide until August 1939—Munich was surely the event that tipped the scales.

Here the fact that alternative history should be careful not to go too far comes into play. There is no question, from what we now know, that the Czechs would have put up a magnificent resistance to Hitler in 1938. But Neville Chamberlain's policy to the war might still have come into play had he been prime minister, and so it is possible that while France might *not* have fallen, that tragedy in 1940 not being entirely inevitable, it is also the case that not much might have actually changed 1938–40 *except* that Hitler would have had to prepare for a two-front war, which he managed in reality to avoid in August 1939.

In the past, as Norman Davies and others have pointed out, we used to ignore most of the war in Europe! Churchill himself was guilty of this—while he did acknowledge all the sacrifices made by the Soviets he can, if one looks at the proportions given to various parts of the war in his six volumes, be as unbalanced in ignoring the Eastern Front as those British and American film producers who ignore the fact that when the UK and United States fought in France they did so with Allies, and not alone!

Norman Davies's statistics, quoted elsewhere in this book, give the true dimensions of the war—Operation Bagration, for example, being not only massively larger than most battles fought in Western Europe or North Africa and Italy but also, in terms of the eventual Allied victory, far more important and critical.

I would therefore want to say, as I think Norman Davies does,[7] that it was the Eastern Front that, as the war truly turned out, was the pivot of the war. In this sense, therefore, Stalin's decision in August 1939 was of the utmost importance, since he thereby, in effect, not only allowed Hitler to carve up Poland with him just a few days later, but also freed the Wehrmacht to conquer western and southern Europe in 1940 in a way that could not otherwise have happened. In this sense, one could say that Stalin enabled the conquest of France, the Low Countries, and Scandinavia that latter year.

All this was, I would argue, the fault of Chamberlain at Munich as much as the chaos of the French military and political leadership in 1940. Had Churchill become or even been prime minister in 1938 none of this would have happened. But that is another counterfactual altogether, and, alas, beyond the scope of this book. What we are dealing with in our work is the way in which Churchill, after May 1940, dealt with the catastrophic hand Chamberlain's arrogance and incompetence had dealt him. This is also why this is a *postrevisionist* book, in that while clear Churchill was a man who made the most terrible blunders, he was actually fully in the right of the key issues of 1938–41.

However...all this is relevant to the key matter of how the Cold War would have begun very differently—if perhaps at all—had the decision to invade in 1943 been made as Marshall wanted and, as this work argues, should have been the case.

For what the events of 1938–41 did was to sow the seeds of a most profound mistrust (to reuse the phrase Chamberlain used in writing to his sisters about Russia) in the minds of Stalin over the West. What I am trying to say is that had the second front been launched *on April 1, 1943*, then the profound and dominating effect of the Molotov-Ribbentrop Pact of 1939 would have been negated, and for several valid reasons.

First, the acute and justifiable suspicion held by the Soviets would not have happened. Stalin would understandably have preferred a second front in 1944, but a *two-year* delay surely made things far worse than one of less than a year—April 1943 would have been only nineteen months after Barbarossa began. Since a growing consensus seems to be that Second World War suspicions played a major role in the atmosphere that created the Cold War (if indeed that event has a post-1945 beginning) then anything that would have lessened Soviet feelings that the West was deliberately bleeding the Red Army to death would surely have been a good thing. Nothing could have prevented someone like Stalin being a *bit* paranoid, but reducing it by removing a major excuse would have been very helpful.

Second, one of the major moral problems the Allied leaders faced during the war might never have occurred if *Western* forces had got to the Vistula first. This was, as we saw, the insistence of Stalin on the *1940* borders, not the far more legitimate Central and Eastern European borders that existed before the betrayal of the Czechs in 1938–39. In asking Eden, the British foreign secretary, to consent to them, the USSR was asking the West to consent to the Soviet borders

during the time the Soviet Union was in league with the Third Reich.
In other words, Stalin wanted the West to recognize Russian aggression only made possible by the Molotov-Ribbentrop Pact with Nazi Germany. Since the West's aim was to defeat Nazism, this was thus a doubly immoral thing to do. It is why Norman Davies, just to take one example, is so correct in saying that the Second World War was only a "good war" from the perspective of the West—from the viewpoint of Central and Eastern Europe, for people such as the Czechs and Poles, it was simply the substitution of one oppressive tyranny for another, and effectively Western consent to decades of tyranny from the Baltic states down to the Balkans. To be fair, Churchill and Eden were not at all happy about this, but felt that the need to have the Soviet Union onside to defeat Hitler overrode all other considerations, as shown by the former's famous remarks on Yugoslavia and Tito defeating more Germans to Fitzroy Maclean.

America, *in theory at least*, did not go along with such blatant appeasement, nominally refusing to recognize the 1940 seizure of the three Baltic states, for example. As we saw, many in the State Department were well aware of what Stalin was capable.

But be that as it may, the unfortunate truth remains that by 1945, in the real world, all the huffing and puffing and moral indignation possible would have done very little indeed to alter the facts on the ground—the Red Army had lost millions of men winning these territories from the Nazis, and it was their boots on the ground in these places, not those of the West. Only with Prague could an actual difference have been made that might have worked had Patton been granted his request.

(With Vienna, since as we have just seen, the Soviets did withdraw voluntarily from there in 1955, an early Western capture of that city would have not changed anything much in the Cold War, except that Austria *might* have been able to join NATO and the EU earlier, to their and everyone's benefit.)

But *the borders of Cold War Europe would have been drastically different if the two sides had met on the Vistula in 1944 instead of on the Elbe in 1945.*

This I think is the real difference that an earlier D-day would have made to the map of Cold War Europe. Austria, as above, would have been in from the start. Hungary, Poland, and Czechoslovakia would similarly have been, as Dean Acheson's memoirs described the origins of NATO, *present at the creation.*

The Allies would never have been able to reach Baltic countries such as Estonia, Latvia, and Lithuania, and it is possible that Romania and Bulgaria would have still suffered their eventual fates. Hungary, as an ally of the Reich against the USSR, would still have had to return Transylvania to Romania, and the parts of Slovakia annexed in 1939, and some other border changes would have gone ahead.

But NATO's borders would have been considerably farther west and, in Cold War terms, that would have given a significant military edge to the Grand Alliance. It would, for example, have had a direct border with the USSR from the beginning, and the psychological impact of that, let alone anything else, would have been enormous. Today Russia resents the fact of NATO's geographical proximity—had that been the case from day one that too would have been different.

Readers will also notice that this book always refers to Central and Eastern Europe as two distinct geographical entities, which historically they have always been—the old German phrase *Mitteleuropa,* or, literally, Middle Europe, expresses not just something geographic but a whole intellectual/historical stream of associations as well, especially since much of that area spent centuries linked to or ruled by the

Hapsburg dynasty based in Vienna and, under Emperor Rudolf II, in Prague.

Alas, though, during the Cold War, Western Europeans, and probably Americans, got into the habit of thinking of Western Europe (free, protected by the United States) and Eastern Europe (not free, and under Soviet yoke). This was, thankfully for the inhabitants, only a temporary and, as it has turned out, entirely Cold War phenomenon, as writers such as Norman Davies and Timothy Garton Ash have reminded us in their various books. Prague is literally and often mentally further west than Vienna, and with the fall of the Iron Curtain in 1989 and dissolution of the USSR in 1991, this idea of a separate *Central Europe* has, for all sorts of wonderful reasons, made a comeback, now that its peoples are once again free and part of the common European home once again.

So, one can say, had Western troops liberated such areas, that false division would not have occurred, and Mitteleuropa would not have died, especially as hundreds of thousands of Jews, who made the region so special a place, might well have survived a much-shortened Holocaust.

However, all this presumes there would still have been a Cold War....

Since we are dealing with counterfactuals here, this question is a hard one to answer, especially since we spurned the notion, for instance, of Churchill giving independence to India in 1940, or supporting de Gaulle against Roosevelt, two things he should have done but which would have been altogether out of character.

Similarly, as John Lewis Gaddis has showed us so conclusively in *Now We Know: Rethinking Cold War History*, written, most significantly, both after the Cold War was over and also in the brief time in which Soviet-era archives were open to Western historians, we should never forget that Stalin and the Soviets *really were Communists*.

This may sound ridiculous to say, like the famous rhetorical joke line "Is the Pope a Catholic?"

But, during the Cold War, it was indeed often forgotten, especially by those who wanted to reduce all policy to *realism*, the notion that everything is competition between nation-states, and which thus altogether eliminated from calculation the powerful *ideological* nature of the USSR.

This is not to say that national borders counted for something with the Soviet leadership. Russia had been invaded by Napoleon, in the Crimean War, and in the First World War, and then in its new Bolshevik guise, again in 1941, the last being the most brutal of all due to Nazi racist ideology and practice. Naturally a country that had suffered on that scale wanted to have buffer states to protect it against what many thought at the time might still be a renascent Germany. It is only now—to paraphrase Gaddis again—that we know, decades after 1945, that the latter state not only never became a threat but is, in any circumstance that we can foresee, not going to be the nation it was from 1870 to 1945.

However, since Stalin and company genuinely were what they professed to be—devout followers of Karl Marx—we can also say that perhaps their *prime* motive was indeed the spread of global Communism, and if the foolishness and utter lack of political foresight of the West during the Second World War enabled them to spread Communism throughout Eastern and Central Europe, then so much the better for the one major Marxist state that then existed, the USSR!

So I think *some* kind of ideological confrontation would have taken place, even if the West had reached the Vistula. Soviet leaders would have, for valid historic reasons, still been paranoid. They would also have been as loyal to their beliefs as ever, and done all they could to have continued the spread of Marxism worldwide, as can only be expected.

But with major sacrifices on both fronts, and a second front launched in 1943, liberating far more of Central Europe, their moral superiority, as they saw it, and as some misguided local inhabitants also saw it, at least for a while, would have either vaporized or for certain been no greater than that of the West. The United States and its allies would have gained the credit for liberating Poland, Hungary, Czechoslovakia, and Austria, and the kudos that instead, in the real world, went to the USSR instead. As Timothy Garton Ash and John Lewis Gaddis remind us, the Soviet bloc collapsed because the internal moral legitimacy of Soviet rule imploded—and, as Gaddis shows, the humongous-scale rapes of German women by Red Army soldiers in 1944–45 meant that the German Democratic Republic never really had any moral legitimacy in the eyes of its unwilling subjects at all.

Central Europe, then, would have been solidly with the West, and all Churchill's actual nightmares, which he tragically had, in reality, far too late into the war, when the die in Eastern and Central Europe was firmly cast in Stalin's favor, would never have been realized. Churchill, the great defender of Czechoslovakia's freedom in 1938, would have been the hero there he should always have been, and would have had the undying gratitude of all the Poles, Czechs, and Slovaks in whose freedom from tyranny he so believed.

So while I think that some version of the Cold War would have happened, the West would have been in a much stronger geographical, moral, and strategic position, since the armies of Poland and Czechoslovakia, to take just two, would have been on the Western not Soviet side of the equation.

NATO came into being as the result of two things: the Communist coup in Prague in 1948 and the Berlin Airlift of 1948–49. One interesting question to ponder is: while there would still have been tension between the USSR and the democracies, would NATO have been necessary? There would have been no Prague coup and, quite possibly, with Poland in the Western camp, maybe no Berlin Airlift either. There might have been a Soviet bloc, but it would have been far smaller, and while the three Baltic states were fully incorporated into the USSR, the so-called satellite states, now reduced in number, might all have been able to follow the successful Yugoslavian path: Communist, but unaligned and certainly no puppet state of Moscow.

So would over four decades of Cold War and nuclear threat, under which anyone reading this except those under twenty would have lived a large part of their lives, have been removed for good? I think possibly not, since that is to deny the Soviet leadership the genuineness of their Marxist beliefs, which I do not think we can do. But the advantage would have been far more with the West (or, one might have said, West/Central), with far more constraints on Soviet behavior than proved to be the reality. It might also have been far shorter, ending in the 1970s, though that too is uncertain, since we do not know how much of a role individuals played in ending Soviet rule, such as Gorbachev with his attempts to reform the system from within. But things would certainly have been better than they actually were in the years 1949–89.

Churchill would still have been Churchill and Stalin a genuine Marxist—what else might have changed with an earlier end to the war?

One interesting thing to ponder is this—what effect would the saving of hundreds of thousands if not millions of Jewish lives have had? In Hungary, where many Jews survived until well into 1944, there is still a comparatively large Jewish population today, and to the astonishment of many people, the number of Jews in Germany is itself growing significantly. Sadly nothing can make up for the supreme horror and tragedy of the Holocaust in terms of numbers, so Europe will never again be so rich in culture, scientific discovery, thought, and more besides as it was when millions of Jews lived there.

But where would those who would now have survived the Holocaust have gone? If, for instance, Poland, Hungary, and Czechoslovakia had all been free democracies following the Allied victory of *1944* (or maybe 1943, if we are being really optimistic, in which case even more Jews would thankfully have been spared), *might those Jews have stayed on in Europe?* If so, what would that have done for the creation of Israel in 1948? Would they have wanted to go there, or stay in Warsaw, Kraków, Prague, Budapest, and other cosmopolitan places enriched over the centuries by their strong cultural presence? It is certainly something to ponder....

Likewise, what if they had after all decided to go to Israel? Since one million inhabitants today would have around five to six million present-day descendants, the state of Israel would, with this huge early influx, have double or even more the number of inhabitants that it actually does today.

Here I think we have to be careful not to let counterfactual speculation run away with us, whether the outcome would have been a twenty-first-century Central Europe with at least six million more Jewish citizens, or an Israel that would, with a far larger population, be economically and militarily far more powerful, and an overwhelmingly European-ancestor Jewish balance that might have caused its internal politics to be rather different as well.

Before we take our alternative history on yet further tracks, one can argue that had Churchill agreed *with clear understanding* to a second front in 1943, the world would have been a much better place. Of course other things could and would have happened—remember all those pre–September 11, 2001, predictions for the early years of the twenty-first century? (We must also recall those pre–fall 1989 prognostications in which pundits predicted that the USSR was sure to keep going....) But I think a note of cautious optimism would be in order, and the sad irony is that it would have been a world that Churchill, of all people, would have preferred to what really happened. That to me is one of the saddest things about the mistakes he made as the *flawed genius of World War II.*

ACKNOWLEDGMENTS

There is a new trend that an author's spouse be thanked at the beginning of the acknowledgments rather than the end. This is a move of which I approve thoroughly, since without my wife Paulette's support I would never get anything written at all, let alone a full-length book such as this. Paulette, a musicologist and music teacher *sans pareil* is my constant inspiration, muse, companion, encourager, best critic and many more things besides. My gratitude to her is more than profound, and she can never be thanked enough.

As I am breaking with tradition in thanking my wife early on, I will do the same with my two literary agents, without whom this book would not have gotten off the ground. Frank Weimann and Jaimee Garbacik are two of the very best, and I am more than fortunate in my link with Literary Group International in New York. The time from concept/synopsis to contract was the fastest ever in my twenty-five-years-plus as a writer, and at a time when contracts are, alas, harder to obtain, this was therefore an especial success.

Thanks therefore naturally go on to my kind and patient editor, Natalee Rosenstein, at Penguin. This book was unfortunately late in arrival, not simply because of the vast wealth of material on Churchill—of which more later—but also because of unforeseen circumstances such as family illness, a massively delayed house reconstruction, and other extraneous factors unrelated to the writing process itself. Thankfully for me, Natalee was kind and merciful to her author, and as I spent time back in the 1980s as an editor myself, I am all the more grateful since I know what a nuisance to the scheduling process that a delay can be. Her assistant, Michelle Vega, has also been a wonderful go-between and warm thanks also go to her.

Very warmest possible thanks go to the delightfully helpful and personally more than kind staff of the Churchill Archives Centre at Churchill College Cambridge. Allen Packwood and his team have been simply splendid beyond the call of duty, and my year delving into the Churchill Archives has been a sheer joy. Allen Packwood, the director, has been the embodiment of helpfulness and has found considerable time to help me not just in the archives themselves, but also abroad, and my links in the United States with the Churchill Memorial Library in Fulton, Missouri, and the Marshall Center at Virginia Military Institute, in Lexington, Virginia, are entirely thanks to him. He has put the Archives on the international map and given it the global status it has long deserved.

The archivists all live up to their reputation as highly knowledgeable and equally personable: the legendary Andrew Riley (famous on television and beyond as the expert on the Thatcher archives, which are also in Churchill), Natalie Adams, Katherine Thompson, and

Sophie Bridges, who is working on the Hailsham papers (those of Quintin Hogg, the winner of the famous 1938 Oxford by-election).

The assistants, the main interface with the general public, have been great in helping with arcane technical matters such as how to use a spool, as well as fetching interminable amounts of archive for me; these are: Sandra Marsh, Elizabeth Wells, and especially, Caroline Herbert, who manages a full-time job helping historians with being (along with her astronomer husband, Peter) one of Cambridge's most popular and highly-considered young church leaders.

The conservator, Sarah Lewery—the lady in the white coat—has done a wonderful job of keeping the archives in a state in which they can still be seen, ably helped by her assistant Bridget Warrington, and, last but not least, Julie Sanderson, the administrator, has done an excellent task of keeping absent-minded historians and archivists connected to the real world. In addition, many of the staff also eat at the College—the dining hall, in memory of Winston Churchill, is the biggest in Cambridge—and they have all been the very best of lunchtime companions. Claire Knight was there at the beginning of the research and she was especially helpful in getting me used to the complex machinery necessary to read the archives on film. The archives staff have become friends as well as colleagues, and I have been blessed in having such a delightful crew of people with whom to work during the research and writing of this book.

In addition, the Roskill Library is in itself a treasure trove, with books on Churchill and on the war all together in one place, whereas in a major university research library they would be spread over many floors and different rooms. The library also has American books not otherwise available in Britain, and all these factors combine together to make it a splendid resource for historians.

Acknowledgments

I must thank Dr. Christopher Tout, the astronomer, for introducing me to helioseismology and for my election as an Associate of the Senior Combination Room and for the many friends I have made there, including the delightful Canadian academic professor Jonathan Hart, Dr. Alice Reid, Dr. Paul Dicken and his partner, Dr. Katrina Gulliver, and many more besides.

I am also very grateful to the Master and Fellows of Churchill College for electing me as a By-Fellow of the College during the writing of this book. (Warm thanks here to my referees—Professor Christopher Andrew of Cambridge University, Dr. Philip Towle, the distinguished international relations specialist, Professor Peter Hennessy of London University, Professor AE Dick Howard of the University of Virginia, and several from the University of Richmond, thanked below.)

This meant that, apart from the delicious free meals I was able to eat, I was part of a dynamic and friendly academic community, and thus not the typical lonely academic working alone in the archives. In Churchill's case *fellowship* is a correct term not just as an academic nomenclature, but also in the wider sense of a body of people who get on with one another in common endeavour. Fortunately for me as a mere historian, the one science subject in which I can bluff my way— astronomy—is one of Churchill's greatest academic strengths (with Nobel Prize winners to prove it), so I was not as lost for conversation over meals as I had feared. The number of Fellows to thank would make too long a list, but they know who they are, and I am grateful to them. I am now an Associate of the Senior Combination Room, so this enjoyable link will continue in the years to come.

My happy links with two other Cambridge colleges continue. I remain a dining member of St. Edmund's College Cambridge, many of whose members I have thanked elsewhere. Here I would like to add one more name, that of Dr. George Wilkes, an internationally renowned expert on Just War theory, a delightful colleague and someone whose students laugh heartily at his jokes not out of the usual nervous politeness but because they really are that funny. More seriously, his seminars have been a model of how such academic discussions should be run and they have provided an intellectual feast for all of us involved.

I am also a Key Supervisor at Homerton College, and Steve Watts has just given me another most enjoyable year in that post, with students as excellent as ever. Through Homerton I have had the leisure of getting to know one of Britain's top Churchill scholars, Richard Toye, now a Senior Lecturer at the University of Exeter, who has been most helpful on all his visits to Cambridge.

I also teach for the Tulane/Wake Forest/Villanova accredited INSTEP course in Cambridge, England, with students from those three and several other universities enrolled each year. The class of 2007–2008 has been especially fun to teach and warmest possible thanks must go to the pupils who gave their professor such an excellent year but also to that legendary and internationally loved Cambridge couple, Geoffrey and Janice Williams, the organizers of the Cambridge INSTEP program, for making teaching such an enjoyable experience.

Five historians have been of especial help and encouragement, and here I must add the usual caveat that all views expressed in this book are my own—astute readers will spot where I agree and upon what I disagree with the distinguished quartet who follow. These are Professor Christopher Andrew of Cambridge, Professor Peter Hennessy of London, Professor Norman Davies at Oxford, Professor Richard Holmes of Cranfield, and finally Professor Paul Kennedy of Yale, who, very fortunately for me, was visiting and using the Churchill archives and Roskill Library during my writing of this book while working on one of his own, and who was able to give me much invaluable wisdom over many a cup of coffee in the SCR nearby at Churchill. I think I saw more of Paul during that time than of my actual supervisor when I was a postgraduate student at Cambridge more than years ago. All four have written books that have inspired me greatly over the decades (Peter and I have known each other for thirty years by now) and I can now add my gratitude to each and every one of them. Many thanks too for Norman Davies and Richard Holmes for seeing me at length and in person and Christopher Andrew for his fascinating weekly seminar in Cambridge.

Eagle eyes will notice how strongly I disagree with the distinguished British historian Professor John Charmley of the University of East Anglia. This is a profound difference of view, but it is also very much a disagreement among friends. John and I had the pleasure of being at Oxford together, both knowing the great historian of the 1930s, RAC Parker, and we were reunited when I completed my PhD at UEA under John's superb supervision, on Churchill's creation of Iraq in 1921 (which is also my book, *Winston's Folly* in the UK, *Churchill's Folly* in the United States). On most of the rest of Churchill's life, John and I are fully in accord, over 1938–1945 we must beg to differ. But John is one of the most delightful people one can meet, a superb encourager and a good friend. My deep-felt divergence on Neville Chamberlain and on Churchill in the period of this book should be seen in the context of what I write here.

Thanks too to Peter Martland and Hugh Bicheno of the seminar I attend in Cambridge.

This is, sadly, the last book that I shall have written partly in the office I have enjoyed for many years in the attic of the fifteenth century wing of my parents' house. My father and mother have owned

Sutton Hall, which ranges from Saxon in the gardens, through the fifteenth century on to some early Victorian architecture, for nearly half a century, or most of my lifetime. Alas the passing of time means that this wonderful place had to be sold, and a home that has seen literally dozens of books written in it over those decades—I am the third generation of a literary family—will be in their hands no more. So for this book, as for so many of mine, and dozens more, I thank them profusely for the fabulous support they have been to my writing in the past quarter century and more. This book comes with fond love and best wishes for their new life in their new home.

Much of the rest of this book has been written in two places. One of these—the Churchill Archives—I have thanked already. The other is that most author-friendly of settings, the History Department of the University of Richmond, in Richmond, Virginia. The president, Ed Ayers, is an historian and gives the campus an air of quiet distinction and inner contentment that makes it so splendid a place to work. Professors John Gordon (and his wife, Susan, and daughter, Sarah) and John Treadway (and his wife, Marina) have been all one could ever wish for in academic colleagues and being a Writer in Residence again in 2008 was especially enjoyable thanks to them.

The Boatwright Library at Richmond has once again proved an idyllic place in which to work, and the staff of its 8:15 café, Maya Vincelli and Kristin Hedgepeth, provided excellent coffee to keep me awake while writing. Every campus has its own National Treasures, people not often high up the hierarchy but who are known and loved by all ranks: Ethel Thomas of the dining hall and Douglass Young of the UR bookstore fulfill this role to the joy and delight of countless generations of student and staff alike. Once more I am most grateful to all the others at the bookstore, for making it such a happy place to browse, and for selling my many books over the years.

I am indebted as always to David Kitchen (and to his wife, Michelle, and daughter, Sarah) and Cheryl Genovese of the School of Continuing Studies; to Kritikka Osanit of International Education for obtaining my J1 visa another year, and to the stellar faculty at the Osher Institute, Jane Dowrick and Debra Guild, for giving me my biggest-ever summer class of thirty-three delightful and highly intelligent pensioners to whom to lecture on Churchill.

Special thanks for accommodation to my brother-in-law Sterling Moore and his family, and to the Midlothian County legend Betsy Weaver Brandt and her husband, Lamar.

The University Library in Cambridge has also proved how vital it is to live near to and be able to use a copyright library.

In Lexington, Virginia, where I worked in the George C. Marshall Archives of Virginia Military Institute I am most grateful for the excellent hospitality there of Reverend Mike Wilkins and his wife, Lucy, two contemporaries of my wife's at the University of Richmond, and, in Mike's case, pastor of the church at which my father-in-law, the late John S. Moore, was the minister for more than twenty-seven years. Paul Barron, the director, was most kind and welcoming, Peggy Dillard, the model of assistance in fetching the manuscripts, and Anne Wells, the current editor of the Marshall Papers, a treasure trove of helpful knowledge about what to look up and where. In addition, VMI is a scenic and delightful place in which to work, and everyone I met there was most kind to a visiting foreigner.

I am most grateful to Caroline Herbert and Allen Packwood of the Churchill Archives Centre for drawing my attention to the Clementine Churchill Picture Album and for doing so much to make their appearance in this book possible.

I am also thankful to my Wednesday support group—the legendary bookseller, prize judge, and internationally appreciated raconteur

Acknowledgments

Richard Reynolds, of Heffers in Cambridge, and his wife, Sally; Matthew and Sara Barling; Jane Hollis; Derek Wright; Juliet Cook; and Max and Julia Halbert. Richard's colleagues at Heffers (and its own Caffe Nero) have been as invaluable as ever, providing me with so many much needed books during the course of writing this one, and many thanks here go to Bruce Dixon for choosing such excellent volumes for the history section.

Notes

The following abbreviations are used in the notes:

CHAR: Chartwell Papers: Churchill Archives, Churchill College Cambridge

CHU: Churchill Papers: Churchill Archives, Churchill College Cambridge

D, M, C, T: Subsets of the above in some of the documents on microfiche

CIGS: Chief of the Imperial General Staff

Churchill SCR: Churchill College Senior Combination [sic] Room, Cambridge

COS: Chiefs of Staff

PREM: Prime Minister's Files, National Archives, Kew, London

CHAPTER ONE: STOPPING HITLER IN 1938

1   As will be evident to anyone who has read their works, I am very indebted to their research and the books that resulted, especially as I do not read Russian myself. These works include Carley's *1939*, a sadly neglected book that makes an outstanding case for how things could have been so very different.

2   Michael Jabara Carley, *1939: The Alliance That Never Was and the Coming of World War II* (Chicago: Ivan R. Dee, 1999), xiv.

3   My own research for another book about Churchill at that time led me to many letters between Churchill and Lloyd George on this subject, which the latter rejected on the basis that Britain was exhausted from war with Germany already. For a more detailed analysis see Clifford Kinvig's *Churchill's Crusade* (London: Hambledon and London, 2006). Kinvig argues that if Britain *had* intervened and nipped the Bolshevik Revolution in the bud, world history would have been very different. While that is true, the fact that by then the United States was becoming increasingly detached from global affairs means that chances of Western victory would have been sadly slight.

4   Carley, *1939*, 256–57.

5   Ibid., 257

6   I am very grateful to informal discussions with Professor Paul Kennedy of Yale University, Sir Basil Liddell Hart's former researcher, for fascinating chats on all these issues, as well as to the works of the Oxford and Yale historian Sir Michael Howard, which I have enjoyed reading for decades now. As always, I should say, though, that the conclusions reached in this chapter are my own, especially since Paul Kennedy, while rightly and zealously anti-appeasement in his writing, gives weight to factors that favor Britain waiting until 1939 to deal with Hitler.

7   The copy of this book in the Churchill Archives is the one given by the author to the great naval historian Captain Stephen Roskill, who felt, as his friend Telford Taylor notes on page 985, that the Munich settlement *did* buy time, a view that Churchill (and your author) rejected.

8   Telford Taylor, *Munich: The Price of Peace* (New York: Doubleday, 1979), 977–1004.

9   Ibid., quoted on p. 989.

10 Ibid., 992.

11 Ibid., 994.

12 Ibid., 995.

13 Conversation about the French army with Paul Kennedy, Cambridge, 2008.

14 Taylor, *Munich*, 211. Churchill's memoirs are devastating in their criticism of Baldwin, whereas Taylor argues, I think correctly, that it was *Chamberlain*, as the chancellor of the exchequer, who was primarily responsible for holding up British rearmament in the 1930s.

15 Correlli Barnett, *Britain and Her Army, 1509–1970* (London: Allen Lane, 1970), 423, in the copy Barnett gave to Stephen Roskill.

16 Ibid., 411 and 415; see also Churchill's cost-cutting mania in my book *Churchill's Folly* (New York: Carroll and Graf, 2004), passim.

17 John Charmley, *Churchill: The End of Glory* (London: Hodder and Stoughton, 1993), 258.

18 Ibid., 343–54.

19 All the speeches Churchill made at the time that are quoted here are from the *Collected Edition*, in several volumes, of his speeches, edited by Sir Rob-

ert Rhodes James, who was a distinguished historian himself and also, like Churchill, a Conservative member of Parliament. British and American editions can be different, so quoting page numbers might be misleading.

20 Charmley, *Churchill: The End of Glory*, 353–56.

21 See for example ibid., 396–98.

22 See for example: Robert Rhodes James, *Anthony Eden* (London: Weidenfeld and Nicolson, 1986); David Dutton, *Anthony Eden* (London: Allen Lane, 1981), and D. R. Thorpe, *Eden* (London: Chatto and Windus, 2003), all of which are excellent.

23 Quoted in the official biography by Keith Feiling: *The Life of Neville Chamberlain* (London: Macmillan, 1946), 416.

24 John Charmley, *Chamberlain and the Lost Peace* (London: Hodder and Stoughton, 1989).

25 Charmley, *Churchill: The End of Glory*, 367.

26 Feiling, *Chamberlain*, 322–25, especially 325.

27 T. K. Derry, *The Campaign in Norway* (London: HMSO, 1952); Captain Stephen Roskill, *The War at Sea* Volume 1 (London: HMSO, 1954), which is not at all praiseworthy of Churchill's brief tenure at the Admiralty.

28 Richard Holmes, *In the Footsteps of Churchill* (London: BBC Books, 2005), 118–20.

29 Ibid., 122–23.

30 Winston Churchill, *The Gathering Storm* (London: Cassell, 1948), 526–27.

CHAPTER TWO: BRITAIN ALONE AND CHURCHILL'S FATAL ERROR

1 Charmley, *Churchill: The End of Glory*, 396.

2 David Reynolds, *In Command of History*, (London), 164.

3 Holmes, *In the Footsteps*, 202.

4 Winston Churchill, *Their Finest Hour* (London: Cassell, 1949), 157.

5 Ibid., *The Gathering Storm*, 524.

6 John Colville, *The Fringes of Power: Downing Street Diaries, 1939–1955* (London: Hodder and Stoughton, 1985), 121.

7 Ibid., 122.

8 Ibid.

9 Holmes, *In the Footsteps*, 205–6.

10 Charmley, *Churchill: The End of Glory*, 396, and Holmes, *In the Footsteps*, 202–3.

11 Churchill, *Their Finest Hour*, 9.

12 Reynolds, *In Command of History*, 169–73 for the helpful details.

13 Quoted from the Robert Rhodes James–edited volume of Churchill's speeches cited earlier.

14 Holmes, *In the Footsteps*, 202.

15 Quoted in Reynolds, *In Command of History*, 172. There is a wonderful picture of Churchill, machine gun in hand, at Dover Castle.

16 Mark Mazower, *Hitler's Empire* (London: Allen Lane, 2008).

17 Reynolds, *In Command of History*, 175, discusses this but my take is slightly different.

18 Ibid., 173.

19 John Keegan, *Churchill* (London: Weidenfeld and Nicolson, 2002), 128.

20 Ibid.

21 Reynolds, *In Command of History*, 175.

22 Ibid., 175–76.

23 Holmes, *In the Footsteps*, 259.

24 Feiling, *Chamberlain*, 325.

25 I am indebted to Richard Holmes for this wonderful and telling reference.

26 Holmes, *In the Footsteps*, 219.

27 I am grateful to Richard Holmes for the statistics that follow.

28 Keegan, *Churchill*, 136.

29 Ibid., 136–37.

30 CHAR 20/36: Prime Minister's Personal Minutes for January 1941 for most of the quotations.

31 Ibid., D 11/1: Note from Churchill to Ismay for subsequent transmission.

32 Ibid., M 46/1.

33 Ibid., M 44/1.

34 Ibid., M 57/1: January 17, 1941; when he took over as acting foreign secretary in Eden's absence overseas in February 1941, he insisted that the august permanent undersecretary Sir Alexander Cadogan did the same. As Churchill put it, "I am going to give myself a treat." M 179/1, February 16, 1941.

35 Ibid. Churchill to the Chiefs of Staff, January 27, 1941: D 27/1.

36 *The Balkans in World War Two* (London: Palgrave Macmillan, 2002).

37 CHAR 20/36: Minute to the CIGS M452/1.

38 CHAR 20/36: Prime Minister's Personal Minutes for February 1941: Note for the Foreign Secretary February 12, 1941.

39 And Turkey too, Churchill added, but the Turks were far too canny to agree to join the war at so perilous a stage.

40 CHAR 20/36: D 42/1.

41 Ibid., M 208/1, February 19, 1941.

42 Ibid., Churchill Memo as Minister of Defence April 14, 1941.

43 Ibid., D 130/1.

44 Ibid., M 455/1.

45 Ibid., Churchill Directive as Minister of Defence April 28, 1941.

46 CHAR 20/36 (continued), Churchill Memo to the Chiefs of Staff.

47 Ibid., D 260/1, September 19, 1941.

48 Victoria Schofield, *Wavell: Soldier and Statesman* (London: John Murray, 2006), and it should be said I am sterner on Churchill than she would be.

49 J. R. M. Butler, *Grand Strategy* Volume II (London: HMSO, 1957), 541.

50 John Strawson, *The Battle for North Africa* (London: Batsford, 1969), especially 43–49 for the quotations that follow.

51 Ibid.

52 Bernard Fergusson, *The Business of War* (London: Hutchinson, 1957), especially xii–xiv and 67–126, and on Greece 77–103.

53 Ibid., 87.

54 Ibid., 81–85.

55 Correlli Barnett, *The Desert Generals* (London: George Allen and Unwin, 1960). I am quoting from the 1983 revised and expanded edition. See especially 60–68.

56 Sir Francis de Guigand, *Generals at War* (London: Hodder and Stoughton, 1964), 15–55, and *Operation Victory* (London: Hodder and Stoughton, 1947), 44–104. See also Barnett, *Britain and Her Army*, 436–40 and also Barrie Pitt, *The Crucible of War* (London: Jonathan Cape, 1980), 160–284 for very considerable detail on these sad events.

57 Tuvia Ben-Moshe, *Churchill: Strategy and History*, (Lynne Reinner Co., 1992), 267.

58 Ibid., 268.

59 Ibid., 272–74.

60 Ibid., 275.

61 Ben-Moshe makes this very clear in his chapter on Churchill's delaying tactics for Overlord: ibid., 245–76.

CHAPTER THREE: GETTING TO KNOW ONE ANOTHER

1 CHAR 23/10: 6–9 (Parts III and IV) December 18, 1941.

2 CHAR 23/10: for his memoranda on this subject.

3 CHAR 23/10: 10–14: Memo to General Ismay for the Chiefs of Staff and Defence Committee, January 4, 1942.

CHAPTER FOUR: CHURCHILL AND THE WAR'S WRONG TURN

1 CHAR 20/77/101.

2 Winston Churchill, *The Hinge of Fate* (London: Cassell, 1951), except for quotations from the US edition as below.

3 Reynolds, *In Command of History.*

4 In the very kind conversations they found time to have with me despite their busy schedule.

5 See CHUR 4/270/109–18.

6 Churchill, *The Hinge of Fate* (Boston: Houghton Mifflin), 322–25, for the Churchill quotations that follow (note: these paginations may differ from the British edition).

7 CHUR 4/270/113–14.

8 CHUR 4/277/7–8.

9 For example by Norman Davies, who points out that it was the Russian and American generals who performed many of the best feats of the Second World War, notably Zhukov on the Eastern Front.

10 This also appears in CHUR 4/272/1.

11 CHUR 4/272/124.

12 As does British historian Keith Sainsbury, who I think is persuasively right.

13 Both in his book and a brief after-dinner conversation at Churchill College, Cambridge.

14 Historians such as Norman Davies and Max Hastings in general, Laurence

Rees and Anthony Beevor on the Eastern Front, and David Reynolds in relation to Churchill.

15   As David Reynolds points out.

16   Churchill, *Hinge of Fate*, 323.

17   Numerous books on the Second World War say this but I am especially grateful to Professor Paul Kennedy of Yale for pointing this out to me in Churchill SCR.

18   Harry Hopkins, *The White House Papers of Harry Hopkins* Volume 2, ed. by Robert Sherwood (London: Eyre and Spottiswoode, 1949), 523–47, for the quotations made in this chapter.

19   The copy in Churchill's own archive is CHUR 4/270/1–3.

20   And also in CHUR 4/270/4–9.

21   Marshall memo again, and the next extract as well.

22   *Churchill in War*, Roskill Library, Churchill College, Cambridge, 920 CHU (box).

23   CHUR 4/270/123–24 and 127–29 for Churchill's detailed views.

24   Page 246.

25   Marshall Archives 61/50 for this meeting—also COS (42) 23.

26   Ibid., and see also Churchill Archives: CHUR 4/270/10–15.

27   For example in his book *Wedemeyer Reports!*

28   Marshall Archives 62/1: Topics for London Talks, April 1942: USP (42) 1st meeting.

29   Ibid., 62/1/o.

30   See the Marshall Archives, Oral Histories Tape 40.

31   Marshall Archives 61/50; otherwise COS (42) 97.

32   Ibid.

33   Marshall Archives 61/50—meeting on April 14, 1943; also COS (42) 118.

34   George Bernard Shaw, the great-twentieth-century writer, thinker, and satirist.

35   Marshall Archives 62/2/Q.

36   "Pug" Ismay (so known because of the canine expression on his face) was the man who coined the famous aphorism that NATO was designed to keep the Germans down, the Russians out, and the Americans in.

37   Marshall Archives, Oral Histories Tape 40, for this and all further Ismay quotations.

38 In Lebanon and in Guatemala.

39 All the quotations from Sir Alan Brooke (later Field Marshal Lord Alanbrooke) are from *War Diaries, 1939–1945*, edited by Alex Danchev and Daniel Todman (London: Weidenfeld and Nicolson, 2001), in this instance pp. 248–49.

40 Ibid.

41 Ibid., 553–54.

42 Ibid. Diary of May 15, 1944, p. 546.

43 Mark Stoler, *George C. Marshall: Soldier-Statesman of the American Century*, (Woodbridge, CT: Twayne Publishers, 1982), 99.

44 Ibid.

45 Ibid.

46 Pogue interview with Ismay (see note 36 above).

47 Stoler, *Marshall*, 101.

48 Ben-Moshe, *Churchill: Strategy and History*, 257–58.

49 Walter Scott Dunn Jr., *Second Front Now, 1943* (University AL: University of Alabama Press, 1980).

50 Ibid., vii.

51 Ibid., 1.

52 Norman Davies, *Rising '44: The Battle for Warsaw* (London: Macmillan, 2003).

53 As proved convincingly in Richard Overy's work *Why the Allies Won*, op. cit.

54 Dunn, 58–74.

55 Ibid., 74.

56 Ibid., 3.

57 Ibid., 3–4; and for the argument that follows, 4–19.

58 Ibid., 9.

59 Ibid., 11.

60 Charles Whiting, *Patton's Last Battle* (Staplehurst: Spellmount, 2002), 171–75. (This book was originally published in the United States in 1987.)

CHAPTER FIVE: WAITING FOR WINSTON

1 See note 2 in chapter 4, above.

2 CHAR 23/10: WP (42) 11: Churchill memo of July 21, 1942.

3 Ibid.

4 CHAR 20/77/88.

5 CHAR 20/77 containing T 990/2.

6 CHAR 20/78/46–47.

7 CHUR 4/271/68 and 104 and 69–91 for what he cut out.

8 For some background see Herbert Feis, *Churchill Roosevelt Stalin* (Princeton, NJ: Princeton University Press, 1957), 73–79.

9 Quoted by David Reynolds, *In Command of History*, 325.

10 Churchill, *The Hinge of Fate*, 428.

11 Reynolds, *In Command of History*, 326.

12 Quoted in *The Diaries of Sir Alexander Cadogan*, ed. David Dilks (London: Cassell, 1971), 471, in the commentary section.

13 Churchill, *Hinge of Fate*, 431.

14 Churchill memo of the talks to the Canadian and Australian prime ministers in CHAR 20/79A/73-77.

15 A translation of Stalin's aide-mémoire is to be found in CHAR 20/79A.

16 Churchill, *Hinge of Fate*, 432.

17 Reynolds, *In Command of History*, 294.

18 Churchill, *Hinge of Fate*, 433.

19 Ibid., 433–35.

20 Ibid., 438.

21 Ibid., 441–42.

22 Ibid., 444.

23 For these details see Reynolds, *In Command of History*, 310–11, and for a proper perspective on the war one cannot beat Norman Davies's panoramic *Europe at War, 1939–1945: No Simple Victory* (London: Macmillan, 2006), to which I have referred elsewhere.

24 Churchill, *Hinge of Fate*, 444.

25 Dunn, *Second Front Now*, 20. Many of the thoughts, suggestions, and discussion in this chapter are based upon my synthesis both of this book and of the more famous work by John Grigg, *1943: The Victory That Never Was*, (London: Eyre Methuen, 1980). I am indebted to both books, and to avoid endless *ibid.*'s in this chapter I will cite them directly only when making actual quotations—those familiar with both these fascinating works will see how much I owe each of them.

26 Dunn, *Second Front Now*, 25.

27 CHAR 23/10/63–64.

28 CHAR 23/10/63–66 for the full correspondence, including Churchill's account of discussions with Stalin.

29 Dunn, *Second Front Now*, 58–74, and Grigg in *1943*.

30 From PREM 3, quoted by Dunn, 26.

31 CHAR 23/10/43–44.

32 Ibid., 44.

33 CHAR 23/10/74–75, which is also COS (42) 435 (O), December 29, 1942.

34 Ibid.

35 Ibid.

36 Churchill's own papers give his account in CHUR 4/275.

37 The conference is described in Churchill's *Hinge of Fate*, 660–95, which includes the preliminaries.

38 Ibid., 671.

39 Grigg, *1943*, 54.

40 Maurice Matloff, *Strategic Planning for Coalition Warfare, 1943–1944* (Department of the Army: Washington DC, 1959), 20.

41 Sir Basil Liddell Hart, *History of the Second World War* (New York: G. P. Putnam and Sons, 1971; first US edition), 438–39. Liddell Hart, it should be added, felt that the correctness of the *British*-led decision to postpone D-day was one "that will hardly be questioned in historical retrospect," and in Britain that has continued to be the majority view to this day.

42 Matloff, *Strategic Planning*, 20.

43 Churchill, *Hinge of Fate*, 679.

44 The essay is in *Studies in War and Peace* (New York: Viking 1971), 122–40; the quotation is on 132.

45 Hart, *Second World War*, 238

46 See Albert Wedemeyer, *Wedemeyer Reports!* (New York: Henry Holt and Company, 1958).

47 See the work for instance of Trumbull Higgins.

48 Mark Stoler, *Allies and Adversaries* (Chapel Hill: University of North Carolina Press, 2000), 110–18.

49 Leonard Mosley, *Marshall: Hero of Our Times* (New York: Hearst Books, 1982), 223–29.

50 Brooke, *War Diaries*, 358–59; and for the official minutes see *Foreign Relations of the United States: Conferences at Washington DC and Casablanca* (Washington DC: State Department, 1968), 483–849, henceforth referred to as *FRUS Washington and Casablanca*.

51 *FRUS Washington and Casablanca*, 559–60.

52 Brooke, *War Diaries*, 359–60; and *FRUS Washington and Casablanca*, 570–73.

53 The Sainsbury argument, which is I think correct.

54 Howard, *Studies in War and Peace*, 133–34.

55 *FRUS Washington and Casablanca*, 572–73.

56 Ibid., 583.

57 Brooke, *War Diaries*, 360.

58 Forrest Pogue, *George C. Marshall: Organizer of Victory* (New York: Viking, 1973), 23–31.

59 Ibid., and see also Mark Stoler, *The Politics of the Second Front* (Westport CT: Greenwood Press, 1973), 75–78.

60 As Grigg argues in *1943*, 60–61.

61 Ibid.

62 Ibid., 63.

63 See his memoir, *Wedemeyer Reports!*

64 Thank you to the Boatwright Library at the University of Richmond, Virginia, for letting me use their wonderful facilities in which biographies of Roosevelt abound.

65 This is well argued by David Reynolds (*In Command of History*, 323–24), who, as usual, shows that Churchill was not entirely candid in his memoirs.

66 Taking David Reynolds's arguments outlined in note 65 above further than Reynolds does himself.

67 As does John Grigg, I think, in *1943: The Victory That Never Was*.

68 Dunn, *Second Front Now*, especially pp. 58–74.

69 CHAR 20/127: Churchill to War Cabinet, January 18, 1941.

70 Ibid., Stratagem 78: Churchill to Eden: Churchill was even worried de Gaulle would bring civil war to France, which is surely a massive exaggeration.

71 Ibid., Stratagem 198: Churchill to War Cabinet.

72 CHAR 20/128/48: Pencil 227, May 24, 1943.

73 Especially in his controversial but well-written *Churchill's Grand Alliance* on Churchill and the evolution of the US-UK "Special Relationship" (US edition: New York: Harcourt Brace, 1995).

74 In the English Civil War of the seventeenth century, the Roundheads, the joke goes, were "right but repulsive" and the Cavaliers, the party of King Charles I, were "wrong but wromantic." Needless to say, the war was a lot more complex than that!

75 See Churchill's thoughts on this in CHAR 23/10/75.

76 CHAR 20/127/34: Stratagem 198 (Section Two).

77 CHAR 20/127/41: Stratagem 255: January 26, 1943.

78 Stoler, *Marshall*, 103–4.

79 Churchill, *Hinge of Fate*, 700.

80 Brooke, *War Diaries*, 398, entry of May 4, 1943.

81 Ibid., 409–10.

82 Ibid., 410 and the next quote as well.

83 Ibid., 406.

84 Forrest Pogue, *Organiser of Victory* (New York: Viking, 1973), 194.

85 See Stoler, *Marshall*, 103–4, and also Pogue, *Organiser of Victory*, 194.

86 Pogue, *Organiser of Victory*, 196.

87 Hopkins, *White House Papers* Volume 2, 427.

88 Detailed by Churchill in *The Hinge of Fate*, 706–25.

89 Ibid., 710, and for the next quotation as well.

90 Pogue, *Organiser of Victory*, 198.

91 Brooke, *War Diaries*, 411—but see Pogue, *Organiser of Victory*, 211–12.

92 Pogue, *Organiser of Victory*, 200–9, for a helpful discussion of the often heated debates.

93 Charmley, *Churchill: The End of Glory*, 538–39.

94 Many writers have pointed this out, from John Charmley on the anti- to Richard Holmes and David Reynolds on the pro-Churchill sides. Here I am following Charmley, *Churchill: The End of Glory*, 538–42, and Reynolds, *In Command of History*, 334–36, to avoid too many *ibid.*'s and *op.cit.*'s in these endnotes, and see also Richard Holmes, *In the Footsteps*, 250.

95 Churchill, *Hinge of Fate*, 504.

96 Hopkins, *White House Papers* Volume 2, 729.

97 This is from chapters 9 and 10 of Pogue's *Organiser of Victory*, 214–40, including all the delicate negotiations between the United States and France in Algiers, and from Churchill's *Hinge of Fate*, 726–40.

98 One imagines this is a reference to Count Lazare Carnot, the organizer of so many of the victories France won during the Revolutionary Wars.

99 Churchill, *Hinge of Fate*, 726.

100 Ibid., 729.

101 Ibid., 730.

102 Pogue, *Organiser of Victory*, 216.

103 Ibid., 218–19.

104 Churchill, *Hinge of Fate*, 733–37.

105 Pogue, *Organiser of Victory*, 220.

106 All quotations taken from Stimson's account are as published in *Foreign Relations of the United States: Conferences at Washington and Quebec, 1943*, 444–52, henceforth referred to as *FRUS Washington and Quebec*.

107 Ibid., 445.

108 Ibid., 446.

109 Ibid., 448.

110 Reynolds, *In Command of History*, 373.

111 *FRUS Washington and Quebec*, 449.

112 A point referred to in Dunn, *Second Front Now*, 32.

113 *FRUS Washington and Quebec*, 452.

114 Ibid., 452.

CHAPTER SIX: CHURCHILL FINALLY HAS TO GIVE IN

1 Churchill Papers, Churchill College, CHAR 23/12, for all Churchill's copies of the Quadrant conclusions.

2 Stoler, *Marshall*, 104.

3 Ibid., 104–5.

4 The full version is in *FRUS Washington and Quebec*, 1024–26.

5 Both quotations are from *Closing the Ring*, (London: Cassell, 1952), 75; see also CHAR 23/12.

6 For these quotations Churchill, *Closing the Ring*, 75–76, and CHAR 23/12.

7 Churchill, *Closing the Ring*, 81–82.

8   The father was the then Prince Louis of Battenberg, who was married to a granddaughter of Queen Victoria; in 1914, in the wave of anti-German feeling prevalent when war began, Churchill, as First Lord of the Admiralty, was forced to make him step down as First Sea Lord.

9   Reynolds, *In Command of History*, 376–77.

10 Quoted in Reynolds, *In Command of History*, 376.

11 Ibid., 376–77.

12 From comments Kennedy made in one of many Churchill SCR conversations with your author.

13 Churchill, *Closing the Ring*, 273–76; see also CHAR 23/12.

14 Ibid., 277.

15 Warren Kimball, *Alliance Forged*, 555–58, C471 and also omitting paragraph 10 in Churchill, *Closing the Ring*, 277–78.

16 Kimball, *Alliance Forged*, 554–55.

17 Charmley, *Churchill: The End of Glory*, 552–57.

18 Quoted by Richard Holmes, *In the Footsteps*, 249.

19 Charmley, *Churchill: The End of Glory*, 552.

20 Holmes, *In the Footsteps*, 258.

21 Quoted in a footnote in the chapter by Sir Ian Jacob in *Action This Day* ed. Sir John Wheeler-Bennett (London: Macmillan, 1958), 96. Lady Violet, now best known as the grandparent of the actress Helena Bonham-Carter, does not mention it in her memoirs, *Winston Churchill As I Knew Him*, but gave the quotation in an interview in 1965. Jacob recalls that Churchill said similar things at other times.

22 *Action This Day*, 209.

23 Ibid.

24 Ibid.

25 A point made by several of his biographers, and which any reading can confirm.

26 This is the major thesis of writers such as John Charmley and Correlli Barnett, as we have seen from the quotes already made from their works.

27 Especially, for example, Charmley in *Churchill's Grand Alliance*, which, though, is surely right to say that Churchill only made this far worse, from Britain's point of view, in rejecting the only way out, namely, forming a

much closer relationship with continental Europe, and, in particular, in ruling out a role as a cofounder of the infant European Union, and thus a leadership that Britain, with Churchill's prestige, could have had for the asking.

28 *Action This Day*, 209–10.

29 Quoted by Stoler, *Second Front*, 87.

30 Ibid., 88.

31 The film *A Bridge Too Far* is an honorable exception since it gives heroic status to both British and American alike, and also to local resistance heroes.

32 Both Hopkins quotations are from Stoler, *Second Front*, 90.

33 Ibid., for quotation.

34 Ibid., for the two Marshall quotations.

35 Ibid., 90–91.

36 Ibid., 91.

37 Holmes, *In the Footsteps*, 258.

38 Charles Bohlen minutes (for reference see next footnote), 486.

39 Apparently no official minutes exist! What we do have, and what *Foreign Relations of the United States: Cairo and Teheran* (Washington DC: State Department, 1961) use, are the minutes taken by Charles Bohlen of the US delegation at the meeting. (Henceforth referred to as *FRUS Cairo and Teheran.*)

40 *FRUS Cairo and Teheran*, 487–97 for the whole meeting: this quotation from p. 488.

41 He was also right to say that Turkey would not enter the war.

42 For details of this see *FRUS Cairo and Teheran*, 514–28, from which any quotations come.

43 Ibid., quoted on p. 523.

44 Some of the Soviet marshal's views are quoted in the British Official History: John Ehrman, *Grand Strategy* Volume 5 (London: HMSO, 1956), 177–79.

45 Once again Bohlen's minutes are the ones used: *FRUS Cairo and Teheran*, 533–40.

46 Ibid., 547.

47 Brooke, *War Diaries*, 487.

48 Ibid., 484.

49 This and the next quote, *FRUS Cairo and Teheran*, 552.

50 Ibid., 552–55.

51 Sellar and Yeatman, *1066 and All That*.

52 Churchill, *Closing the Ring*, 330.

53 *Struggle for Survival*, 140–41, for both quotations.

54 Ibid., 144, and Holmes, *In the Footsteps*, 262.

55 Holmes, *In the Footsteps*, 261–62 for this and the next two quotations.

56 Churchill, *Closing the Circle*, 321, and 331–60 for the rest of the conference.

57 Holmes, *In the Footsteps*, 263.

58 Douglas Hurd, Foreign and Commonwealth Secretary 1989–95.

59 I am thinking in particular of Davies's books *Rising 44* and *No Simple Victory*.

60 See especially pp. 348–54 and 359–60, where Churchill's defensiveness is clearer still.

61 Bohlen minutes of plenary session on December 1, *FRUS Cairo and Teheran*, 598–99 for this and the next quotation.

62 Ibid., 599.

63 Ibid., 598.

64 Churchill, *Closing the Circle*, 360.

CHAPTER SEVEN: CHURCHILL AND AMERICA AT WAR

1 See especially Chester Wilmot, *The Struggle for Europe*, (London: William Collins, 1952), 788–99.

2 Marshall Archives: Pogue Interviews (Oral Archives) Tape 104: George Kennan—and for the quotations that follow on Kennan's views.

3 Norman Davies, *Europe at War, 1939–1945: No Simple Victory*; (London: Macmillan, 2004), I am here quoting from the 2007 Pan edition, 119–20, and see also 189.

4 *Churchill and Roosevelt*, Warren Kimball ed., (Princeton: Princeton University Press, 1984) 280–83, including commentary by Kimball and the Roosevelt-Churchill correspondence on that tragedy, and 292–96.

5 Pogue Oral History Interviews: Averell Harriman, who makes what I think is the somewhat limp excuse that the Soviet Army of the Vistula stopped in order to refuel. If that had been the case, why did they forbid Western Allies to come to the rescue of the Poles?

6 For details see below.

7 Winston Churchill, *Triumph and Tragedy*, 208.

8 *Churchill and Roosevelt III* C-755, 278–79.

9 Ibid., 297.

10 Churchill, *Triumph and Tragedy*, 217–18, and in *Churchill and Roosevelt III* C-789, 340–41.

11 Churchill, *Triumph and Tragedy*, 217 and 219–20.

12 Ibid., 226–29; the original documents of the meeting can be found in the National Archive in the PREM 3 files.

13 Reynolds, *In Command of History*, 459.

14 Ibid., 458–61, for Reynolds's analysis.

15 Churchill, *Triumph and Tragedy*, 231–35.

16 Reynolds, *In Command of History*.

17 Ibid., 462–63.

18 Radovan Gajer to the author in around 1981.

19 Reynolds, *In Command of History*, 463.

20 For much of what follows I am grateful to Albert Resis, "The Churchill-Stalin Secret 'Percentages' Agreement on the Balkans," in the *American Historical Review* vol. 83 no. 2 (April 1978), 368–87, and also to another article, by Joseph Siracusa, "The Night Stalin and Churchill Divided Europe: The View from Washington," in the *Review of Politics* vol. 43 no. 3 (July 1981), 381–409. The latter disagrees with the former author on points of analysis—I am not sure why since I found both articles equally helpful. Let the reader decide....I think it is the Resis statement that the Cold War began on October 4, 1944, when Roosevelt told Stalin that the United States demanded full and *sole* rights over Western Europe's future. But I would disagree—one could argue that it really began with the Molotov-Ribbentrop Pact of 1939 and the drastically delayed second front. Then there is the theory of my good friend and Cambridge colleague Geoffrey Williams, who argues, with much cogency, that it *actually* began in 1917, in the October Revolution. Either way, we can argue about this until the cows come home, as there is a lack of consensus both on when the Cold War began and indeed on when it ended.

21 See the thesis by Christopher Catherwood on this issue in the University Library in Cambridge, on Britain and Turko-Soviet relations 1935–41.

22 Resis, op. cit. (see note 20, above), 375–76.

23 Ibid., 381.

24 Charles Bohlen, head of the Eastern Europe desk at the State Department, quoted in Siracusa (see note 20, above), 386.

25 See especially the articles in note 20, above, for what follows.

26 Siracusa quoting the late Elizabeth Barker.

27 Max Hasting's book *Nemesis* is particularly helpful in examining the key issues of the Japanese war.

28 Siracusa, 385, quoting the Harriman memoirs.

29 *Churchill and Roosevelt III* C-687, Churchill to Roosevelt, May 31, 1944. "Roumanian" is an alternative and now archaic British spelling.

30 Siracusa, 393–409, and for what follows.

31 *Churchill and Roosevelt III* C-712, 23 June 1944, 202–3.

32 Quoted by Siracusa, 406.

33 Quoted in the Siracusa article.

34 Grigg, in the conclusion to his book *1943: The Victory That Never Was.*

35 Sellers and Yeatman, *1066 and All That*, which came out just after the First World War.

36 To use the phrase made famous in this context by John Lewis Gaddis of Yale University in his book of that name.

37 There is an enormous literature on this, one of the most contentious disagreements of the Second World War and a major source of dissent between Churchill and both Americans and his fellow Britons, as this chapter will have made clear. So for much of what follows in this chapter I am very grateful to my hosts in Lexington, Virginia, at the Virginia Military Institute, where the excellent *Journal of Military History* is located—see my thanks to current assistant editor Anne S. Wells in the acknowledgments. In particular much time and effort was saved by my discovering in that journal an article in the January 1992 issue by Thomas M. Barker: "The Ljubljana Gap Strategy: Alternative to Anvil/Dragoon or Fantasy?" vol. 56 no. 1: 57–85; the maps are particularly helpful and, as is the case with your author, this is a part of the world that Barker has visited in person—see 73–84 for a usefully detailed topographical study.

38 Wilmot, *Struggle for Europe*, 502.

39 Ibid., 496–508, the chapter called "Roosevelt and the Balkans," for an actual direct discussion in Wilmot's work of the Ljubljana Gap possibility, and a helpful map on page 451 (of the American edition).

40 D. J. Markwell in *English Historical Review* vol. 107 no. 423 (April 1992), 549.

41 Barker, "Ljubljana Gap," 83.

42 Forrest Pogue Oral History Interview with Beddell Smith, Marshall Archives.

43 Barker, "Ljubljana Gap," 84.

44 Marshall Archives, Xerox File 768, Eisenhower to War Department (in effect to Marshall, as with the other telegrams).

45 Ibid.

46 Marshall Papers, Xerox 769, Marshall to Eisenhower WAR 55794, June 24, 1944.

47 Marshall Papers, Xerox 770, Eisenhower to Marshall S54760, June 29, 1944.

48 Ibid.

49 This version Marshall Papers, Xerox 771.

50 Marshall Papers, Xerox 772, Eisenhower to Marshall S54849.

51 FPOHI with Alanbrooke (of which Reel 1 is missing), Marshall Archives.

52 For example, by Thomas Barker, "Ljubljana Gap."

53 FPOHI interview with Field Marshal Lord Wilson.

54 Ibid., same interview.

EPILOGUE

1 I do understand Cambridge Professor Richard Evans's caveat on such things, since so many British counterfactual historians are on the political right. Your author is a political *centrist* who has voted for different British political parties over the years, so I trust Evans's caution does not apply to this book in the way that it might well to others.

2 In a review in *International Affairs* vol. 57 no. 1 (Winter 1980–81), 148–49.

3 In a chat in Churchill College, Cambridge, with the author.

4 The historian Michael Burleigh is an honorable exception, for which he has got in trouble in some of his writing.

5 It is worth saying here that the Thirty Years War in Germany (1618–48) had

a similar horrific civilian death toll, which set German population growth, and probably more besides, back for decades if not centuries.

6   Your author was raised in Ealing, the Polish district of West London.

7   I am including my talk with him in 2007 in Wolfson College, Cambridge, as well as his books.

INDEX

Index

Index

Index